AAT

INTERACTIVE TEXT

Intermediate Unit 5

Financial Records and Accounts

<table>
<tr><td>

In this May 2002 edition

- Text updated in the light of the assessor's review of the previous edition of this Text.

- Numerous activities have been added

- The section on bookkeeping has been made more user friendly

- The chapters on manufacturing and club accounts and incomplete records have been simplified and made more assessment-focused.

- Thorough reliable updating of material to 1 April 2002

FOR 2002 AND 2003 ASSESSMENTS

</td></tr>
</table>

BPP Publishing
May 2002

First edition 1998
Fifth edition May 2002

ISBN 07517 6275 X (Previous edition ISBN 0 7517 6508 2)

British Library Cataloguing-in-Publication Data
A catalogue record for this book
is available from the British Library

Published by

BPP Publishing Limited
Aldine House, Aldine Place
London W12 8AW

www.bpp.com

Printed in Great Britain by W M Print
45-47 Frederick Street
Walsall WS2 9NE

We are grateful to the Lead Body for Accounting for permission to reproduce extracts from the Standards of Competence for Accounting, and to the AAT for permission to reproduce extracts from the Mapping and Guidance Notes.

Page

BPP PUBLISHING

HOW TO USE THIS INTERACTIVE TEXT

Aims of this Interactive Text

> To provide the knowledge and practice to help you succeed in the assessments for Intermediate Unit 5 *Maintaining Financial Records and Preparing Accounts.*

To pass the devolved assessment you need a thorough understanding in all areas covered by the standards of competence.

> To tie in with the other components of the BPP Effective Study Package to ensure you have the best possible chance of success.

Interactive Text

This covers all you need to know for central and devolved assessment for Unit 5 *Financial Records and Accounts.* Icons clearly mark key areas of the text. Numerous activities throughout the text help you practise what you have just learnt.

Assessment Kit

When you have understood and practised the material in the Interactive Text, you will have the knowledge and experience to tackle the Assessment Kit for Unit 5 *Financial Records.* This aims to get you through the assessment, whether in the form of the AAT simulation or in the workplace. It contains the AAT's sample simulations for Unit 5 plus other simulations. The Kit also contains numerous past Central Assessments set by the AAT.

Passcards

These short memorable notes are focused on key topics for Unit 5, designed to remind you of what the Interactive text has taught you.

Recommended approach to this Interactive Text

- To achieve competence in Unit 5 (and all the other units), you need to be able to do **everything** specified by the standards. Study the text very carefully and do not skip any of it.

- Learning is an **active** process. Do **all** the activities as you work through the text so you can be sure you really understand what you have read.

- After you have covered the material in the Interactive Text, work through the **Assessment Kit**.

- Before you take the assessments, check that you still remember the material using the following quick revision plan for each chapter.

   ° Read through the **chapter learning objectives**. Are there any gaps in your knowledge? If so, study the section again.

   ° Read and learn the **key terms**.

   ° Look at the **assessment alerts.** These show the sort of things that are likely to come up.

   ° Read and learn the **key learning points**, which are a summary of the chapter.

   ° Do the **quick quiz** again. If you know what you're doing, it shouldn't take long.

This approach is only a suggestion. Your college may well adapt it to suit your needs.

Remember this is a **practical** course.

- Try to relate the material to your experience in the workplace or any other work experience you may have had.

- Try to make as many links as you can to your study of the other Units at Intermediate level.

- Keep this Text - you will need it as you move on to Technician, and (hopefully) you will find it invaluable in your everyday work too!

Stop press

The AAT is planning to change the terminology used for assessments in the following ways:

(a) Central assessments to be called exam based testing
(b) Devolved assessments to be called skills based testing

As the plans had not been finalised at the time of going to press, the 2002 editions of BPP titles will continue to refer to central and devolved assessments.

INTERMEDIATE QUALIFICATION STRUCTURE

The competence-based Education and Training Scheme of the Association of Accounting Technicians is based on an analysis of the work of accounting staff in a wide range of industries and types of organisation. The Standards of Competence for Accounting which students are expected to meet are based on this analysis.

The Standards identify the **key purpose** of the accounting occupation, which is **to operate, maintain and improve systems to record, plan, monitor and report on the financial activities of an organisation,** and a number of **key roles** of the occupation. Each key role is subdivided into **units of competence,** which are further divided into **elements of competences**. By successfully completing assessments in specified units of competence, students can gain qualifications at NVQ/SVQ levels 2, 3 and 4, which correspond to the AAT Foundation, Intermediate and Technician stages of competence respectively.

Below we set out the overall structure of the Intermediate (NVQ/SVQ Level 3) stage, indicating how competence in each Unit is assessed. In the next section there is more detail about the Central and Devolved Assessments for Unit 5.

Intermediate qualification structure

NVQ\SVQ Level 3 - Intermediate
All units are mandatory

Unit of competence

Elements of competence

	5.1 Maintain records relating to capital acquisition and disposal
Unit 5 Maintaining financial records and preparing accounts	5.2 Record income and expenditure
	5.3 Collect and collate information for the preparation of final accounts
	5.4 Prepare the extended trial balance

Central *and* Devolved Assessment

	6.1 Record and analyse information relating to direct costs
Unit 6 Recording cost information	6.2 Record and analyse information relating to the allocation, apportionment and absorption of overhead costs
	6.3 Prepare and present standard cost reports

Central *and* Devolved Assessment

	7.1 Prepare and present periodic performance reports
Unit 7 Preparing reports and returns	7.2 Prepare reports and returns for outside agencies
	7.3 Prepare VAT returns

Devolved Assessment *only*

	21.1 Obtain information from a computerised Management Information System
Unit 21 Using information technology	21.2 Produce spreadsheets for the analysis of numerical information
	21.3 Contribute to the quality of the Management Information System

Devolved Assessment *only*

	22.1 Monitor and maintain health and safety within the workplace
Unit 22 Monitor and maintain a healthy, safe and secure workplace (ASC)	22.2 Monitor and maintain the security of the workplace

Devolved Assessment *only*

UNIT 5 STANDARDS OF COMPETENCE

The structure of the Standards for Unit 5

The Unit commences with a statement of the **knowledge and understanding** which underpin competence in the Unit's elements.

The Unit of Competence is then divided into **elements of competence** describing activities which the individual should be able to perform.

Each element includes:

(a) A set of **performance criteria** which define what constitutes competent performance.

(b) A **range statement** which defines the situations, contexts, methods etc in which competence should be displayed.

(c) **Evidence requirements**, which state that competence must be demonstrated consistently, over an appropriate time scale with evidence of performance being provided from the appropriate sources.

(d) **Sources of evidence**, being suggestions of ways in which you can find evidence to demonstrate that competence. These fall under the headings: 'observed performance; work produced by the candidate; authenticated testimonies from relevant witnesses; personal account of competence; other sources of evidence.' They are reproduced in full in our Devolved Assessment Kit for Unit 5.

The elements of competence for Unit 5: *Maintaining Financial Records and Preparing Accounts* are set out below. Knowledge and understanding required for the unit as a whole are listed first, followed by the performance criteria, range statements and evidence requirement for each element. Performance criteria and areas of knowledge and understanding are cross-referenced below to chapters in this Unit 5 *Financial Records and Accounts* Interactive Text.

Unit 5: Maintaining financial records and preparing accounts

What is the unit about?

This unit is concerned with the **collecting and recording of information for the purpose of preparing accounts and maintaining effective records**. It involves identifying the types of information that are required, recording it, making any appropriate calculations or adjustments and maintaining the appropriate records.

The unit requires you to have responsibility for collecting all the relevant information for preparing accounts and presenting it to your supervisor in the form of a trial balance or an extended trial balance. Also required are communication responsibilities relating to handling queries, making suggestions for improvements and maintaining confidentiality.

Knowledge and understanding

The business environment

- Types and characteristics of different assets and key issues relating to the acquisition and disposal of capital assets (Element 5.1)

- Relevant legislation and regulations (Elements 5.1, 5.2, 5.3 & 5.4)

- Main requirements of relevant SSAPs (Elements 5.1, 5.2, 5.3 & 5.4)

- Methods of recording information for the organisational accounts of: sole traders; partnerships; manufacturing accounts; club accounts (Element 5.2)

- Understanding the structure of the organisational accounts of: sole traders; partnerships; manufacturing accounts; club accounts (Element 5.2)

- The need to present accounts in the correct form (Element 5.3)

- The importance of maintaining the confidentiality of business transactions (Elements 5.1, 5.2, 5.3 & 5.4)

Accounting techniques

- Methods of depreciation: straight line; reducing balance (Element 5.1)

- Accounting treatment of capital items sold, scrapped or otherwise retired from service (Element 5.1)

- Use of plant registers and similar subsidiary records (Element 5.1)

- Use of transfer journal (Elements 5.1, 5.2, 5.3 & 5.4)

- Methods of funding: part exchange deals (Element 5.1)

- Accounting treatment of accruals and prepayments (Elements 5.2, 5.3 & 5.4)

- Methods of analysing income and expenditure (Element 5.2)

- Methods of restructuring accounts from incomplete evidence (Element 5.3)

- Identification and correction of different types of error (Elements 5.3 & 5.4)

- Making and adjusting provisions (Elements 5.3 & 5.4)

Accounting principles and theory

- Basic accounting concepts and principles - matching of income and expenditure within an accounting period, historic cost, accruals, consistency, prudence, materiality (Elements 5.1, 5.2, 5.3 & 5.4)

- Principles of double entry accounting (Elements 5.1, 5.2, 5.3 & 5.4)

- Distinction between capital and revenue expenditure, what constitutes capital expenditure (Element 5.1)

- Function and form of accounts for income and expenditure (Element 5.2)

- Function and form of a trial balance, profit and loss account and balance sheet for sole traders, partnerships, manufacturing accounts and club accounts (Elements 5.3 & 5.4)

- Basic principles of stock valuation: cost or NRV; what is included in cost (Elements 5.3 & 5.4)

- Objectives of making provisions for depreciation and other purposes (Elements 5.3 & 5.4)

- Function and form of final accounts (Element 5.4)

The organisation

- Understanding of the ways the accounting systems of an organisation are affected by its organisational structure, its administrative systems and procedures and the nature of its business transactions (Elements 5.1, 5.2, 5.3 & 5.4)

Element 5.1 Maintain records relating to capital acquisition and disposal

Performance criteria		Chapters in this Text
1	Relevant details relating to capital expenditure are correctly entered in the appropriate records	5
2	The organisation's records agree with the physical presence of capital items	5
3	All acquisition and disposal costs and revenues are correctly identified and recorded in the appropriate records	5
4	Depreciation charges and other necessary entries and adjustments are correctly calculated and recorded in the appropriate records	5
5	The records clearly show the prior authority for capital expenditure and disposal and indicate the approved method of funding and disposal	5
6	Profit and loss on disposal is correctly calculated and recorded in the appropriate records	5
7	The organisation's policies and procedures relating to the maintenance of capital records are adhered to	5
8	Lack of agreement between physical items and records are identified and either resolved or referred to the appropriate person	5
9	When possible, suggestions for improvements in the way the organisation maintains its capital records are made to the appropriate person	5

Range statement

1	Methods of calculating depreciation: straight line; reducing balance	5
2	Records: asset register; ledger	5

Element 5.2 Record income and expenditure

Performance criteria		Chapters in this Text
1	All income and expenditure is correctly identified and recorded in the appropriate records	2
2	Relevant accrued and prepaid income and expenditure is correctly identified and adjustments are made	8
3	The organisation's policies, regulations, procedures and timescales in relation to recording income and expenditure are observed	2
4	Incomplete data is identified and either resolved or referred to the appropriate person	10

Range statement

1	Records: day book; journal; ledger	1, 2, 7

BPP PUBLISHING

Element 5.3 Collect and collate information for the preparation of final accounts

Performance criteria		Chapters in this Text
1	Relevant accounts and reconciliations are correctly prepared to allow the preparation of final accounts	7
2	All relevant information is correctly identified and recorded	6
3	Investigations into business transactions are conducted with tact and courtesy	6
4	The organisation's policies, regulations, procedures and timescales relating to preparing final accounts are observed	6
5	Discrepancies and unusual features are identified and either resolved or referred to the appropriate person	10
6	The trial balance is accurately prepared and, where necessary, a suspense account is opened and reconciled	2, 7
Range statement		
1	Sources of information: ledger; bank reconciliation; creditors' reconciliation; debtors' reconciliation	6, 7
2	Discrepancies and unusual features: insufficient data has been provided; inconsistencies within the data	10

Element 5.4 Prepare the extended trial balance

Performance criteria		Chapters in this Text
1	Totals from the general ledger or other records are correctly entered on the extended trial balance	12
2	Material errors disclosed by the trial balance are identified, traced and referred to the appropriate authority	12
3	Adjustments not dealt with in the ledger accounts are correctly entered on the extended trial balance	12
4	An agreed valuation of closing stock is correctly entered on the extended trial balance	9, 12
5	The organisation's policies, regulations, procedures and timescales in relation to preparing extended trial balances are observed	12
6	Discrepancies, unusual features or queries are identified and either resolved or referred to the appropriate person	12
7	The extended trial balance is accurately extended and totalled	12
Range statement		
1	Adjustments relating to: accruals; prepayments	12

ASSESSMENT STRATEGY

This unit is assessed by both **central/exam based testing** and **devolved/skills based testing.**

Central Assessment

A central assessment is a means of collecting evidence that you have the **essential knowledge and understanding** which underpins competence. It is also a means of collecting evidence across the **range of contexts** for the standards, and of your ability to **transfer skills,** knowledge and understanding to different situations. Thus, although central assessments contain practical tests linked to the performance criteria, they also focus on the underpinning knowledge and understanding. You should in addition expect each central assessment to contain tasks taken from across a broad range of the standards.

*Each Unit 5 central assessment will last for **three hours** plus 15 minutes reading time and will be divided into two sections. The case studies on which the two sections are based will be unconnected.*

Section 1: Accounting exercises

This section will include one or more accounting exercises from the following.

* *Trial balance*

    Example task: Preparation of a trial balance from a list of balances given

* *Extended trial balance*

    Example tasks: Completion of the adjustments columns from information given. Extension of relevant figures into profit and loss and balance sheet columns

* *Identification and correction of errors*

    Example task: You are given a number of transactions and entries made. Errors and correcting journal entries are to be identified

* *Suspense accounts*

    Example tasks: Suspense account required to balance a trial balance. Correcting entries to be identified to eliminate the suspense account balance

* *Bank reconciliation statements*

    Example tasks: Preparation of a statement to reconcile the opening balances and preparation of a further statement to reconcile the closing balances of a cash book and a bank statement

* *Control accounts*

    Example tasks: Preparation of a debtors control account from information given and reconciliation with the total of the sales ledger balances

Section 2: Practical exercise(s)

This section will comprise one or more practical exercises concerned with the processing, restructuring and production of information for different types of organisations. You will be expected to be able to produce:

- Manufacturing accounts from data given
- Information from data given and/or incomplete records for sole traders, partnerships and clubs

The processing, restructuring and production of information includes, for example:

- Calculation of opening and/or closing capital (accumulated fund for clubs)
- Restructuring the cash and/or bank account.
- Preparation of total debtors account and total creditors account to calculate, for example, sales and purchases.
- Production of simple statements showing the calculation of gross profit and/or net profit and listing assets, liabilities and capital (or equivalent for clubs); these statements to summarise figures or to ascertain missing items of information.
- Use of mark-up and margin (the use of other ratios is outside the scope of this unit).
- Production of other statements and/or restructured ledger accounts, for example to calculate expenses paid, expense profit and loss figures, accruals and prepayments, profit or loss on the sale of an asset, provisions and subscriptions for the period.

Short-answer questions

Both sections will contain a number of short-answer questions (usually three or four) designed to assess knowledge, understanding and communication skills. The tasks will be drawn from across the whole range of the standards for Unit 5 and may require brief explanations, calculations, accounting entries, selection from a number of given possible answers or similar responses. One or more of the tasks will required a memo, letter or notes to be written.

Devolved Assessment (*more detail can be found in the Assessment Kit*)

Devolved assessment is a means of collecting evidence of your ability to carry out **practical activities** and to **operate effectively in the conditions of the workplace** to the standards required. Evidence may be collected at your place of work or at an Approved Assessment Centre by means of simulations of workplace activity, or by a combination of these methods.

If the Approved Assessment Centre is a **workplace**, you may be observed carrying out accounting activities as part of your normal work routine. You should collect documentary evidence of the work you have done, or contributed to, in an **accounting portfolio**. Evidence collected in a portfolio can be assessed in addition to observed performance or where it is not possible to assess by observation.

Where the Approved Assessment Centre is a **college or training organisation**, devolved assessment will be by means of a combination of the following.

(a) Documentary evidence of activities carried out at the workplace, collected by you in an **accounting portfolio**.

(b) Realistic **simulations** of workplace activities. These simulations may take the form of case studies and in-tray exercises and involve the use of primary documents and reference sources.

(c) **Projects and assignments** designed to assess the Standards of Competence.

If you are unable to provide workplace evidence you will be able to complete the assessment requirements by the alternative methods listed above.

Part A

Accounting principles

1 Double entry accounting

This chapter contains

1   Recording and summarising transactions

2   Assets and liabilities

3   Double entry accounting

4   Posting from the day books

Learning objectives

- Understand and use the day books to record income and expenditure
- Understand the principles of double entry accounting

Performance criteria

5.2.1 All income and expenditure is correctly identified and recorded in appropriate records

Range statement

5.2.1 Records: day book; journal; ledger

Knowledge and understanding

Principles of double entry accounting

BPP PUBLISHING

IMPORTANT

If you are exempt from Foundation and have not studied double entry before, we recommend that you go on a bookkeeping course or use the BPP *Introduction to Bookkeeping*. This chapter is an overview for revision purposes.

1 RECORDING AND SUMMARISING TRANSACTIONS

Source documents

KEY TERM

Source documents are the source of all the information recorded by a business.

1.1 Here are some source documents with which you should be familiar already.

• Invoices	• Cheques received
• Credit notes	• Cheque stubs (for cheques paid out)
• Petty cash vouchers	• Wages, salary and PAYE records

1.2 You should be familiar with all of these documents. Learn the following definitions.

KEY TERMS

- An **invoice** is a request for payment.

- A **credit note** is issued by a seller to cancel part or all of a previously issued invoice(s).

Recording source documents

1.3 A company sends out and receives *many* source documents. The details on these source documents need to be recorded, otherwise the business may lose track of receipts and payments. It needs to **keep records of source documents** – of transactions – so that it can keep tabs on what is going on.

1.4 Such records are made in **books of prime entry**, sometimes called the **books of original entry**.

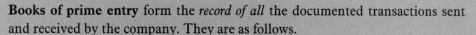

> **KEY TERM**
>
> **Books of prime entry** form the *record of all* the documented transactions sent and received by the company. They are as follows.
>
> - Sales day book
> - Purchase day book
> - Journal (see Chapter 2)
> - Cash book
> - Petty cash book

The sales day book

> **KEY TERM**
>
> The **sales day book** is a list of the invoices sent out to **customers** each day.

1.5 An extract from a sales day book, ignoring VAT for the moment, might look like this.

SALES DAY BOOK

Date 20X7	Invoice number (2)	Customer	Sales ledger folio (1)	Total amount invoiced £
Sept 10	540	Socco Shops	SL22	207.45
	541	Richards Ltd	SL31	42.77
	542	Sandy & Co	SL04	113.82
	543	Bits and Pieces Co	SL42	2,409.00
				2,773.04

(1) The 'sales ledger folio' column refers to a page (called a **folio**) for the individual customer in the **sales ledger**. For example, the sale to Socco Shops Ltd for £207.45 is also recorded on page 22 of the sales ledger.

(2) The invoice number is the **unique number** given on each sales invoice. Listing them out sequentially shows us that all the invoices are included.

Sales analysis

1.6 Most businesses 'analyse' their sales. Suppose that the business sells books and other stationery, and that the sale to Richards Ltd was entirely books, the sale to Sandy & Co was entirely stationery, and the other two sales were a mixture of both.

1.7

SALES DAY BOOK

Date 20X7	Invoice	Customer	Sales ledger folio	Total amount invoiced £	Book sales £	Stationery sales £
Sept 10	540	Socco Shops	SL 22	207.45	159.09	48.36
	541	Richards Ltd	SL 31	42.77	42.77	
	542	Sandy & Co	SL 04	113.82		113.82
	543	Bits and Pieces Co	SL 42	2,409.00	1,861.80	547.20
				2,773.04	2,063.66	709.38

This analysis gives the managers of the business useful information which helps them to decide how best to run the business.

The sales returns day book

> ### KEY TERM
>
> The **sales returns day book** records goods returned by customers.

1.8   An extract from the sales returns day book might look like this. Not all sales returns day books **analyse** what goods were returned, but it helps to keep a complete record.

SALES RETURNS DAY BOOK

Date 20X7	Customer and goods	Sales ledger folio	Amount £
31 Oct	Johnson & Sons		
	10 copies 'Jurassic Park'	SL 27	48.40

1.9   Sales returns could alternatively be shown as **bracketed figures in the sales day book,** so that a sales returns day book would not be needed.

The purchase day book

> ### KEY TERM
>
> The **purchase day book** is a record of the invoices received from **suppliers**.

1.10   An extract from a purchase day book might look like this (again, we have ignored VAT).

PURCHASE DAY BOOK

Date 20X7	Supplier (2)	Purchase ledger folio (1)	Total amount invoiced £	Purchases (3) £	Expenses £
Sept 15	R Dysan Ltd	PL 14	177.50	177.50	
	Peters and Co	PL 07	221.08	221.08	
	Western Electric	PL 23	49.00		49.00
	Regally Ltd	PL 19	380.41	380.41	
			827.99	778.99	49.00

(1) The 'purchase ledger folio' refers to a page for the individual supplier in the purchase ledger. We will see the purpose of this later in the chapter.

(2) There is no 'invoice number' column, as the purchase day book records **other people's invoices**, which have all sorts of different numbers. However, a purchase day book may allocate an internal number to an invoice.

(3) The purchase day book analyses the invoices which have been sent in. Here, three of the invoices related to goods which the business intends to re-sell (**purchases**). The fourth invoice was an electricity bill.

The purchase returns day book

KEY TERM

The **purchase returns day book** records credit notes relating to goods the business sends back to its suppliers.

1.11 A business might expect a credit note from the supplier. However, it might issue a **debit note** to the supplier, indicating the amount its total debt to the supplier should be reduced by.

An extract from the purchase returns day book might look like this. Again, purchase returns could be shown as **bracketed figures** in the purchase day book.

PURCHASE RETURNS DAY BOOK

Date 20X7	Supplier and goods	Purchase ledger folio	Amount £
31 Oct	Covering Co Ltd 40 rolls plastic packaging	PL 47	142.87

The cash book

KEY TERM

The **cash book** is a book of prime entry, used to keep a cumulative record of money received and money paid out by the business via its bank account.

1.12 This includes money received **on the business premises** in notes, coins and cheques which are subsequently banked. Also, receipts and payments made by bank transfer, standing order, direct debit and BACS. Bank interest and charges, go directly through the bank.

1.13 One part of the cash book is used to record **receipts of cash** and receipts made by bank transfer. Another part is used to **record payments**. To see how the cash book works we will use an example. In this example, we continue to ignore VAT.

BPP
PUBLISHING

1.14 EXAMPLE: CASH BOOK

At the beginning of 10 January, Peter Jeffries had £2,100 in the bank. During 10 January 20X8, he had the following receipts and payments.

(a) Cash sale: receipt of £220

(b) Payment from credit customer Khan: £3,100 less discount allowed £100 (S/L folio 07)

(c) Payment from credit customer Likert: £1,480 (S/L folio 12)

(d) Payment from credit customer Lee: £2,400 less discount allowed £70 (S/L folio 10)

(e) Cash sale: receipt of £190

(f) Cash received for sale of machine: £370

(g) Payment to supplier Price: £1,250 (P/L folio 27)

(h) Payment to supplier Burn: £2,420 (P/L folio 16)

(i) Payment of telephone bill: £235

(j) Payment of gas bill: £640

(k) Payment of £3,400 to Fawcett for new plant and machinery

If you look through these transactions, you will see that six of them are receipts and five of them are payments.

1.15 SOLUTION

The cash book entries would be as shown on the next page. Do not worry about the details – we will follow them through later in this text.

1.16 • Receipts and payments are listed out on either side of the cash book – **receipts** on the **left** (debit **asset**) and **payments** on the **right** (credit reduction of **asset**).

• Both sides have columns for these details.

  o Date   o Folio reference
  o Narrative   o Total

• Each side has a number of **columns for further analysis** – receipts from debtors, cash sales and other receipts; payments to creditors, expenses and payments for fixed assets.

Balancing the cash book

1.17 At the beginning of the day there is a debit **opening balance** of £2,100. During the day, the total receipts and payments were as follows.

	£
Opening balance	2,100
Receipts	7,590
	9,690
Payments	(7,945)
Closing balance	1,745

PETER JEFFRIES: CASH BOOK

RECEIPTS

Date 20X8	Narrative	Folio	Discount allowed	Total	Receipts from debtors	Cash sales	Other
10-Jan	Balance b/d (= opening bal)			2,100			
	(a) Cash sale			220		220	
	(b) Debtor pays: Khan	SL07	100	3,000	3,000		
	(c) Debtor pays: Likert	SL12		1,480	1,480		
	(d) Debtor pays: Lee	SL10	70	2,330	2,330		
	(e) Cash sale			190		190	
	(f) Fixed asset sale			370			370
			170	9,690	6,810	410	370
11-Jan	Balance b/d (= new opening bal)			1,745			

PAYMENTS

Date 20X8	Narrative	Folio	Total	Payments to creditors	Expenses	Fixed assets
10-Jan	(g) Creditor paid: Price	PL27	1,250	1,250		
	(h) Creditor paid: Bum	PL16	2,420	2,420		
	(i) Telephone expense		235		235	
	(j) Gas expense		640		640	
	(k) Plant & machinery purchase		3,400			3,400
			7,945	3,670	875	3,400
	Balance c/d		1,745			
			9,690	3,670	875	3,400

The **closing balance** of £1,745 is the excess of receipts over payments. Peter Jeffries still has cash available, so he 'carries it down' at the end of 10 January from the payments side of the cash book, and 'brings it down' to the beginning of 11 January on the receipts side of the cash book. 'Balance brought down' and 'balance carried down' are generally used instead of 'opening balance' and 'closing balance'. (You will have met these terms in your Foundation or bookkeeping studies.)

Balance b/d	Balance brought down	Opening balance
Balance c/d	Balance carried down	Closing balance

Petty cash book

KEY TERM

The **petty cash book** is the book of prime entry which records the small amounts of cash received into and paid out of the cash float.

1.18 Most businesses keep cash on the premises to make occasional **small payments** – eg to pay the milkman, or to buy a few postage stamps. This is often called the **cash float**; it is also used for **occasional small receipts**, such as cash paid by a visitor to take some photocopies.

1.19 There are usually more payments than receipts, and petty cash must be 'topped-up' from time to time with cash from the business bank account.

Activity 1.1

State which books of prime entry the following transactions would be entered into.

(a)   Your business pays J Sunderland (a supplier) £6,200
(b)   You send Hall & Co (a customer) an invoice for £1,320
(c)   You receive an invoice from J Sunderland for £1,750
(d)   You pay Hall & Co £1,000
(e)   Sarti Ltd (a customer) returns goods to the value of £100
(f)   You return goods to Elphick & Co to the value of £2,400
(g)   Sarti Ltd pays you £760

The general ledger

KEY TERM

The **general ledger** is the accounting record which summarises the financial affairs of a business. It contains details of assets, liabilities and capital, income and expenditure and so profit and loss. It consists of a large number of different **ledger accounts**, each account having its own purpose or 'name' and an identity or code. Another name for the general ledger is the **nominal ledger**.

1.20 Transactions are **posted** to accounts in the general ledger from the books of prime entry.

> ## KEY TERM
>
> **Posting** means to enter transactions in ledger accounts in the general ledger from books of prime entry. Often this is done in total (ie all sales invoices in the sales day book for a day are added up and the total is posted to the debtors control account) but individual transactions are also posted (eg fixed assets).

1.21   Examples of ledger accounts in the general ledger include the following.

- Plant and machinery at cost
- Motor vehicles at cost
- Proprietor's capital
- Stocks: raw materials
- Stocks: finished goods
- Total debtors
- Total creditors
- Wages and salaries
- Rent and rates

- Advertising expenses
- Bank charges
- Motor expenses
- Telephone expenses
- Sales
- Cash
- Bank overdraft
- Bank loan

The format of a ledger account

1.22   If a ledger account were to be kept manually rather than as a computer record, its **format** might be as follows.

ADVERTISING EXPENSES

Date	Narrative	Folio	£	Date	Narrative	Folio	£
20X8							
15 Jan	WBSC Agency for quarter to 31 Dec 20X7	PL 97	4,000				

One account entry is shown here to illustrate the general format of a ledger account.

There are two sides to the account, and an account heading on top. It is a 'T' account:

(a)   On top of the account is its name.
(b)   There is a left hand side, or **debit** side.
(c)   There is a right hand side, or **credit** side.

We have already seen this with Peter Jeffries' cash book.

NAME OF ACCOUNT

DEBIT SIDE	£	CREDIT SIDE	£

Discounts, rebates and allowances

> ### KEY TERM
>
> A **discount** is a reduction in the price of goods below the amount at which those goods would normally be sold.

1.23 There are two types of discount. The distinction between **trade and cash discounts** is important as they are accounted for differently.

Type of discount	Description	Timing	Status
Trade discount	A reduction in the **cost of goods** owing to the nature of the trading transaction. It usually results from buying goods in bulk. For example: (a) A customer is quoted a price of £1 per unit for an item, but a price of 95 pence per unit if the item is bought in quantities of 100 units or more at a time. (b) A customer might be offered a discount on all the goods he buys, regardless of the size of each individual order, because the total volume of his purchases is so large. Customers who receive trade discounts are often other business customers.	Given on supplier's invoice	Permanent
Cash (sometimes called settlement) discount	A reduction in the **amount payable** to the supplier, in return for immediate or prompt payment, rather than purchase on credit. A supplier might charge £1,000 for goods, but offer a cash discount of, say, 10% if the goods are paid for immediately in cash, 5% if they are paid for within 7 days of the invoice date but payment anyway within 30 days. In this case the invoice would indicate these terms.	Given for immediate or very prompt payment	Withdrawn if payment not received within time period expected

1.24 EXAMPLE: DISCOUNTS

Trent Marcus has three major suppliers.

(a) Parker is in the same business as Trent and offers 5% trade discount.

(b) Scott offers a trade discount of 6% on amounts *in excess of* £200 (ie the trade discount does not apply to the first £200).

(c) Alan offers a 10% cash discount for immediate payment or a 5% cash discount for all items paid for within 30 days of purchase.

In January 20X8, Trent makes purchases of goods worth the following amounts before discounts have been deducted.

(a) From Parker: £600
(b) From Scott: £850

(c)   From Alan: £280 cash

£920 to be paid on 14.1.X8 for goods purchased on 3.1.X8

Calculate how much Trent has received as discounts in January. How much were trade and cash discounts?

1.25   SOLUTION

		£	
From Parker	£600 × 5%	30	Trade
From Scott	(£850 – £200) × 6%	39	Trade
From Alan	£280 × 10%	28	Cash: immediate
£920 × 5%		46	Cash: prompt
		143	

Activity 1.2

Champer Ltd purchases goods with a list price of £30,000. The supplier offers a 10% trade discount, and a 2½% cash discount for payment within 10 days. *Note.* Ignore VAT.

Task

(a)   Calculate the amount Champer Ltd will have to pay if it delays longer than 10 days before paying.

(b)   Calculate the amount the company will pay if it pays within 10 days.

---

2   ASSETS AND LIABILITIES

Assets

> **KEY TERM**
>
> An **asset** is something of value which a business owns or has the use of.

2.1   Examples of assets are land, buildings, vehicles, plant and machinery, computer equipment, office furniture, cash and stock.

Fixed and current assets

2.2   Some assets are held and used in operations for a **long time**. A building might be occupied for years; similarly, a machine might have a productive life of many years. These are usually referred to as **fixed assets**. These are covered in detail in Part B of this text.

2.3   Other assets are held temporarily. Newsagents sell newspapers on the same day that they get them, and weekly newspapers and monthly magazines also have a short shelf life. The quicker a business can sell goods the more profit it is likely to make. We usually call these **current assets**.

Liabilities

> ### KEY TERM
>
> A **liability** is something which is owed to somebody else.

2.4 '**Liabilities**' is the accounting term for the debts of a business. Debts are owed to **creditors.** Here are some examples of liabilities.

Liability	Description
A **bank loan** or **bank overdraft**	The **liability** is the amount which must eventually be repaid to the **bank**.
Amounts owed to **suppliers** for purchases not yet paid for	A boat builder buys timber on credit from a **timber merchant**. He does not have to pay for the timber until after it has been delivered. Until the boat builder pays what he owes, the timber merchant will be his **creditor**.
Taxation owed to the **government**	Tax is paid on profits. There is a time lag between when profits arise and when tax is due. The **government** is the business's **creditor** during this time.

3   DOUBLE ENTRY ACCOUNTING

> ### ASSESSMENT ALERT
>
> You must expect to be thoroughly assessed on double entry at the Intermediate stage in both Central and Devolved Assessments. It is *vital* that you have a sound knowledge and understanding of double entry and confidence in using it.

3.1 Double entry accounting or book-keeping allows us to keep the accounting equation balanced, because **every financial transaction gives rise to two accounting entries, one a debit and the other a credit.**

DEBIT To own/have ↓	CREDIT To owe ↓
AN ASSET INCREASES eg new office furniture	AN ASSET DECREASES eg pay out cash
CAPITAL/ A LIABILITY DECREASES eg pay a creditor	CAPITAL/A LIABILITY INCREASES eg buy goods on credit
INCOME DECREASES eg cancel a sale	INCOME INCREASES eg make a sale
AN EXPENSE INCREASES eg incur advertising costs	AN EXPENSE DECREASES eg cancel a purchase
Left hand side	**Right hand side**

THE ACCOUNTING EQUATION

Assets = Capital + Liabilities

15

Cash transactions: double entry

3.2   Remember that the **cash book** is a book of prime entry while the **cash account** is the ledger account in the general ledger. **It is the cash account which is part of the double entry system**.

Book of prime entry		Ledger account in general ledger
Cash book	*Summary posted to*	Cash account

Many businesses use computerised accounts systems which have an integrated cash book meaning it is both a book of prime entry **and** a ledger account.

3.3   The rule to remember about the cash account is as follows.

     (a)   A **cash payment** is a **credit entry** in the cash account. Here the **asset** (cash) **is decreasing**. Cash may be paid out to pay an expense (such as rates) or to purchase an asset (such as a machine). The **matching debit entry** is therefore made in the appropriate **expense** account or **asset** account.

     (b)   A **cash receipt** is a **debit entry** in the cash account. Here the **asset** (cash) **is increasing**. Cash might be received by a retailer who makes a cash sale. The **matching credit entry** is made in the **sales** account.

Cash transactions	DR	CR
Sell goods for cash	Cash	Sales
Buy goods for cash	Purchases	Cash

3.4   EXAMPLE: DOUBLE ENTRY FOR CASH TRANSACTIONS

In the cash book of a business, the following transactions have been recorded.

(a)   A cash sale (ie a receipt) of £40
(b)   Payment of an electricity bill totalling £270
(c)   Buying some goods for cash at £150
(d)   Paying cash of £320 for an office desk

How would these four transactions be posted to the ledger accounts? Which ledger accounts should they be posted to? Don't forget that each transaction will be posted twice, in accordance with the rule of double entry.

3.5   SOLUTION

     (a)   The two sides of the transaction are:

         (i)   Cash is received (**debit** entry in the cash account).
         (ii)   Sales increase by £40 (**credit** entry in the sales account).

CASH ACCOUNT

	£		£
Sales a/c	40		

SALES ACCOUNT

	£		£
		Cash a/c	40

(The entry in the cash account is cross-referenced to the sales account and vice-versa. Finding where the other half of the double entry is, is therefore possible.)

(b) The two sides of the transaction are:

    (i)   Cash is paid (**credit** entry in the cash account).

    (ii)   Electricity expense increases by £270 (**debit** entry in the electricity account).

CASH ACCOUNT

	£		£
		Electricity a/c	270

ELECTRICITY ACCOUNT

	£		£
Cash a/c	270		

(c) The two sides of the transaction are:

    (i)   Cash is paid (**credit** entry in the cash account).

    (ii)   Purchases increase by £150 (**debit** entry in the purchases account).

CASH ACCOUNT

	£		£
		Purchases a/c	150

PURCHASES ACCOUNT

	£		£
Cash a/c	150		

(d) The two sides of the transaction are:

    (i)   Cash is paid (**credit** entry in the cash account).

    (ii)   Assets increase by £320 (**debit** entry in office furniture account).

CASH ACCOUNT

	£		£
		Office furniture a/c (desk)	320

OFFICE FURNITURE (ASSET) ACCOUNT

	£		£
Cash a/c	320		

The **summary cash account** for these transactions would be.

CASH ACCOUNT

	£		£
Sales a/c	40	Electricity a/c	270
		Purchases a/c	150
		Office furniture a/c	320

Activity 1.3

In the cash book of a business, the following transactions have been recorded on 7 December 20X7.

(a)   Received £37 for a cash sale
(b)   Paid a rent bill of £6,000
(c)   Paid £1,250 cash for some goods
(d)   Paid £4,500 cash for some office shelves

Task

Draw up the appropriate ledger ('T') accounts and show how these four transactions would be posted to them.

Credit transactions: double entry

3.6   Not all transactions are settled immediately in cash. Goods might be purchased on **credit terms**, so that the suppliers would be **creditors** of the business until settlement was made in cash. Equally, the business might grant credit terms to its customers who would then be **debtors** of the business. No entries are made in the cash book when a credit transaction occurs, because no cash has been received or paid. Where are the details of the transactions entered?

3.7   The solution to this problem is to use **ledger accounts for debtors and creditors.**

CREDIT TRANSACTIONS	DR	CR
Sell goods on credit terms	Debtors	Sales
Receive cash from debtor	Cash	Debtors
Net effect = cash transaction	Cash	Sales
Buy goods on credit terms	Purchases	Creditors
Pay cash to creditor	Creditors	Cash
Net effect = cash transaction	Purchases	Cash

The net effect is the same as for a cash transaction – the only difference is that there has been a time delay during which the debtor/creditor accounts have been used.

3.8   EXAMPLE: CREDIT TRANSACTIONS

Recorded in the sales day book and the purchase day book are the following transactions.

(a)   The business sells goods on credit to a customer Mr Ahmed for £3,200.
(b)   The business buys goods on credit from a supplier Blip Ltd for £2,000.

How and where are these transactions posted in the general ledger accounts?

17

3.9 SOLUTION

(a)

DEBTORS ACCOUNT

	£		£
Sales a/c	3,200		

SALES ACCOUNT

	£		£
		Debtors account	3,200

(b)

CREDITORS ACCOUNT

	£		£
		Purchases a/c	2,000

PURCHASES ACCOUNT

	£		£
Creditors a/c	2,000		

3.10 EXAMPLE CONTINUED: WHEN CASH IS PAID TO CREDITORS OR BY DEBTORS

Suppose that the business paid £2,000 to Blip Ltd a month later. The two sides of this new transaction are:

(a) Cash is paid (**credit** entry in the cash account)

(b) The amount owing to creditors is reduced (**debit** entry in the creditors account).

CASH ACCOUNT

	£		£
		Creditors a/c	2,000

CREDITORS ACCOUNT

	£		£
Cash a/c	2,000		

3.11 If we now bring together the two parts of this example, the original purchase of goods on credit and the eventual settlement in cash, we find that the accounts appear as follows.

CASH ACCOUNT

	£		£
		Creditors a/c	2,000

PURCHASES ACCOUNT

	£		£
Creditors a/c	2,000		

CREDITORS ACCOUNT

	£		£
Cash a/c	2,000	Purchases a/c	2,000

3.12 The **two entries in the creditors account cancel each other out**, showing that no money is owing to creditors any more. We are left with a credit entry of £2,000 in the cash account and a debit entry of £2,000 in the purchases account. These are the entries which would have been made to record a **cash** purchase of £2,000. After the business has paid off its creditors it is in the same the position as a business which has made cash purchases of £2,000. The accounting records reflect this similarity.

3.13 This also applies when a **customer settles his debt**. In the example above when Mr Ahmed pays his debt of £3,200 the two sides of the transaction are:

(a) Cash is received (**debit** entry in the cash account).

(b) The amount owed by debtors is reduced (**credit** entry in the debtors account).

CASH ACCOUNT

	£		£
Debtors a/c	3,200		

DEBTORS ACCOUNT

	£		£
		Cash a/c	3,200

The accounts recording this sale to, and payment by, Mr Ahmed now appear as follows.

CASH ACCOUNT

	£		£
Debtors a/c	3,200		

SALES ACCOUNT

	£		£
		Debtors a/c	3,200

DEBTORS ACCOUNT

	£		£
Sales a/c	3,200	Cash a/c	3,200

3.14 The **two entries in the debtors account cancel each other out**, while the entries in the cash account and sales account reflect the same position as if the sale had been made for cash.

Activity 1.4

Identify the **debit** and **credit** entries in the following transactions.

(a) Bought a machine on credit from Angelo, cost £6,400
(b) Bought goods on credit from Barnfield, cost £2,100
(c) Sold goods on credit to Carla, value £750
(d) Paid Daris (a creditor) £250
(e) Collected £300 from Elsa, a debtor
(f) Paid wages of £5,000
(g) Received rent bill of £1,000 from landlord Graham
(h) Paid rent of £1,000 to landlord Graham
(i) Paid an insurance premium of £150

Activity 1.5

Your business has the following transactions.
(a) The sale of goods on credit
(b) Credit notes to credit customers upon the return of faulty goods
(c) Daily cash takings paid into the bank

Task

For each transaction identify clearly:

(a) The original document(s).
(b) The book of prime entry for the transaction.
(c) The way in which the data will be incorporated into the double entry system.

4 POSTING FROM THE DAY BOOKS

Sales day book to debtors control account

4.1 Here is an example of a sales day book.

SALES DAY BOOK

Date 20X7	Invoice	Customer	Sales ledger folio	Total amount invoiced £	Book sales £	Stationery sales £
Sept 10	540	Socco Shops	SL 22	207.45	159.09	48.36
	541	Richards Ltd	SL 31	42.77	42.77	
	542	Sandy & Co	SL 04	113.82		113.82
	543	Bits and Pieces Co	SL 42	2,409.00	1,861.80	547.20
				2,773.04	2,063.66	709.38

4.2 How do we post these transactions to the general ledger, and which accounts do we use in the general ledger?

4.3 We post the total of the **total amount invoiced column** to the **debit** side of the **debtors control account** (often called the **sales ledger control account,** or simply **debtors account**). The **credit** entries go to the **sales accounts,** in this case, book sales and stationery sales.

DEBTORS CONTROL ACCOUNT

	£		£
Book sales	2,063.66		
Stationery sales	709.38		
	2,773.04		

BOOK SALES

	£		£
		Debtors control	2,063.66

STATIONERY SALES

	£		£
		Debtors control	709.38

4.4 That is why the analysis of sales is kept. The same reasoning lies behind the analyses kept in other books of prime entry.

4.5 So how do we know how much individual debtors owe? We keep two sets of accounts running in parallel – the **debtors control account** in the general ledger and the memorandum **sales ledger** (individual debtor accounts). **Only the debtors control account is actually part of the double entry system,** but **individual** debtors' transactions are posted to the sales ledger from the sales day book.

Purchases day book to creditors control account

4.6 Here is the page of the purchases day book which we saw earlier.

PURCHASE DAY BOOK

Date 20X7	Supplier (2)	Purchase ledger folio (1)	Total amount invoiced £	Purchases (3) £	Expenses £
Sept 15	R Dysan Ltd	PL 14	177.50	177.50	
	Peters and Co	PL 07	221.08	221.08	
	Western Electric	PL 23	49.00		49.00
	Regally Ltd	PL 19	380.41	380.41	
			827.99	778.99	49.00

4.7 We post the **total** of the **total amount invoiced column** to the **credit** side of the **creditors control account** (or **purchase ledger control account**, or simply **creditors account**) in the general ledger. The **debit** entries are to the different expense accounts, in this case purchases and electricity.

CREDITORS CONTROL ACCOUNT

	£		£
		Purchases	778.99
		Electricity	49.00
			827.99

BPP PUBLISHING

PURCHASES

	£		£
Total creditors	778.99		

ELECTRICITY

	£		£
Total creditors	49.00		

4.8 We keep a separate record of how much we owe individual creditors by keeping two sets of accounts running in parallel – the **creditors control account** in the general ledger, part of the double-entry system, and the memorandum **purchase ledger** (individual creditors' accounts). Individual creditors' transactions are entered in their purchase ledger account from the purchase day book.

4.9 Section summary

CREDIT TRANSACTIONS	DR		CR	
	Memorandum	*General ledger**	*General ledger**	*Memorandum*
Sell goods to Bits & Pieces Co	Sales ledger: Bits & Pieces	Debtors control a/c	Sales	–
Receive cash from Bits & Pieces Co	–	Cash a/c	Debtors control a/c	Sales ledger: Bits & Pieces
Buy goods from R Dysan Ltd	–	Purchases	Creditors control a/c	Purchase ledger: R Dysan Ltd
Pay cash to R Dysan Ltd	Purchase ledger: R Dysan Ltd	Creditors control a/c	Cash a/c	–

* Individual transactions included in **totals** posted from books of prime entry.

Key learning points

- Business transactions are initially recorded on source documents. Records of the details on these documents are made in books of prime entry.

- Invoices and credit notes are important documents which must contain specific information.

- The main books of prime entry are as follows.
    - Sales day book
    - Purchase day book
    - Journal
    - Cash book
    - Petty cash book

- Most accounts are contained in the general ledger (or nominal ledger).

- There are two kinds of discount.
    - **Trade discount**: a reduction in the cost of goods
    - **Cash (or settlement) discount**: a reduction in the amount payable to the supplier

- An **asset** is something of value which a business owns or has the use of.

- A **liability** is something which is owed to somebody else.

- The rules of double entry state that every financial transaction gives rise to two accounting entries, one a debit, the other a credit. It is vital that you understand this principle, which we will investigate in more depth in the next chapter.

- A **debit** is one of the following.
    - An increase in an asset
    - An increase in an expense
    - A decrease in a liability

- A **credit** is one of the following.
    - An increase in a liability
    - An increase in income
    - A decrease in an asset

Quick quiz

1   What are books of prime entry?

2   What is recorded in the sales day book?

3   What is a trade discount?

4   What is a cash discount?

5   Does a debit entry on an asset account increase or decrease the asset?

6   What is the double entry when goods are sold for cash?

7   What is the double entry when goods are purchased on credit?

Answers to quick quiz

1   The books of prime entry record all the documented transactions undertaken by the company.

2   The sales day book records the list of invoices sent out to customers each day.

3   A reduction in the amount of money demanded from a customer.

4   An optional reduction in the amount of money repayable by a customer.

5   It increases the asset balance.

6   *Debit* Cash; *Credit* Sales.

7   *Debit* Purchases; *Credit* Creditors account.

2 From ledger accounts to the trial balance

This chapter contains

1   The sales ledger

2   The purchase ledger

3   Control accounts

4   VAT

5   The journal

6   The trial balance

7   Computerised systems

Learning objectives

- Identify and record in ledgers all income and expenditure in accordance with the organisation's policies, regulations, procedures and timescales

- Prepare relevant control accounts

- Use the transfer journal

- Produce a trial balance

- Understand and know how to record information in ledger accounts

- Analyse income and expenditure

- Understand the function and form of accounts recording income and expenditure

Performance criteria

5.2.1 All income and expenditure is correctly identified and recorded in the appropriate records

5.2.3 The organisation's policies, regulations, procedures and timescales in relation to recording income and expenditure are observed

5.3.1 Relevant accounts and reconciliations are correctly prepared to allow the preparation of final accounts

5.3.6 The trial balance is accurately prepared and, where necessary, a suspense account is opened and reconciled

Range statement

5.2.1 Records: day book; journal; ledger

5.3.1 Sources of information: ledger; bank reconciliation; creditors' reconciliation; debtors' reconciliation

5.3.2 Discrepancies and unusual features: insufficient data has been provided; inconsistencies within the data

Knowledge and understanding

Use of transfer journal; methods of analysing income and expenditure; principles of double entry accounting; function and form of a trial balance, profit and loss account and balance sheet for sole traders, partnerships, manufacturing accounts and club accounts

ASSESSMENT ALERT

This is an important chapter. It describes how to record income and expenditure (in the ledgers) and then collect and collate information for the completion of final accounts (via the trial balance). Make sure you study it carefully, work through each example and make good attempts at activities.

1 THE SALES LEDGER

IMPORTANT

You should have covered the sales and purchase ledgers in your Foundation or bookkeeping studies. Sections 1 and 2 are for revision purposes.

Impersonal accounts and personal accounts

1.1 Accounts in the general ledger (ledger accounts) relate to types of income, expense, asset, liability – rent, rates, sales, debtors, creditors etc – rather than to the person to whom the money is paid or from whom it is received. They are therefore called **impersonal accounts**. However, there is also a need for **personal accounts,** mostly for debtors and creditors. These are contained in the sales ledger and purchase ledger.

> **KEY TERM**
>
> **Personal accounts** include details of transactions which have already been summarised in ledger accounts (eg sales invoices are recorded in sales and total debtors, payments to creditors in the cash and creditors control accounts). **The personal accounts do not form part of the double entry system**, as otherwise transactions would be recorded twice over (ie two debits and two credits for each transaction). They are **memorandum** accounts.

Personal accounts in the sales ledger

> **KEY TERM**
>
> The **sales ledger** consists of a number of personal **debtor** accounts. They are separate accounts for each individual customer, and they enable a business to keep a continuous record of how much a debtor owes the business at any time. The sales ledger is often also known as the **debtors ledger**.

1.2 The **sales day book** provides a chronological record of invoices sent out by a business to credit customers. This might involve large numbers of invoices per day or per week. A customer might appear a number of times in the sales day book, for purchases made on credit on different occasions. At any one time, a customer may owe money on several unpaid invoices.

1.3 A business should also keep a record of how much money each individual credit customer owes, and what this total debt consists of. The need for a **personal account for each customer** is therefore a practical one.

  (a) A customer might ask how much is owed. Staff must be able to tell him.

  (b) **Statements** are usually sent to credit customers at the end of each month, showing how much they owe, and itemising new invoices sent out and payments received during the month.

  (c) Managers want to keep a check on the **credit position** of individual customers, and to ensure that no customer is exceeding his credit limit by purchasing more goods.

  (d) Most important is the need to **match payments received against debts owed**. A business must be able to set off a payment against the customer's debt and establish how much is still owed.

1.4 Sales ledger accounts are written up as follows.

  (a) When individual entries are made in the **sales day book** (invoices issued), they are also made in the **debit side** of the relevant customer account in the sales ledger.

  (b) When individual entries are made in the **cash book** (payments received), or sales returns day book, they are also made in the **credit side** of the relevant customer account.

1.5 Each customer account has a reference or code number. It is the reference which is the 'sales ledger folio' in the **sales day book** and the **cash book**. Amounts are **entered** from the sales day book and the cash book into the sales ledger.

1.6 Here is an example of how a sales ledger account is laid out.

	BITS & PIECES			A/c no: SL 42
		£		£
10.9.X2 Balance b/d		670.50		
10.9.X2 Sales: SDB 253				
(invoice no 543)		2,409.00	10.9.X2 Balance c/d	3,079.50
		3,079.50		3,079.50
11.9.X2 Balance b/d		3,079.50		

1.7 The debit side shows amounts owed by Bits & Pieces. When Bits & Pieces pays some of the money it owes it will be recorded in the cash book (receipts). This receipt will be posted individually to the **credit** side of the personal account, the **credit** side of the debtors control account (as part of a total) and the **debit** side of the cash account (as part of a total). If Bits & Pieces paid £670.50 on 10.9.X2, it would appear as follows.

	BITS & PIECES			A/c no: SL 42
		£		£
10.9.X2 Balance b/d		670.50	10.9.X2 Cash	670.50
10.9.X2 Sales: SDB 253				
(invoice no 543)		2,409.00	10.9.X2 Balance c/d	2,409.50
		3,079.50		3,079.50
11.9.X2 Balance b/d		2,409.50		

The balance owed on 11.9.X2 is now £2,409.50 instead of £3,079.50, due to the receipt of £670.50 which came in on 10.9.X2.

2 THE PURCHASE LEDGER

KEY TERM

The **purchase ledger**, like the sales ledger, consists of a number of **personal creditor accounts**. These are separate accounts for each individual supplier, and they enable a business to keep a continuous record of how much it owes each supplier at any time. The purchase ledger is often known as the **bought ledger** or the **creditors ledger**.

2.1 After transactions are recorded in the purchase day book, cash book, or purchase returns day book – ie after entries are made in the books of prime entry – they are also entered in the relevant supplier account in the purchase ledger. The **double entry posting**, however, is to the **creditors control account** and the **cash account**.

2.2 Here is an example of how a purchase ledger personal account is laid out.

R DYSAN		A/c no: PL 14	
	£		£
		15.9.X2 Balance b/d	320.00
15.9.X2 Balance c/d	497.50	15.9.X2 Purchases: PDB 258	177.50
	497.50		497.50
		16 9.X2 Balance b/d	497.50

2.3 The credit side of this personal account shows amounts owing to R Dysan. If a payment was made it would be entered into the cash book (payments) and subsequently be entered individually into the **debit** side of the personal account, and posted to the **debit** side of the creditors control account (as part of a total) and the **credit** side of the cash account (as part of a total). If the business paid R Dysan £150 on 15 September 20X2, it would appear as follows.

R DYSAN		A/c no: PL 31	
	£		£
15.9.X2 Cash	150.00	15.9.X2 Balance b/d	320.00
15.9.97 Balance c/d	347.50	15.9.X2 Purchases: PDB 258	177.50
	497.50		497.50
		16.9.X2 Balance b/d	347.50

2.4 The balance owed on 16.9.X2 is now £347.50 due to the £150 payment made during 15.9.X2.

3 CONTROL ACCOUNTS

3.1 The debtors control and the creditors control accounts are part of the double entry system in the general ledger, and effectively duplicate the entries to the sales ledger and purchase ledger respectively. So why do we need them? They act as a **control.**

> **KEY TERMS**
>
> • A **control account** is an account in the *general ledger* in which a record is kept of the **total** value of a number of similar but individual items. Control accounts are used chiefly for debtors and creditors. **They should agree with the total of the individual balances** and act as a check to ensure that all transactions have been recorded correctly in the individual ledger accounts.
>
> • The **debtors control account** (also known as the **sales ledger control account, or simply the debtors account**) is a control account in which records are kept of transactions involving all debtors **in total**. It is posted with **totals** from the **sales day book, sales returns day book** and the **cash book**. The balance on the debtors control account at any time will be the total amount due to the business at that time from its debtors, and will agree with the total of the sales ledger accounts.
>
> • The **creditors control account** (also known as the **purchase ledger control account, or simply the creditors account**) is an account in which records are kept of transactions involving all creditors **in total**, being posted with **totals** from the **purchase day book, purchase returns day book** and the **cash book**. The balance on the creditors control account at any time will be the total amount owed by the business at that time to its creditors, and will agree with the total of the purchase ledger accounts.

3.2 It is the **control account balances** which will appear in the **final accounts** of the business; the sales ledger and purchase ledger act as memoranda for the list of individual account balances.

3.3 Although control accounts are used mainly in accounting for debtors and creditors, they can also be kept for other items, such as **stocks** of goods, **wages and salaries** and **VAT**. The same principles apply to all the other control accounts in the general ledger.

3.4 **Section summary**

Control accounts	Posted from	With	Agrees with	Part of general ledger double entry?
Debtors control	Sales day book Sales returns day book Cash book	Totals	Sales ledger balances in total	✓
Creditors control	Purchase day book Purchase returns day book Cash book	Totals	Purchase ledger balances in total	✓

Memorandum accounts	Posted from	With	Agrees with	Part of general ledger double entry?
Sales ledger	As for control a/c	Individual transactions	Debtors control a/c	×
Purchase ledger	As for control a/c	Individual transactions	Creditors control a/c	×

CENTRAL ASSESSMENT ALERT

In Central Assessments you can assume, unless told otherwise, that the debtors control/sales ledger control account, and the creditors control/purchase ledger control account are contained in the general ledger and form part of the double entry. The individual accounts of debtors and creditors will be in the debtors' ledger and creditors' ledger (sales ledger and purchase ledger) and will therefore be regarded as memorandum accounts.

Activity 2.1

Janet Andrew is a sole trader. She has an integrated manual system of accounting, divided into various accounts to form a Cash Book, a Sales Ledger, a Purchases Ledger (all of which are part of the double entry) and a General Ledger. The following transactions have taken place.

(a) The landlord, is paid £2,300 rent by cheque.

(b) £475 of goods are sold to R Sobers on credit.

(c) A credit note for £105 is issued to M Felix for goods returned.

(d) £3,175 of goods are purchased for resale from Rachet Ltd on credit.

(e) Equipment costing £15,000 is purchased by the business by cheque.

(f) A £75 installation charge invoice is received for the equipment. A cheque is issued for this amount.

(g)   The £3,175 owing to Rachet Ltd is paid by cheque.

Task

For each transaction identify clearly:

(a)   The name of the account to be debited.
(b)   The ledger in which the account to be debited would be located.
(c)   The name of the account to be credited.
(d)   The ledger in which the account to be credited would be located.

Activity 2.2

(a)   Name **five** accounts which may be found in the general ledger.
(b)   Explain what **control accounts** are and what they are used for.

---

4   VAT

4.1   Many business transactions include VAT. Most invoices show any VAT charged separately.

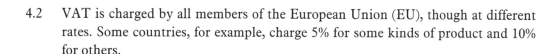

> **KEY TERMS**
>
> • **VAT** is a tax levied on the sale of goods and services. It is administered by HM Customs & Excise, but most of the work of collecting the tax falls on VAT-registered businesses, which hand the tax they collect over to the authorities.
>
> • **Output tax**: VAT charged on goods and services sold by a business.
>
> • **Input tax**: VAT paid on goods and services bought in by a business.

4.2   VAT is charged by all members of the European Union (EU), though at different rates. Some countries, for example, charge 5% for some kinds of product and 10% for others.

4.3   In the UK there are two rates of VAT.

(a)   **Standard rate**. This is (usually) $17\frac{1}{2}\%$ of the value of the goods. If you sell a standard rated item for £100 you must charge £17.50 in tax, so that the total paid by your customer is £117.50. (Note that the prices you pay in shops generally **include** VAT.)

(b)   **Zero-rate**. This is 0%.

Not all goods and services have VAT on them. **Exempt items** are not part of the VAT system.

Calculating VAT

4.4   If a product has a **net price** of, say £120 and VAT is to be added, then it is just a question of working out $17\frac{1}{2}\%$ of £120.

$$\text{VAT} = £120 \times 17.5/100$$
$$= £21$$

4.5 The **gross price** of the product is therefore £120 + £21 = £141. **It is always true that gross price = net price + VAT.**

	£
Purchaser pays gross price	141
Customs and Excise take VAT	(21)
Seller keeps net price	120

4.6 If you are given the gross price of a product (say, £282), then you can work out the VAT included by multiplying by 17.5/117.5 (or 7/47).

£282 × 17.5/117.5 = £42

Therefore the net price must be £282 – £42 = £240.

Activity 2.3

The gross price of Product A is £705 and the net price of Product B is £480. What is the VAT charged on each product?

Input and output VAT

4.7 Usually output VAT (on sales) exceeds input VAT (on purchases). The excess is paid over to **Customs & Excise**. If output VAT is less than input VAT in a period, Customs & Excise will refund the difference to the business. So, if a business pays out more in VAT than it receives from customers it will receive the difference.

Output tax received	Input tax paid	Total	Treatment
£1,000	£(900)	£100 received	Pay to C&E
£900	£(1,000)	£(100) paid	Refund from C&E

4.8 EXAMPLE: INPUT AND OUTPUT TAX

A company sells goods for £127,350 including VAT in a quarter (three months of a year). It buys goods for £101,290 including VAT. What amount will it pay to or receive from HM Customs & Excise for the quarter (round to the nearest £)?

4.9 SOLUTION

The **output tax** will be:

	£
£127,350 × $\dfrac{17.5}{117.5}$ =	18,967

The **input tax** will be:

£101,290 × $\dfrac{17.5}{117.5}$ =	15,086

The tax **payable** is the output tax less the input tax = | 3,881 |

ASSESSMENT ALERT

If you come up with a figure which runs to more than two decimal places when you apply the VAT fraction, simply **round down** to the nearest penny unless told otherwise. (You will become competent in the full VAT rounding rules when you study Unit 7 at Intermediate.)

Discounts and VAT

4.10 If a **cash discount** is offered for prompt payment of the invoice, VAT is computed on the amount **after** deducting the discount (at the highest rate offered), even if the discount is not taken.

Accounting for VAT

4.11 We now outline how VAT is accounted for. (The principles will be similar for most types of sales tax, in most countries, although the rates may differ.)

Sales revenue

4.12 VAT charged is not kept – it is paid back to Customs & Excise. It follows that the **record of sales revenue should not include VAT.**

4.13 EXAMPLE: ACCOUNTING FOR OUTPUT VAT

If a business sells goods for £600 + £105 VAT, ie for £705 gross price, the sales account should only record the £600 excluding VAT. The accounting entries for the sale would be as follows.

DEBIT	Cash **or** debtors	£705	
CREDIT	Sales		£600
CREDIT	VAT account (output VAT)		£105

4.14 Input VAT paid on purchases is not shown as a cost of the business – if it is reclaimed from C&E. However, input VAT is included in purchases if it is **not recoverable.**

(a) If input VAT is **recoverable,** the cost of purchases should exclude the VAT. If a business purchases goods on credit for £400 + recoverable VAT £70, the transaction would be recorded as follows.

DEBIT	Purchases	£400	
DEBIT	VAT account (input VAT)	£70	
CREDIT	Trade creditors		£470

(b) If the input VAT is **not recoverable,** the cost of purchases must include the tax, because it is the business itself which must bear the cost of the tax.

DEBIT	Purchases	£470	
CREDIT	Trade creditors		£470

This topic is covered in more detail in Unit 7 *Reports and Returns*

When is VAT accounted for?

4.15 VAT is accounted for **when it first arises** – when recording **credit purchases/sales in credit transactions**, and when recording **cash received or paid in cash transactions**.

VAT in credit transactions

4.16 For credit sales the total amount invoiced, including VAT, will be recorded in the **sales day book**. The analysis columns separate the VAT from sales income as follows.

Date	Total	Sales income	VAT
	£	£	£
Johnson & Co	2,350	2,000	350

4.17 Supplier invoices are recorded in total, including VAT, in the **purchase day book**. The analysis columns separate the recoverable input VAT from the purchase cost as follows.

Date	Total	Purchase cost	VAT
	£	£	£
Mayhew (Merchants)	564	480	84

4.18 When debtors pay, or creditors are paid, there is no need to show the VAT in an analysis column of the cash book, because the VAT was recorded **when the sale or purchase was made, not when the debt was settled**.

VAT in cash transactions

4.19 VAT charged on **cash sales** or VAT paid on **cash purchases will be analysed in a separate column of the cash book**. Output VAT, having arisen from the cash sale, must be credited to the VAT account. Similarly, input VAT paid on cash purchases, must be debited to the VAT account. The cash book for Peter Jeffries (Chapter 1, 1.18) would be written up as shown on page 37 if items (a), (e) and new item (l) were cash transactions involving VAT.

The VAT account

4.20 The VAT paid to or recovered from the authorities each quarter is the **balance on the VAT account**. This is the control account to which these items are posted.

- The total input VAT in the purchases day book (**debit**)
- The total output VAT in the sales day book (**credit**)
- VAT on cash sales (**credit**)
- VAT on cash purchases (**debit**)

4.21 If Peter Jeffries is invoiced for input VAT of £175 on his credit purchases and charges £450 VAT on his credit sales on 10 January 1998, his VAT account would be as follows.

PETER JEFFRIES: CASH BOOK

RECEIPTS

Date 20X8	Narrative	Folio	Discount allowed	Total	Output VAT on cash sales	Receipts from debtors	Cash sales	Other
10-Jan	Balance b/d			2,100.00				
	(a) Cash sale			220.00	32,77		187.23	
	(b) Debtor pays: Khan	SL07	100.00	3,000.00		3,000.00		
	(c) Debtor pays: Likert	SL12		1,480.00		1,480.00		
	(d) Debtor pays: Lee	SL10	70.00	2,330.00		2,330.00		
	(e) Cash sale			190.00	28,30		161.70	
	(f) Fixed asset sale			370.00				370.00
			170.00	9,690.00	61.07	6,810.00	348.93	370.00
11-Jan	Balance b/d			1,595.25				

PAYMENTS

Date 20X8	Narrative	Folio	Total	Input VAT on cash purchases	Payments to creditors	Expenses	Fixed assets
10-Jan	(g) Creditor paid: Price	PL27	1,250.00		1,250.00		
	(h) Creditor paid: Burn	PL16	2,420.00		2,420.00		
	(i) Telephone expense		235.00			235.00	
	(j) Gas expense		640.00			640.00	
	(k) Plant & machinery purchase		3,400.00				3,400.00
	(l) Cash purchase: Stationery		149.75	22.30		127.45	
			8,094.75	22.30	3,670.00	1,002.45	3,400.00
	Balance c/d		1,595.25				
			9,690.00	22.30	3,670.00	1,002.45	3,400.00

VAT ACCOUNT

	£		£
Purchase day book (input VAT)	175.00	Sales day book (output VAT)	450.00
Cash (input VAT)	22.30		
		Cash (output VAT)	61.05
Balance c/d (owed to Customs & Excise)	313.75		
	511.05		511.05

4.22 Payments to or refunds from Customs and Excise do not usually coincide with the end of the accounting period of a business. At the end of the period there will be a VAT account balance owing to or from Customs and Excise.

CENTRAL ASSESSMENT ALERT

Unless you are told otherwise you should make the following postings for VAT transactions.

CREDIT TRANSACTIONS	DR		CR	
	Memorandum	*General ledger*	*General ledger*	*Memorandum*
Sell goods on credit	Sales ledger 117.50	Debtors control 117.50	Sales 100.00 VAT 17.50	–
Receive cash in settlement	–	Cash 117.50	Debtors control 117.50	Sales ledger 117.50
Buy goods on credit	–	Purchases 100.00 VAT 17.50	Creditors control 117.50	Purchase ledger 117.50
Pay cash in settlement	Purchase ledger 117.50	Creditors control 117.50	Cash 117.50	–
CASH TRANSACTIONS				
Sell goods for cash	–	Cash 117.50	Sales 100.00 VAT 17.50	–
Buy goods for cash	–	Purchases 100.00 VAT 17.50	Cash 117.50	–

Activity 2.4

The following transactions were recorded in a company's books during one week of its trading year.

	£
Trade purchases (at list price)	4,500
Sales on credit (at list price)	6,000
Purchase of a van	10,460
Entertaining	360
Purchase of a car for a sales representative	8,600

A cash discount of £300 is available on the sales. All items are given exclusive of VAT at 17.5%. If the balance on the VAT account was £2,165 at the beginning of the week, what is the balance at the end of the week?

SSAP 5

4.23 **SSAP 5 Accounting for value added tax** states the following.

(a) Sales shown in the profit and loss account should **exclude VAT on taxable outputs (sales).** If gross sales must be shown then the VAT in that figure must also be shown as a deduction in arriving at the sales exclusive of VAT.

(b) **Irrecoverable VAT** relating to fixed assets and other items separately disclosed should be included in their cost where material and practical.

(c) The **net amount due to (or from) HM Customs & Excise** should be included in the total for creditors (or debtors), and need not be separately disclosed.

Activity 2.5

A VAT registered trader, made the following transactions during the year ended 31 March 20X8.

	£
Sales taxable at standard rate	500,000
Sales taxable at zero rate	25,000
Exempt sales	75,000
Expenses subject to input tax	300,000

Included in expenses is the purchase of a motor car for £8,000 and a delivery van for £10,000. All figures are given **exclusive** of VAT. No particular purchase is attributable to any particular sale.

How much input tax can be reclaimed by the trader?

---

5 THE JOURNAL

5.1 You should remember that one of the **books of prime entry** is the **journal**.

> **KEY TERM**
>
> The **journal** is a record of unusual movements between accounts. It records any double entries made which do not arise from the other books of prime entry.

5.2 Whatever type of transaction is being recorded, the **format of a journal entry** is:

Date		Folio		
			£	£
DEBIT	Account to be debited		X	
CREDIT	Account to be credited			X
Narrative to explain the transaction				

(Remember: the ledger accounts are written up to include the transactions listed in the journal.)

5.3 A narrative explanation **must** accompany each journal entry. It is required for audit and control, to indicate the purpose and authority of every transaction which is not first recorded in a book of prime entry.

5.4 EXAMPLE: JOURNAL ENTRIES

The following is a summary of the transactions of the Manon Beauty Salon of which David Blake is the sole proprietor.

1 October	Put in cash of £5,000 as capital
	Purchased brushes, combs , clippers and scissors for cash of £485
	Purchased hair driers from Juno Ltd on credit for £240
30 October	Paid three months rent to 31 December of £500
	Collected and paid in to the bank takings of £1,000
31 October	Gave Mrs Sweet a perm and manicure on credit for £100.

Show the transactions by means of journal entries.

5.5 SOLUTION

JOURNAL

			£	£
1 October	DEBIT	Cash	5,000	
	CREDIT	David Blake: capital account		5,000
		Initial capital introduced		
1 October	DEBIT	Brushes, combs and scissors account	485	
	CREDIT	Cash		485
		The purchase for cash of brushes etc as fixed assets		
1 October	DEBIT	Hair dryer account	240	
	CREDIT	Sundry creditors account		240
		The purchase on credit of hair driers as fixed assets		
30 October	DEBIT	Rent account	500	
	CREDIT	Cash		500
		The payment of rent to 31 December		
30 October	DEBIT	Cash	1,000	
	CREDIT	Sales (or takings account)		1,000
		Cash takings		
31 October	DEBIT	Debtors account	100	
	CREDIT	Sales account (or takings account)		100
		The provision of a hair-do and manicure on credit		

The correction of errors

5.6 The journal is most commonly used to record **corrections of errors that have been made** in writing up the general ledger accounts. Errors corrected by the journal **must be capable of correction by means of a double entry** in the ledger accounts. The error must not have caused total debits and total credits to be unequal. (When errors are made which break the double entry rule – that debits equal credits – a suspense account is used, covered later in this text.)

Journal vouchers

5.7 Journal entries might be logged, not in a single 'book' or journal, but on a separate slip of paper, called a **journal voucher**.

> ### KEY TERM
>
> A **journal voucher** is used to record the equivalent of one entry in the journal.

5.8 The use of journal vouchers is fairly widespread because of:

- The **repetitive nature** of certain journal entries (vouchers can be pre-printed to standardise the narrative of such entries, and to save time in writing them out)

- A voucher is able to hold **more information** than a conventional journal record

6 THE TRIAL BALANCE

6.1 There is no foolproof method for making sure that all entries have been posted to the correct ledger account, but a technique which shows up the more obvious mistakes is to prepare a **trial balance**.

> ### KEY TERM
>
> A **trial balance** is a list of ledger balances shown in debit and credit columns. It is frequently known as the **list of balances.**

Collecting together the ledger accounts

6.2 Before you draw up a trial balance, you must have a **collection of ledger accounts**. These are the ledger accounts of James McHugh, a sole trader.

CASH

	£		£
Capital: James McHugh	10,000	Rent	4,200
Bank loan	3,000	Shop fittings	3,600
Sales	14,000	Trade creditors	7,000
Debtors	3,300	Bank loan interest	130
		Incidental expenses	2,200
		Drawings	1,800
			18,930
		Balancing figure: the amount of cash left over after payments have been made	11,370
	30,300		30,300

BPP
PUBLISHING

CAPITAL (JAMES McHUGH)

	£		£
		Cash	10,000

BANK LOAN

	£		£
		Cash	3,000

PURCHASES

	£		£
Trade creditors	7,000		

TRADE CREDITORS

	£		£
Cash	7,000	Purchases	7,000

RENT

	£		£
Cash	4,200		

SHOP FITTINGS

	£		£
Cash	3,600		

SALES

	£		£
		Cash	14,000
		Debtors	3,300
			17,300

DEBTORS

	£		£
Sales	3,300	Cash	3,300

BANK LOAN INTEREST

	£		£
Cash	130		

OTHER EXPENSES

	£		£
Cash	2,200		

DRAWINGS ACCOUNT

	£		£
Cash	1,800		

The first step is to 'balance' each account.

Balancing ledger accounts

6.3 At the end of an accounting period, a balance is struck on each account in turn. This means that all the **debits** on the account are totalled and so are all the **credits**.

- If the **total debits exceed the total credits** the account has a **debit balance**

- If the **total credits exceed the total debits** then the account has a **credit balance**

Action		Eg James McHugh's Cash a/c
Step 1	Calculate a total for both sides of each ledger account.	Dr £30,300, Cr £18,930
Step 2	Deduct the lower total from the higher total.	£(30,300 – 18,930) = £11,370
Step 3	Insert the result of Step 2 as the balance c/d on the side of the account with the lower total.	Here it will go on the credit side, because the total credits on the account are less than the total debits
Step 4	Check that the totals on both sides of the account are now the same	Dr £30,300, Cr £(18,930 + 11,370) = £30,300
Step 5	Insert the amount of the balance c/d as the new balance b/d on the other side of the account. The new balance b/d is the balance on the account.	The balance b/d on the account is £11,370 Dr

6.4 In our simple example, there is very little balancing to do.

(a) Both the trade creditors account and the debtors account balance off to zero.
(b) The cash account has a debit balance (the new balance b/d) of £11,370.
(c) The total on the sales account is £17,300, which is a credit balance.

The other accounts have only one entry each, so there is no totalling to do.

Collecting the balances on the ledger accounts

6.5 If the basic principle of double entry has been correctly applied throughout the period the **credit balances will equal the debit balances** in total. This is illustrated by collecting together the balances on James McHugh's accounts.

	Debit	*Credit*
	£	£
Cash	11,370	
Capital		10,000
Bank loan		3,000
Purchases	7,000	
Trade creditors	–	–
Rent	4,200	
Shop fittings	3,600	
Sales		17,300
Debtors	–	–
Bank loan interest	130	
Other expenses	2,200	
Drawings	1,800	
	30,300	30,300

6.6 The order of the various accounts listed in the **trial balance** does not matter, it is not a document that a company *has* to prepare. It is just a method used to test the accuracy of the double entry bookkeeping.

What if the trial balance shows unequal debit and credit balances?

6.7 If the trial balance does not **balance** there must be an **error in recording of transactions in the accounts**. A trial **balance** will **not** disclose the following types of errors.

- The **complete omission** of a transaction, because neither a debit nor a credit is made

- A posting to the correct side of the ledger, but to a **wrong account** (also called **errors of commission**)

- **Compensating errors** (eg debit error of £100 is cancelled by credit £100 error elsewhere)

- **Errors of principle** (eg cash received from debtors being debited to the debtors control account and credited to cash instead of the other way round)

We shall see how to deal with these types of problem later in this text.

6.8 EXAMPLE: TRIAL BALANCE

As at the end of 29 November 20X1, your business High & Mighty has the following balances on its ledger accounts.

Accounts	*Balance* £
Bank loan	15,000
Cash	13,080
Capital	11,000
Rates	2,000
Trade creditors	14,370
Purchases	16,200
Sales	18,900
Sundry creditors	2,310
Debtors	13,800
Bank loan interest	1,000
Other expenses	12,500
Vehicles	3,000

During 30 November the business made the following transactions.

(a) Bought materials for £1,400, half for cash and half on credit
(b) Made £1,610 sales, £1,050 of which were for credit
(c) Paid wages to shop assistants of £300 in cash

You are required to draw up a trial balance showing the balances as at the end of 30 November 20X1.

6.9 SOLUTION

Step 1 Put the opening balances into a trial balance, so decide which are debit and which are credit balances.

Account	Debit £	Credit £
Bank loan		15,000
Cash	13,080	
Capital		11,000
Rates	2,000	
Trade creditors		14,370
Purchases	16,200	
Sales		18,900
Sundry creditors		2,310
Debtors	13,800	
Bank loan interest	1,000	
Other expenses	12,500	
Vehicles	3,000	
	61,580	61,580

Step 2 Take account of the effects of the three transactions which took place on 30 November 20X1.

			£	£
(a)	DEBIT	Purchases	1,400	
	CREDIT	Cash		700
		Trade creditors		700
(b)	DEBIT	Cash	560	
		Debtors	1,050	
	CREDIT	Sales		1,610
(c)	DEBIT	Other expenses	300	
	CREDIT	Cash		300

Step 3 Amend the trial balance for these entries.

HIGH & MIGHTY: TRIAL BALANCE AT 30 NOVEMBER 20X1

	12/11/20X1 DR	12/11/20X1 CR		Transactions DR	Transactions CR		30/11/20X1 DR	30/11/20X1 CR
Bank loan		15,000						15,000
Cash	13,080		(b)	560	700	(a)	12,640	
					300	(c)		
Capital		11,000						11,000
Rates	2,000						2,000	
Trade creditors		14,370			700	(a)		15,070
Purchases	16,200		(a)	1,400			17,600	
Sales		18,900			1,610	(b)		20,510
Sundry creditors		2,310						2,310
Debtors	13,800		(b)	1,050			14,850	
Bank loan interest	1,000						1,000	
Other expenses	12,500		(c)	300			12,800	
Vehicles	3,000						3,000	
	61,580	61,580		3,310	3,310		63,890	63,890

Activity 2.6

Bailey Hughes started trading as a wholesale bookseller on 1 June 20X7 with a capital of £10,000 with which he opened a bank account for his business.

During June the following transactions took place.

June	1	Bought warehouse shelving for cash from Warehouse Fitters Ltd for £3,500
	2	Purchased books on credit from Ransome House for £820
	4	Sold books on credit to Waterhouses for £1,200
	9	Purchased books on credit from Big, White for £450
	11	Sold books on credit to Books & Co for £740
	13	Paid cash sales of £310 from the warehouse shop intact into the bank
	16	Received cheque from Waterhouses in settlement of their account
	17	Purchased books on credit from RUP Ltd for £1,000
	18	Sold books on credit to R S Jones for £500
	19	Sent cheque to Ransome House in settlement of their account
	20	Paid rent of £300 by cheque
	21	Paid delivery expenses of £75 by cheque
	24	Received £350 from Books & Co on account
	30	Drew cheques for personal expenses of £270 and assistant's wages £400
	30	Settled the account of Big, White

Task

(a) Record the foregoing in appropriate books of original entry.
(b) Post the entries to the ledger accounts.
(c) Balance the ledger accounts where necessary.
(d) Extract a trial balance at 30 June 20X7.

Tutorial note. You are not required to complete any entries in personal accounts, nor are folio references required.

Activity 2.7

Refer back to the analysed sales day book in paragraph 1.7 of Chapter 1, and the cash book extract below.

CASH BOOK: RECEIPTS

Date	Details	Folio	Discount allowed	Total	Receipts from debtors
			£	£	£
20X7					
10/9	Richards Ltd	SL 31	12.50	672.09	672.09
10/9	Socco Shops	SL 22	15.00	829.02	829.02
10/9	Sandy & Co	SL 04	5.00	267.00	267.00
			32.50	1,768.11	1,768.11

Post the relevant amounts to the sales ledger account below and calculate a balance.

SOCCO SHOPS					A/c no: SL 22
Date 20X7	Details	Amount £	Date 20X7	Details	Amount £
9/9	Balance b/d	1,209.76			

Activity 2.8

Refer back to the analysed purchases day book in paragraph 1.10 of Chapter 1, and the cash book extract below.

CASH BOOK: PAYMENTS

Date	Details	Folio	Discount received £	Total £	Payments to suppliers £
20X7					
10/9	Western Electric	PL 23	70.00	3,097.92	3,097.92
10/9	Regally Ltd	PL 19	13.00	780.35	780.35
10/9	Peters & Co	PL 07	–	2,781.09	2,781.09
			83.00	6,659.36	6,659.36

Post the relevant amounts to the purchases ledger account below and calculate a balance.

REGALLY LTD					A/c no: PL 19
Date 20X7	Details	Amount £	Date 20X7	Details	Amount £
			9/9	Balance b/d	7,109.82

BPP PUBLISHING

Activity 2.9

Make the appropriate postings from the cash book and the day books in Activities 2.7 and 2.8 to the sales ledger control account and the purchases ledger control account below.

	SALES LEDGER CONTROL ACCOUNT				
Date 20X7	Details	Amount £	Date 20X7	Details	Amount £
9/9	Balance b/d	202,728.09			

	PURCHASES LEDGER CONTROL ACCOUNT				
Date 20X7	Details	Amount £	Date 20X7	Details	Amount £
			9/9	Balance b/d	189,209.76

Activity 2.10

The following totals have been extracted from the day books as at 18 June 20X6:

Day book	Transaction	Net £	VAT £	Total £
Sales day book	Sales (SDB)	52,728.19	9,227.43	61,955.62
Sales returns day book	Sales returns (SRDB)	7,209.87	1,261.72	8,471.59
Purchases day book	Purchases (PDB)	72,290.29	12,650.80	84,941.09
Purchases returns day book	Purchases returns (PRDB)	15,287.35	2,675.28	17,962.63
Cash book	Sales (CB)	726.76	127.18	853.94
	Purchases (CB)	829.19	145.10	974.29
	Receipts from debtors (CB)			72,109.29
	Payments to creditors (CB)			45,290.02
Petty cash book	Purchases (PCB)	56.00	9.80	65.80

Post these transactions to the relevant ledger accounts below and carry down balances. Post both sales and sales returns to the same account, and purchases and purchases returns to the same account.

VAT ACCOUNT					
Date 20X6	Details	Amount £	Date 20X6	Details	Amount £
			17/6	Balance b/d	45,029.83

SALES					
Date 20X6	Details	Amount £	Date 20X6	Details	Amount £
			17/6	Balance b/d	459,945.09

PURCHASES					
Date 20X6	Details	Amount £	Date 20X6	Details	Amount £
17/6	Balance b/d	290,673.87			

DEBTORS CONTROL					
Date 20X6	Details	Amount £	Date 20X6	Details	Amount £
17/6	Balance b/d	423,900.92			

CREDITORS CONTROL					
Date 20X6	Details	Amount £	Date 20X6	Details	Amount £
			17/6	Balance b/d	215,876.09

PETTY CASH					
Date 20X6	Details	Amount £	Date 20X6	Details	Amount £
17/6	Balance b/d	200.00			

CASH					
Date 20X6	Details	Amount £	Date 20X6	Details	Amount £
17/6	Balance b/d	23,907.35			

7 COMPUTERISED SYSTEMS

7.1 So far we have looked at the way an accounting system is organised. You should note that all of the books of prime entry and the ledgers may be either **hand-written books** or **computer records**. Most businesses use computers, ranging from one **PC** to huge **mainframe computer systems**.

7.2 All computer activity can be divided into three processes.

Areas	Activity
Input	Entering data from original documents
Processing	Entering up books and ledgers and generally sorting the input information
Output	Producing any report desired by the managers of the business, including financial statements

Activity 2.11

Your friend Lou Dight believes that computerised accounting systems are more trouble than they are worth because 'you never know what is going on inside that funny box'.

Required

Explain briefly why computers might be useful in accounting.

7.3   Computers and computing are covered in detail in your studies for Unit 20 **Information Technology.**

Batch processing and control totals

KEY TERM

Batch processing: similar transactions are gathered into batches, then sorted and processed by the computer.

7.4   Inputting individual invoices into a computer for processing (**transaction processing**), is time consuming and expensive. Invoices can be gathered into a **batch** and **input and processed all together**. Batches can vary in size, depending on the type and volume of transactions and on any limit imposed by the system on batch sizes.

KEY TERM

Control totals are used to ensure there are no errors when the batch is input. They are used to ensure the total value of transactions input is the same as that previously calculated.

7.5   Say a batch of 30 sales invoices has a manually calculated total value of £42,378.47. When the batch is input, the computer adds up the total value of the invoices and produces a total of £42,378.47. The control totals agree, therefore no further action is required.

7.6   If the control total does **not agree** then checks have to be carried out until the difference is found. An invoice might not have been entered or the manual total incorrectly calculated.

Key learning points

- The accounts in the general ledger are **impersonal accounts**. There are also **personal accounts** for debtors and creditors and these are contained in the sales ledger and purchase ledger.

- A **control account** is in the general ledger. It is a record of the total value of a number of similar but individual items.

  - A **debtors control account** records transactions involving all debtors in total. It is posted with totals from the sales day book, sales returns day book and the cash book.

  - A **creditors control account** records transactions involving all creditors in total, being posted with totals from the purchases daybook, purchase returns day book and the cash book.

- VAT rules can be quite complex, but the main points to remember are:

  - **Output VAT** is charged on sales and **input VAT** is charged on purchases.

  - To analyse the VAT on a VAT-inclusive figure, multiply this figure by 17.5/117.5.

- A **journal** is a record of unusual movements between accounts. The journal format is:

Date		Folio	£	£
DEBIT	Account to be debited		X	
CREDIT	Account to be credited			X

  Narrative to explain the transaction

- Balances on ledger accounts can be collected in a **trial balance**. The debit and credit balances should be **equal**.

- **Computer accounting systems** perform the same tasks as manual accounting systems, but they can cope with greater volumes of transactions and process them at a faster rate.

Quick quiz

1   Personal accounts form part of the double entry system. True or false?

2   How do control accounts act as a check?

3   What is the double entry for goods sold on credit which are standard-rated for VAT and whose price excluding VAT is £100?

4   Why must a journal include a narrative explanation?

5   A journal can be used to correct errors which cause the total debits and credits to be unequal. True or false?

6   What is the other name for a trial balance?

7   If the total debits in an account exceed the total credits, will there be a debit or credit balance on the account?

8   What types of error will *not* be discovered by drawing up a trial balance?

9   What are the advantages of batch processing?

Answers to quick quiz

1   False. They are memoranda accounts only.

2   Control accounts should agree with the total of the individual balances of debtors or creditors to show all transactions have been recorded correctly.

3   *Debit* Trade debtors £117.50; *Credit* Sales £100.00; *Credit* VAT £17.50.

4   The narrative is required for audit and control, to show the purpose and authority of the transaction.

5   False. The error must be capable of correction by double entry.

6   The trial balance is also sometimes called the 'list of account balances'.

7   There will be a debit balance on the account.

8   There are four types, summarised as: complete omission; posted to wrong account; compensating errors; errors of principle.

9   Batch processing is faster than transaction processing and checks on input can be made using control totals.

3 Content of accounts

This chapter contains

1   What is a business?

2   A business is separate from its owner(s)

3   The accounting equation

4   The business equation

5   Creditors and debtors

6   The balance sheet: an overview

7   Fixed assets

8   Current assets

9   Liabilities

10   The trading, profit and loss account: an overview

11   Capital and revenue items

Learning objectives

- Understand the distinction between capital and revenue expenditure

- Understand the types and characteristics of different assets

- Identify the function and form of final accounts for sole traders

- Appreciate the function and form of a balance sheet and a trading, profit and loss account

- Appreciate the need to present accounts in the correct form

Performance criteria

5.3.2 All relevant information is correctly identified and recorded

Knowledge and understanding

Principles of double entry accounting; distinction between capital and revenue expenditure, what constitutes capital expenditure

BPP PUBLISHING

1 WHAT IS A BUSINESS?

1.1 To prepare final accounts effectively we need to understand that a **business** invests money in resources (eg it buys buildings, machinery etc; it pays employees) in order to make money for its owners – a **profit**. Business enterprises vary in character, size and complexity. They range from small businesses (the local shopkeeper or plumber) to large ones (Microsoft). But the **profit objective** applies to all of them.

KEY TERM

Profit is the excess of income over expenditure. When expenditure exceeds income, the business is running at a **loss**.

1.2 One of the jobs of an accountant is to **measure** income, expenditure and profit. This can be an inexact science, although the accounting fundamentals of **double entry accounting** make sure that there is a firm set of principles underlying this process.

1.3 Learning to account for a business involves building a clear picture of what a business consists of. A thorough revision of what a business **owns** and **owes** – its **assets** and **liabilities**, is needed.

2 A BUSINESS IS SEPARATE FROM ITS OWNER(S)

2.1 In accounting terms, a business is **always a separate entity from its owner(s)**; but there are two aspects to this situation: the strict legal position and the convention adopted by accountants.

The legal position

2.2 Many businesses are carried on in the form of **limited companies**. The owners of a limited company are its **shareholders**, who may be few in number (as with a small, family-owned company) or numerous (ie a public company whose shares are quoted on the Stock Exchange).

2.3 **The law recognises a company as a legal entity, quite separate from its owners.**

(a) A company may, **in its own name**, acquire assets, incur debts, and enter into contracts.

(b) If a company **owns** less than it **owes** (its assets are not enough to meet its liabilities), the company as a separate entity might become 'bankrupt', but the owners of the company would not usually be required to pay the debts from their own private resources. The company's debts are not debts of the shareholders.

This is **limited liability**: the shareholder's liability is **limited** to the amount they 'put in' to the company (how much the company asked for their shares on issue).

2.4 The case is different, in law, when a business is carried on by an individual (a **sole trader**) or by a group of individuals (a **partnership or a club**). Suppose Fiona Middleton sets up a hairdressing business trading as 'Hair by Fiona'. The law makes no distinction between Fiona, the individual, and the business known as 'Hair by Fiona'. Any debts of the business which cannot be met from business assets must be met by Fiona.

2.5 The **law recognises no distinction between the business of a sole trader, partnership – or club – and its owner(s).**

Activity 3.1

Distinguish between the terms 'enterprise', 'business', 'company' and 'firm'.

The accounting convention

2.6 **A business must always be treated as a separate entity from its owners when preparing accounts.** This applies whether or not the business is recognised in law as a separate entity, whether the business is carried on by a company, a sole trader a partnership or a club.

Activity 3.2

Fill in the missing words to make sure you understand the concept of the business as a separate entity and how the law differs from accounting practice.

A business is a _____ entity, distinct from its _____ . This applies to _____ businesses. However, the law only recognises a _____ as a legal entity separate from its _____ . The liability of shareholders to the company is _____ to the amount the company asks them to pay for their shares.

---

3   THE ACCOUNTING EQUATION

3.1 Since a business is a separate entity from its owners, it follows that:

- The business can owe money to, or be owed money by, its owners
- The assets and liabilities of the business are separate to those of the owners

This is a fundamental rule of accounting. **The assets and liabilities of a business must always be equal (the accounting equation)**, we saw this in Chapter 1. Let's demonstrate this with an example, which we will build up during this chapter.

3.2 EXAMPLE: THE ACCOUNTING EQUATION

On 1 September 20X9, Courtney opens a mail order business at home, to sell CDs. He has saved £5,000 for this purpose.

When the business is set up, an 'accountant's picture' can be drawn of what it **owns** and what it **owes**. The business begins by **owning** the cash that Courtney has provided, £5,000, and, because it is a separate entity in accounting terms, **it owes this amount of money to its owner**. If Courtney changed his mind about going into business, the business would be dissolved by the 'repayment' of the cash by the business to Courtney.

3.3 **Accountants treat capital as money owed to the proprietor by the business**.

KEY TERM

Capital is an investment of money (funds) with the intention of earning a return. A business proprietor invests capital with the intention of earning **profit**. The business owes the capital and the profit to the proprietor.

3.4 Capital invested is a form of **liability**. As liabilities and assets are always equal amounts, we can state the accounting equation as follows.

THE ACCOUNTING EQUATION 1

Assets = Capital + Liabilities

3.5 For Courtney, as at 1 September 20X9:

Assets	=	*Capital*	+	*Liabilities*
£5,000 cash		£5,000 owed to Courtney		£0

3.6 EXAMPLE CONTINUED: DIFFERENT ASSETS

Courtney purchases a computer system from George at a cost of £1,600, cash. He also purchases CDs from a Soho trader for £720. Of the original £5,000, £2,680 remains after paying for the database and CDs. Courtney keeps £2,500 in the bank and draws £180 as petty cash. He is ready for his first mail drop on 3 September 20X7. How does the accounting equation look now?

3.7 SOLUTION

The assets and liabilities of the business have now altered, and at 3 September, before trading begins, the state of his business is as follows.

Assets	£	=	*Capital*	+	*Liabilities*
Computer system	1,600		£5,000		£0
CDs	720				
Cash at bank	2,500				
Cash in hand	180				
	5,000				

3.8 EXAMPLE CONTINUED: PROFIT INTRODUCED

In the week after 3 September Courtney does well. He sells all of the CDs for £1,500 cash.

Since Courtney has sold goods costing £720 to earn revenue of £1,500, he has earned a **profit** of £(1,500 – 720) = £780 on the week's trading to 10 September. How is this reflected in the accounting equation?

3.9 SOLUTION

Profit, like capital, belongs to the owner of a business: it is why he invested. The £780 belongs to Courtney. So long as the **business retains the profits, and does not pay anything to its owner, the retained profits are accounted for as an addition to the proprietor's capital.**

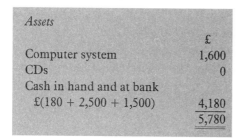

Assets		=	Capital		+	Liabilities
	£			£		
Computer system	1,600		Capital			
CDs	0		introduced	5,000		
Cash in hand and at bank			Retained			
£(180 + 2,500 + 1,500)	4,180		profit	780		
	5,780			5,780		£0

3.10 So we could expand the accounting equation as follows.

THE ACCOUNTING EQUATION 2

Assets = (Capital introduced + Retained profits) + Liabilities

Increase in net assets

KEY TERM

Net assets = Total assets – Total liabilities

3.11 We can re-arrange the accounting equation to calculate the total capital balance, which is the sum of capital introduced plus retained profit.

Assets – Liabilities	=	Capital
Net assets	=	Capital

3.12 At the beginning and end of the first week in September 20X9 Courtney's financial position was.

	Net assets	=		Capital
(a) At 3 September:	£(5,000 – 0)	=		£5,000
(b) At 10 September:	£(5,780 – 0)	=		£5,780
Increase in net assets	780	=	Retained profit for week	780

3.13 We can now state the following principles.

- A business's **net assets** represent **capital introduced** by the owner plus **retained profits** at any point in time.

- An **increase** in the business's net assets represents additional **profit made**.

- **Total** net assets at a later point represent capital introduced by the owner plus **increased** retained profit.

For example:

		£m			£m			£m
1 Jan	Net assets	170	= Capital introduced		20	+ Retained profit		150
1 Jan-31 Dec	Increase in net assets	34	=			Profit made in year		34
31 Dec	Total net assets	204	= Capital introduced		20	+ Total retained profit		184

Drawings

KEY TERM

Drawings are amounts of money taken out of a business by its owner(s).

3.14 EXAMPLE CONTINUED: DRAWINGS

Since Courtney has made a profit of £780 in the first week, he might draw some of the profits out of the business. Business owners need income for living expenses. Courtney decides to pay himself £500 as a 'wage', as a reward for his work.

As he is the business's **owner,** the £500 is **not** an expense to be deducted before arriving at the profit figure. It is **incorrect** to calculate the profit earned by the business as follows.

	£
Profit on sale of CDs	780
Less 'wages' paid to Courtney	500
Profit earned by business (incorrect)	280

Any amounts paid by a business to its owner are treated by accountants as withdrawals of profit (drawings), not as expenses incurred by the business. For Courtney's business, the true position is that the profit **earned** is the £780 surplus on the sale of CDs, but the profit **retained** in the business is £(780 – 500) = £280.

	£
Profit earned by business	780
Less profit withdrawn by Courtney as drawings	500
Profit retained in the business	280

The drawings are taken in cash, so the business loses £500 of its cash assets. After the drawings are made, the accounting equation would be restated as follows.

Assets	£	*Capital*	£	*Liabilities*
Database	1,600	Capital introduced	5,000	
CDs	0	Profit earned	780	
Cash £(4,180 – 500)	3,680	Less drawings	(500)	
	5,280		5,280	£0

The increase in net assets since trading operations began is now only £(5,280 − 5,000) = £280, which is the amount of the retained profits.

3.15 **Profits are capital as long as they are retained in the business**. When drawings are made, the business suffers a **reduction in capital**. We can therefore restate the accounting equation as:

THE ACCOUNTING EQUATION 3

Assets = Capital introduced + (Earned profit − Drawings) + Liabilities

3.16 These examples illustrate that the basic equation (Assets = Capital + Liabilities) always applies. Transactions affecting the business have a **dual effect** as shown in the table below.

	Asset	=	*Capital*	+	*Liabilities*
	Increase		Increase		
or	Increase				Increase
or			Increase		Decrease
or			Decrease		Increase
or	Decrease		Decrease		
or	Decrease				Decrease

Activity 3.3

Considering each transaction mark on the grid which area will be increased and which decreased. The first is done for you.

(a) The bank tells the business it no longer owes the bank £100 in bank charges.
(b) The business finds it has been overcharged £50 for some furniture it bought on credit.
(c) A gas bill of £200 is received by the business.
(d) The owner withdraws £500 from the business.
(e) Cash is introduced into the business by its owner.
(f) A car is bought by the business, for payment in 1 month's time.

Transaction	=	*Assets*	=	*Capital*	+	*Liabilities*
(a)				Increase		Decrease
(b)						
(c)						
(d)						
(e)						
(f)						

4 THE BUSINESS EQUATION

4.1 The business equation is an elaboration of the accounting equation which gives a definition of profits earned. The example of Courtney shows that **the profit earned in a time period is related to the increase in net assets of the business, the drawings of profits by the owner and the introduction of new capital.**

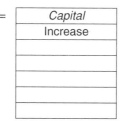

4.2   We know that: *Accounting equation*

| Assets | = | Capital | + | Liabilities | 1 |

which is the same as:

| Assets | = | Capital introduced
+ Retained profits | + | Liabilities | 2 |

which is the same as:

| Assets | = | Capital introduced
+ Profit earned
– Drawings | + | Liabilities | 3 |

4.3   Over time, **retained profit** (profit earned less drawings) increases the amount of capital in the business – it becomes **part of the opening balance of capital**. After another period of trading, additional profit will (hopefully) be earned. We should restate the accounting equation:

> ## THE ACCOUNTING EQUATION 4
>
> Assets =   Capital introduced   +   Liabilities
>   + Profit retained in previous periods
>   + Profit earned in current period
>   – Drawings

4.4   EXAMPLE CONTINUED: MORE PROFIT EARNED

On 11 September Courtney purchases more CDs for £2,000 cash. He employs Sheila agreeing a wage of £250 at the end of the week.

Trading for the week ended 17 September is again very brisk. Courtney and Sheila sell all the CDs for £4,200 cash. Courtney pays Sheila £250 and draws £500 himself. How do these transactions affect Courtney's capital?

4.5   SOLUTION

The accounting equation before trading begins on 11 September, and after trading ends on 17 September, can be set out as follows.

(a)   *Before trading begins* (11 September)

Assets		=	*Capital*		+	*Liabilities*
	£			£		
Database	1,600		Capital introduced	5,000		
CDs	2,000		Retained profit	280		
Cash £(3,680 – 2,000)	1,680			———		
	5,280			5,280		£0

(b) *After trading ends* (17 September)

The profit for the week is £1,950, computed as follows.

	£	£
Sales		4,200
Less: cost of goods sold	2,000	
Sheila's wage	250	
		2,250
Profit		1,950

Courtney withdraws £500 of this profit for his personal use.

Assets		=	Capital		+	Liabilities
	£			£		
Database	1,600		At 11 Sept	5,280		
CDs	0		Profits earned to 17 Sept	1,950		
Cash £(1,680 + 4,200			Less drawings	(500)		
– 250 – 500)	5,130					
	6,730			6,730		£0

More capital introduced

4.6   If a business is doing well, the owner may **invest more money** in the expectation of generating greater profit. If we include this in our accounting equation we will arrive at the **business equation**, which allows us to compute profit from the increase in net assets of the business, drawings and new capital introduced.

4.7   EXAMPLE: MORE CAPITAL INTRODUCED

On 17 September, in addition to the above, Courtney rents a lockup for £150 to store the CDs during the week. He pays the rent from his own pocket. How would this affect the accounting equation at the end of 17 September?

4.8   SOLUTION

After trading ends (17 September)

Profit for the week is now £1,800:

	£	£
Sales		4,200
Less: cost of goods sold	2,000	
Sheila's wage	250	
lockup rent	150	
		2,400
		1,800

Courtney withdraws £500 for his personal use and introduces £150 capital.

Assets		=	Capital		+	Liabilities
	£			£		
Database	1,600		At 11 Sept	5,280		
Goods	0		Capital introduced	150		
Cash £(1,680 + 4,200 –	5,130		Profits earned 17 Sept	1,800		
250 – 500)			Drawings	(500)		
	6,730			6,730		£0

4.9 So new capital introduced should also be brought into the accounting equation.

> ### THE ACCOUNTING EQUATION 5
>
> Assets = Capital introduced in previous periods + Liabilities
> + Profit retained in previous periods
> + Profit earned in current period
> + Capital introduced in current period
> – Drawings in current period

4.10 If we put Courtney's figures from Paragraph 5.8 into this, we get:

				£		£		£
Assets	6,730	=	Capital introduced in previous periods		5,000	+	0
			+ Profit retained in previous periods		280		
			+ Profit earned in current period		1,800		
			+ Capital introduced in current period		150		
			– Drawings in current period		(500)		
	6,730				6,730		0

The business equation

4.11 Profit earned in a period can be expressed in terms of transactions within the period.

PREVIOUS PERIODS	Assets at start of period	= Capital introduced in previous periods + Liabilities at start of period + Profit retained in previous periods

+

CURRENT PERIOD	Increase/decrease in assets (**I**)	= Profit earned in current period (**P**) + Increase/decrease in liabilities (**I**) + Capital introduced in current period (**C**) – Drawings in current period (**D**)

=

END OF CURRENT PERIOD	Total assets at end of period	= Total capital at end of period + Liabilities at end of period

4.12 Looking at the current period box above, we can state the business equation as follows.

> ### THE BUSINESS EQUATION
>
> Profit earned in current period
>
> = Increase/decrease in net assets in current period* + Drawings in current period – Capital introduced in current period
>
> P = I + D – C
>
> *This is the increase/decrease in assets less the increase/decrease in liabilities.

4.13 Let's see how Courtney's figures for 17 September plug into this equation.

Profit = Increase in net assets + Drawings – Capital introduced
= £(6,730 – 5,280) + £500 – £150
= £1,800

5 CREDITORS AND DEBTORS

Credit transactions

5.1 So far we have looked at **capital** (including profits) and certain types of **asset** (cash, goods for resale, fixed assets). We now look at two items which arise when goods and services are purchased or sold in a **credit transaction: debtors and creditors**.

5.2 Sales and purchases occur in two different ways, by cash or on credit.

    (a) A **sale** takes place at one of two points in time.

        (i) **Cash sales**. If the sale is for cash, the sale occurs when goods or services are given in exchange for immediate payment.

        (ii) **Credit sales** (goods are ordered and delivered before payment is received). The sale occurs when the business sends out an invoice for the goods or services supplied.

    (b) A **purchase** also takes place at one of two points in time.

        (i) **Purchases for cash**. The purchase occurs when the goods and cash exchange hands.

        (ii) **Purchases on credit**. The purchase occurs when the business receives the goods, accompanied by an invoice from the supplier.

5.3 With credit transactions, the **point in time when a sale or purchase is recognised in the accounts of the business** is *not* the same as **the point that cash is received or paid**. There is a **gap** in time between the sale or purchase and the eventual cash settlement. (Also, something might happen which results in the amount of cash paid (if any) being different from the original value of the sale or purchase on the invoice.)

> **KEY TERMS**
>
> - A **creditor** is a person from whom a business has **purchased** items and to whom a business **owes** money. A creditor is a **liability** of the business.
>
> - A **trade creditor** is a person a business owes money to for debts incurred in the course of trading operations. The term might refer to debts outstanding from the purchase of materials, components or goods for resale.
>
> - A **debtor** is a person to whom the business has **sold** items and by whom the business is **owed** money. A debtor is an **asset** of a business.
>
> - A **trade debtor** is a person who owes the business money for debts incurred in the course of trading operations ie because the business has sold its goods or services.

5.4   This should serve as a useful summary.

CREDIT TRANSACTIONS	
SALES by the business to a customer	PURCHASES by the business from a supplier
↓ creates a DEBTOR a customer who owes money to the business	↓ creates a CREDITOR a supplier who is owed money by the business
↓ recorded as an ASSET of the business	↓ recorded as a LIABILITY of the business
↓ settled when the business RECEIVES CASH	↓ settled when the business PAYS CASH

5.5   EXAMPLE CONTINUED: DEBTORS AND CREDITORS

The example of Courtney's mail order business will be continued further, by looking at the following transactions in the week to 23 September 20X9.

(a)   Courtney needs even more money in the business as he wants to move into mail order of portable CD players as well. He makes the following arrangements.

    (i)   He invests immediately a further £500 of his own capital.

    (ii)   Gary lends him £1,000 immediately. Gary tells him that he can repay the loan whenever he likes, but he must pay him interest of £10 per week. They agree that it will probably be quite a long time before the loan is eventually repaid.

(b)   Courtney is pleased with the progress of his business, so he buys a second-hand van to pick up CDs and CD players from his supplier and bring them to his lockup. Carver agrees to sell him a van on credit for £1,200. Courtney agrees to pay for the van after 30 days' trial use.

(c)   During the week to 23 September, Viv telephones him to ask whether he would sell him some special sound equipment. Courtney tells him that he will look for a supplier. After some investigations, he buys what Viv has asked for, paying £1,000 in cash to the supplier. Viv accepts delivery of the goods and agrees to pay £1,600 at a later date.

(d)   Courtney buys CDs and CD players costing £6,000. Of these purchases £5,000 are paid in cash, with the remaining £1,000 on 14 days' credit.

(e)   By 23 September, Courtney sells all his goods, earning £11,340 (all in cash). He takes drawings of £700 for his week's work. He pays Sheila £250 in cash. He decides to make the interest payment to Gary the next time he sees him.

(f)   There were no van or lockup expenses.

First of all we want to state the accounting equations:

- After Courtney and Gary have put more money into the business

- After the purchase of the van

- After the sale of goods to Viv

- After the purchase of goods for the week

- At the end of the week's trading on 23 September, and after drawings have been withdrawn from profit

Then we will state the business equation showing profit earned during the third week.

5.6 SOLUTION

There are a number of transactions to deal with here. We deal with them one at a time in chronological order, the numbers that change each time are in **bold type**.

(a) **The addition of Courtney's extra capital and Gary's loan**

Gary's loan is long term, but he is not an owner of the business, even though he has made a loan investment to it. He would only become an owner if he was offered a partnership in the business. To the business, Gary is a long-term creditor, and his investment is a **liability** of the business – it is not business capital.

The accounting equation after £(500 + 1,000) = £1,500 cash is introduced will be:

Assets	£	=	Capital	£	+	Liabilities	£
Database	1,600		As at end of 17 Sept	6,730		Loan	**1,000**
Goods	0		Additional capital	**500**			
Cash £(5,130+ 1,500)	**6,630**						
	8,230			7,230			1,000

(b) The **purchase of the van** (cost £1,200) is on credit.

Assets	£	=	Capital	£	+	Liabilities	£
Database	1,600		As at end of 17 Sept	6,730		Loan	1,000
Van	**1,200**		Additional capital	500		Creditor	**1,200**
Cash	6,630						
	9,430			7,230			2,200

(c) The **sale of goods to Viv** is on credit (£1,600), the cost to the business being £1,000 (cash paid). Viv, because he is paying later, is shown as a debtor.

Assets	£	=	Capital	£	+	Liabilities	£
Database	1,600		As at end of 17 Sept	6,730		Loan	1,000
Van	1,200		Additional capital	500		Creditor	1,200
Debtor	**1,600**		Profit on sale to Viv	**600**			
Cash £(6,630 – 1,000)	**5,630**						
	10,030			7,830			2,200

(d) **Purchase of goods for the week** (£5,000 cash and £1,000 on credit).

Assets		=	Capital		+	Liabilities	
	£			£			£
Database	1,600		As at end of 17 Sept	6,730		Loan	1,000
Van	1,200		Additional capital	500		Creditor for van	1,200
Goods	**6,000**		Profit on sale to Viv	600		Creditor for	
Debtor	1,600			7,830		goods	**1,000**
Cash £(5,630 – 5,000)	630						3,200
	11,030						

(e) After trading in the week to 23 September, **sales of goods** costing £6,000 earned **revenues** of £11,340. **Sheila's wages** were £250 (paid), Gary's **interest charge** is £10 (not paid yet) and **drawings** out of profits were £700 (paid). The profit for the week to 23 September may be calculated as follows, taking the full £10 of interest as a cost on that day.

	£	£
Sales		11,340
Cost of goods sold	6,000	
Wages	250	
Interest	10	
		6,260
Profits earned by 23 September		5,080
Profit on sale of goods to Viv		600
Total profit for the week		5,680

Assets		=	Capital		+	Liabilities	
	£			£			£
Database	1,600		As at end of 17 Sept	6,730		Loan	1,000
Van	1,200		Additional capital	500		Creditor for van	1,200
Goods	0		Profit on sale to			Creditor for	
Debtor	1,600		Uncle Viv	600		goods	1,000
Cash £(630 +			Profit for week	**5,080**		Creditor for	
11,340 – 250 – 700)	**11,020**		Drawings	**(700)**		interest payment	**10**
	15,420			12,210			3,210

5.7 The increase in the net assets of the business during the week was as follows.

	£
Net assets as at 23 September £(15,420 – 3,210)	12,210
Net assets as at 17 September	6,730
Increase in net assets in week	5,480

The business equation for the week ended 23 September is as follows. (Remember that extra capital of £500 was invested by Courtney.)

$$P = I + D - C$$
$$= £5,480 + £700 - £500$$
$$= £5,680$$

This confirms the calculation of total profit for the week.

Activity 3.4

Ann has £2,500 of capital invested in her business. Of this, only £1,750 has been provided by herself, the rest is a loan of £750 from Tim. What are the implications of this for the accounting equation?

Hint. The answer is not clear cut. There are different ways of looking at Tim's investment.

5.8 Since the **total of liabilities plus capital is always equal to total assets**, any transaction has a **dual effect** – if total assets changes then total liabilities plus capital changes, and *vice versa*. Alternatively, a transaction might decrease an asset whilst increasing other assets by the same value. If a business pays £50 cash for goods, its total assets will be unchanged, but as the amount of cash falls by £50, the value of goods in stock rises by £50.

5.9 There are **two sides to every business transaction** – we have seen this in the 'double entry' system of accounting. Every transaction is recorded twice in the accounts.

KEY TERM

Double entry accounting is the system of accounting which reflects the fact that:

- Every financial transaction gives rise to two accounting entries, one a **debit** and the other a **credit**

- The total value of **debit entries** is always equal to the total value of **credit entries**

5.10 Each asset, liability, expense item or income item has a **ledger account** in which debits and credits are made. Which account receives the credit entry and which receives the debit depends on the **nature of the transaction**, as we have seen above and in Chapters 1 and 2.

Activity 3.5

Try to explain the dual effects of each of the following transactions.

(a) A business receives a loan of £5,000 from its bank
(b) A business pays £800 cash to purchase a stock of goods for resale
(c) The proprietor of a business removes £50 from the till to buy her husband a birthday present
(d) A business sells goods costing £300 at a profit of £140
(e) A business repays a £5,000 bank loan, plus interest of £270

Activity 3.6

Draw up the ledger accounts for Courtney for the period 1 September 20X9 to 23 September 20X9, and extract a trial balance. Assume Courtney retains a petty cash float of £180 throughout and banks all receipts immediately. You will need the following ledger accounts: Cash, Capital, Retained profit, Fixed assets, Petty cash, Loan creditor, Debtor, Creditor for van, Creditors for purchases, Profit, Sales, Purchases, Lockup expense, Wages, Interest.

6 THE BALANCE SHEET: AN OVERVIEW

ASSESSMENT ALERT

You **do not** need to have to be able to **prepare** a balance sheet for Unit 5. However, an understanding of what it is and how it is made up, is very useful to you in showing what the ultimate aim of accounting is.

6.1 If you understand the accounting and business equations, you should have little difficulty in getting to grips with the **balance sheet** and **profit and loss account**.

KEY TERM

A **balance sheet** is a statement of the assets, liabilities and capital of a business at a given time. It is like a 'snapshot', since it records a still image of something which is continually changing. Typically, a balance sheet is prepared to show the assets, liabilities and capital at the **end** of the accounting period to which the financial statements relate.

6.2 A **balance sheet** is very similar to the **accounting equation** being:

Assets – Liabilities = Capital introduced + Retained profit

There are only two differences between a balance sheet and the accounting equation.

(a) The manner or **format** in which the assets and liabilities are presented
(b) The extra **detail** which is contained in a balance sheet

6.3 A balance sheet is divided into two halves, usually showing **capital** in one half and **net assets** (assets less liabilities) in the other.

NAME OF BUSINESS
BALANCE SHEET AS AT (DATE)

	£
Assets	X
Less liabilities	X
Net assets	X
Capital	X

The total value in one half of the balance sheet will equal the total value in the other half. You should readily understand this from the **accounting equation**.

6.4 The way assets and liabilities are categorised and presented in a balance sheet is a matter of choice. You may come across different formats. A typical balance sheet format is shown below. (It is a simplified version of the format prescribed for limited companies.)

BUSINESS NAME
BALANCE SHEET AS AT 31 DECEMBER 20X9

	£	£
Fixed assets		
Land and buildings	X	
Plant and machinery	X	
Fixtures and fittings	X̲	
		X
Current assets		
Stock	X	
Debtors	X	
Cash at bank and in hand	X̲	
	A̲	
Current liabilities		
Bank overdraft	X	
Trade creditors	X̲	
	B̲	
Net current assets (A − B)		X
Long-term creditors		(X)
Net assets		C̲
Capital		
Proprietor's capital		X
Retained profits (including previous and current period profits)		X̲
		C̲

Activity 3.7

Produce a simple balance sheet from Courtney's trial balance prepared in Activity 3.6 above.

---

7 FIXED ASSETS

7.1 Assets in the balance sheet are divided into **fixed** and **current** assets.

> ### KEY TERM
>
> A **fixed asset** is an asset acquired for use within the business (rather than for selling to a customer), with a view to earning income or making profits from its use, either directly or indirectly, over more than one accounting period.

The following examples are only ideas; you may come up with other assets for both.

Industry	Example of fixed asset
Manufacturing	A production machine, as it makes goods which are then sold.
Service	Equipment used by employees giving service to customers, such as testing machines and ramps in a garage, and furniture in a hotel.

7.2 To be a fixed asset in the balance sheet an item must satisfy two further conditions.

(a) It must be **used by the business**. For example, the proprietor's own house would not normally appear on the business balance sheet.

(b) The asset must have a **'life' in use of more than one year** (strictly, more than one 'accounting period', which might be more or less than one year).

8 CURRENT ASSETS

KEY TERM

Current assets are

- Items owned by the business with the intention of turning them into cash within one year (stocks of goods, and debtors)

- Cash, including money in the bank, owned by the business

Assets are 'current' in that they are flowing through the business.

Activity 3.8

The type of asset held by a business depends on the nature of its trading activities. Try to imagine what the main assets might be in the accounts of:

(a) A steel manufacturer
(b) A bank

8.1 EXAMPLE: TURNING STOCK AND DEBTORS INTO CASH WITHIN ONE YEAR

A trader, Boxer, runs a business selling farm and other machinery, and has a showroom which he stocks with machines for sale. He obtains the machines from a manufacturer, and pays for them cash on delivery (COD).

(a) If he sells a machine in a **cash sale**, the 'goods' are immediately converted back into cash. This cash might then be used to buy more machinery for re-sale.

(b) If he sells a machine in a **credit sale**, expecting payment in 30 days time, the machine will be given to the customer who then becomes a **debtor** of the business. The debtor will then pay what he owes, and Boxer will receive cash.

8.2 The machines, debtors and cash are all current assets. Why?

(a) The machines (**goods**) held in stock for re-sale are current assets, because Boxer intends to sell them within one year, in the normal course of trade.

(b) The **debtor** is a current asset, as he is expected to pay what he owes in 30 days.

(c) **Cash** is a current asset.

8.3 The transactions described above could be shown as a **cash cycle**.

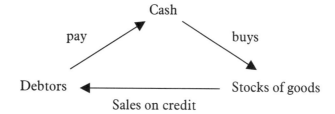

Cash is used to buy goods which are sold. Sales on credit create debtors, but eventually cash is earned from the sales. Some of the cash will then be used to replenish stocks.

Activity 3.9

Which of the following assets falls into the 'fixed' category and which should be treated as 'current'?

Asset	Business	Current or fixed
Van	Delivery firm	
Machine	Manufacturing business	
Car	Car trader	

---

9 LIABILITIES

9.1 In the case of liabilities, the main distinction is made between:

- **Current** liabilities
- **Long-term** liabilities

Current liabilities

> **KEY TERM**
>
> **Current liabilities** are debts of the business that must be paid within a year.

9.2 Examples of current liabilities include **loans** repayable in one year, **bank overdrafts, trade creditors** and **taxation payable**.

9.3 Some may argue that a **bank overdraft** is not a current liability, because a business can negotiate an overdraft facility for a long period of time. If an overdraft becomes a more permanent source of borrowing, it is really a long-term liability. However, you should normally expect to account for an overdraft as a current liability, since banks usually reserve the right to have repayment on demand, even if this rarely happens in practice.

Activity 3.10

Classify these items as long-term assets ('fixed assets'), short-term assets ('current assets') or liabilities.

	Fixed asset	Current asset	Liabilities
(a) A PC used in the accounts department of a retail store			
(b) A PC on sale in an office equipment shop			
(c) Wages due to be paid to staff at the end of the week			
(d) A van for sale in a motor dealer's showroom			
(e) A delivery van used in a grocer's business			
(f) An amount owing to a bank for a loan for the acquisition of a van, to be repaid over 9 months			

Long-term liabilities

KEY TERM

Long-term liabilities are debts which are not payable within the 'short term'. Any liability which is not current must be long-term. Just as 'short-term' by convention means one year or less, 'long-term' means more than one year.

9.4 Examples of long-term liabilities are bank loans **repayable after more than one year**.

Capital

9.5 The make-up of the 'capital' section of the balance sheet will vary, depending on the legal nature of the business. It will include **amounts invested** by the owner(s) in the business, plus **profits earned and retained** by the business.

Activity 3.11

Reproduced below is an example of a balance sheet.

CARLO
BALANCE SHEET AS AT 31 DECEMBER 20X7

	£	£
Fixed assets		
Land and buildings	57,000	
Plant and machinery	32,500	
Fixtures and fittings	6,000	
		95,500
Current assets		
Stocks	8,300	
Debtors	5,600	
Cash at bank and in hand	1,800	
	15,700	
Current liabilities		
Bank overdraft	2,100	
Trade creditors	3,900	
	6,000	
Net current assets		9,700
Total assets less current liabilities		105,200
Capital		
Proprietor's capital		40,000
Retained profits		65,200
		105,200

Required

Using the figures in the balance sheet above, check that the accounting equation holds good in the form: Assets = Capital + Liabilities.

10 THE TRADING, PROFIT AND LOSS ACCOUNT: AN OVERVIEW

ASSESSMENT ALERT

As with the balance sheet, you will **not** need to **prepare** a profit and loss account. We include this information so you can see where your Unit 5 studies fit into the whole picture.

KEY TERM

The **trading, profit and loss account** is a statement which matches the **revenue** earned in a period with the **costs** incurred in earning it. It is usual to distinguish between a **gross profit** (sales revenue less the cost of goods sold) and a **net profit** (being the gross profit less the expenses of selling, distribution, administration etc). If costs exceed revenue the business has made a **loss**.

10.1 Any organisation needs income (or revenue) from one or more sources. A **business** will **sell** its **goods or services** to **customers** in exchange for **cash**.

10.2 The income generated will be used to finance the activities of the business which incur **costs**: purchasing raw materials for use in manufacturing goods, purchasing ready-made goods for onward sale, purchasing equipment, paying expenses such as staff salaries, stationery, lighting and heating, rent and so on. **Revenue** less **costs** result in a **profit or loss**.

10.3 Many businesses try to distinguish between a **gross profit** earned on trading, and a **net profit**. They therefore prepare a statement called a **trading, profit and loss account.**

(a) In the first part of the statement (the **trading account**) revenue from selling goods and services is compared with **costs of acquiring, producing or supplying the goods** sold to arrive at a **gross profit figure**.

(b) From this, deductions are made in the second half of the statement (the **profit and loss account**) in respect of **expenses** to arrive at a **net profit figure**.

10.4 As with the balance sheet earlier in this chapter, it may help you to focus on the content of the trading, profit and loss account if you have an example in front of you.

BUSINESS NAME
TRADING, PROFIT AND LOSS ACCOUNT
FOR THE PERIOD ENDED (DATE)

	£
Sales	X
Cost of sales	X
Gross profit	X
Expenses	(X)
Net profit	X

The trading account

> ### KEY TERMS
>
> The **trading account** shows the gross profit for the accounting period.
>
> **Gross profit** is the difference between:
>
> - The value of sales
>
> - And the purchase cost or production cost of the goods sold

10.5 Different businesses will have different items shown as the cost of goods sold.

Business	Cost of goods sold
Retail	Purchase cost of goods bought from suppliers
Manufacturing	Cost of raw materials in the finished goods made, plus the cost of the labour required to make the goods, and often plus an amount of production 'overhead' costs (We shall look at manufacturing accounts in more detail in Chapter 11.)

The profit and loss account

> ## KEY TERMS
>
> The **profit and loss account** shows the net profit of the business.
>
> The **net profit** is:
>
> - The gross profit
>
> - **Plus** any other income from sources other than the sale of goods
>
> - **Minus** expenses which are not included in the cost of goods sold

11 CAPITAL AND REVENUE ITEMS

11.1 You have seen how the profit and loss account and balance sheet are developed, and how they are linked via the accounting equation. But, how do we distinguish between items which appear in the **calculation of profit**, and those which belong on the **balance sheet**?

11.2 Consider the following examples.

(a) A business sells goods worth £50,000 (for cash) during a month, and also borrows £20,000 from a bank. Its total receipts for the month are therefore £70,000.

(b) A business spends £25,000 buying some land, and receives £2,500 rent from the tenant farmer in the year.

How should these items be accounted for in the profit and loss account and balance sheet?

11.3 The answer is as follows. Note that there are always two entries.

(a) (i) The £50,000 of sales appear as **sales** in the **trading, profit and loss account** and as an **asset** (cash) in the **balance sheet**.

(ii) The £20,000 borrowed will not appear in the profit and loss account, but will be shown as an **asset** (cash) and a **liability** (loan) of £20,000 in the **balance sheet**.

(b) (i) The cost of the land will not be an expense in the profit and loss account. It will appear as a **fixed asset** in the **balance sheet**. The cash payment will decrease an **asset** (cash) in the **balance sheet**.

(ii) The rent of £2,500 will appear as **income** of the business in the **profit and loss account,** and as an **asset** (cash) in the **balance sheet**.

11.4 So how do we make these decisions? We must now turn our attention to the distinction between **capital** and **revenue** items.

Capital expenditure and revenue expenditure

11.5 EXAMPLE: REVENUE EXPENDITURE

If a bathroom business buys ten sinks for £4,000 (£400 each) and sells eight of them during an accounting period, it will have two sinks left at the end of the period. The full £4,000 is **revenue expenditure** but only (8 × £400) = £3,200 is a cost of goods sold during the period. The remaining £800 (cost of two sinks) will be included in the **balance sheet** in the stock of goods held – as a **current asset** valued at £800.

Capital income and revenue income

Additional capital, additional loans and the repayment of existing loans

11.6   The categorisation of capital and revenue items given above does not mention raising additional capital from the owner of the business, or raising and repaying loans. These are transactions which either:

(a)   add to cash **assets** creating corresponding **capital** or a **liability**; or

(b)   when a loan is repaid, reduce **liabilities** (loan) and **assets** (cash).

From your understanding of the accounting equation, you should see that these transactions would be reported on the balance sheet, **not** the profit and loss account.

Why is the distinction between capital and revenue items important?

11.7   Since **revenue expenditure** and **capital expenditure** are accounted for separately (in the **profit and loss account** and **balance sheet** respectively), the correct and consistent calculation of profit depends on the correct and consistent classification of items of revenue or capital. Failure to classify items correctly will lead to misleading profit figures.

ASSESSMENT ALERT

The distinction between revenue and capital items is fundamental to accounting properly for a business's transactions. You must be able to identify, record and account for revenue and expenditure accurately.

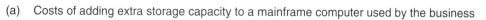

Activity 3.12

State whether each of the following items should be classified as 'capital' or 'revenue' expenditure or income for the purpose of preparing the trading, profit and loss account and the balance sheet.

(a)   Costs of adding extra storage capacity to a mainframe computer used by the business

(b)   Computer repair and maintenance costs

(c)   Sales by credit card

(d)   Cost of new machinery

(e)   Wages of the machine operators

BPP PUBLISHING

Key learning points

- It is vital that you acquire a thorough understanding of the **principles of double entry accounting** and are able to identify the characteristics of the balance sheet and the trading, profit and loss account.

- A **business** may be defined in various ways. Its purpose is to make a **profit** for its owner(s).

- **Profit** is the excess of income over expenditure.

- A business **owns assets** and **owes liabilities**.

- For accounting purposes it is important to keep business assets and liabilities **separate** from the personal assets and liabilities of the proprietor(s).

- **Assets** are items owned by a business and used by the business. They may be **fixed** (such as machinery or office premises), or **current** (such as stock, debtors and cash).

- **Liabilities** are amounts owed by a business to outsiders such as a bank or a trade creditor.

- **Assets = Capital + Liabilities** (the accounting equation).

- $P = I + D - C$ (the business equation).

- Double entry book-keeping requires that every transaction has two accounting entries, a **debit** and a **credit**.

- A **balance sheet** is a statement of the financial position of a business at a given moment in time.

- A **trading, profit and loss account** is a financial statement showing in detail how the profit or loss of a period has been made.

- A distinction is made in the balance sheet between **long-term liabilities** and **current liabilities**, and between **fixed assets** and **current assets**.

- **Fixed assets** are those acquired for long-term use within the business.

- 'Current' means 'within one year'. **Current assets** are expected to be converted into cash within one year. **Current liabilities** are debts which are payable within one year.

- An important distinction is made between **capital** and **revenue** items. If these are not identified correctly, then the resulting **profit figure** will be wrong and misleading.

Quick quiz

1   What is a business's prime objective?

2   Define profit.

3   What is an asset?

4   What is a liability?

5   How does the accounting view of the relationship between a business and its owner differ from the strictly legal view?

6   State the basic accounting equation.

7   What is capital?

8   What are drawings? Where do they fit in the accounting equation?

9   What does the business equation attempt to show?

10   What is the main difference between a cash and a credit transaction?

11   What is a creditor? What is a debtor?

12   Define double entry accounting.

13   What is a balance sheet?

14   How long does a business keep a fixed asset?

15   What are current liabilities?

16   Is a bank overdraft a current liability?

17   What is a trading, profit and loss account?

18   Distinguish between the trading account and the profit and loss account.

19   Distinguish between capital expenditure and revenue expenditure.

Answers to quick quiz

1   A business's prime objective is earning a profit.

2   Profit is the excess of income over expenditure.

3   An asset is something valuable which a business owns or has the use of.

4   A liability is something which is owed to someone else.

5   In accounting a business is always treated as a separate entity from its owners, even though in law there is not always a distinction (in the cases of a sole trader and a partnership).

6   Assets = Capital + Liabilities.

7   Capital is the investment of funds with the intention of earning a profit.

8   Drawings are the amounts of money taken out of a business by its owner. In the accounting equation drawings are a reduction of capital.

9   The business equation describes the relationship between a business's increase in net assets in a period, the profit earned, drawings taken and capital introduced.

10   The main difference between a cash and a credit transaction is timing – cash changes hands immediately in a cash transaction, with credit it changes hands some time after the initial sale/purchase.

11   A creditor is a person from whom a business has purchased items and to whom it owes money. A debtor is a person to whom the business has sold items and by whom it is owed money.

12   Double entry book-keeping is a system of accounting which reflects the fact that every financial transaction gives rise to two equal accounting entries, a debit and a credit.

13 A balance sheet is a listing of asset and liability balances on a certain date. The balance sheet gives a 'snapshot' of the net worth of the company at a single point in time.

14 At least one accounting period and usually several.

15 Amounts owed which must be paid soon, usually within one year.

16 Yes, usually, because it is repayable on demand (in theory at least).

17 A trading, profit and loss account matches revenue with the costs incurred in earning it.

18 The trading account shows the gross profit; the profit and loss account shows net profit (gross profit plus non-trading income, less expenses).

19 Capital expenditure results in a fixed asset appearing on the balance sheet. Revenue expenditure is trading expenditure or expenditure in maintaining fixed assets, which appears in the profit and loss account.

4 Accounting concepts and standards

This chapter contains

1   Introduction: accounting concepts and principles

2   The going concern concept

3   The prudence concept

4   The accruals concept or matching concept

5   The consistency concept

6   The materiality concept

7   Development of accounting standards

8   Relevant accounting standards

Learning objectives

- Understand basic accounting concepts and principles relating to matching, historic cost, accruals, consistency, prudence and materiality

Knowledge and understanding

Relevant legislation and regulations; main requirements of relevant SSAPs; basic accounting concepts and principles - matching of income and expenditure within an accounting period, historic cost, accruals, consistency, prudence, materiality

BPP PUBLISHING

1 INTRODUCTION: ACCOUNTING CONCEPTS AND PRINCIPLES

ASSESSMENT ALERT

The definitions given in this chapter as key terms are *very important*. You will be asked to explain some of them in the central assessment. They are key to your competence in this unit.

1.1 So far we have gone through various mechanical procedures of basic bookkeeping. Did you understand **why** things were done in the way they were? You may be pleased to know that it is *not* always clear how certain items should be treated in a set of accounts.

1.2 We need to think a little bit more about **why** certain items are treated in specific ways and, where there is a choice of treatment, **how to decide** which treatment to use.

1.3 To some extent at least, the decision is made for you when preparing financial statements for publication by one or both of two authorities.

   (a) **Legal regulation.** In the UK the Companies Act 1985 governs the form and content of **company** accounts and this has filtered down, as best practice, to the accounts of sole traders, partnerships and clubs.

   (b) **Accounting standards.** In the UK these are called Financial Reporting Standards (FRSs) and Statements of Standard Accounting Practice (SSAPs). Accounting standards are produced by the Accounting Standards Board and are discussed further in Sections 7 and 8 of this chapter.

1.4 When there is no specific legal regulation or accounting standard which covers an item in the accounts, you must decide on its accounting treatment by applying **fundamental accounting concepts**. These are the basis of the law and accounting standards.

What are accounting concepts?

1.5 Accounting concepts are covered in FRS 18 *Accounting policies*. The main focus at this stage is on the four accounting concepts we cover in detail in the first five sections of this chapter.

1.6 Accounting practice developed gradually over a long time. Many procedures are operated automatically by accounting personnel and those in common use imply the **acceptance of certain concepts**. These concepts are not necessarily obvious, nor are they the only possible concepts which could be used to build up an accounting framework, but they are the concepts which our current system is based upon.

KEY TERM

Accounting concepts are the broad basic assumptions which underlie the periodic financial accounts of business enterprises.

1.7 The following important concepts and conventions are covered in detail in the next few sections.

- The **going concern concept**
- The **prudence concept**
- The **accruals or matching concept**
- The **consistency concept**
- The **materiality concept**

2 THE GOING CONCERN CONCEPT

> **KEY TERM**
>
> The **going concern concept** implies that the business will continue in operational existence for the foreseeable future, and that there is no intention to put the company into liquidation or to make drastic cutbacks to the scale of operations.

2.1 FRS 18 states that the financial statements **must** be prepared under the going concern basis unless the entity is being (or is going to be) liquidated or if it has ceased (or is about to cease) trading. The directors of a company must also disclose any significant doubts about the company's future if and when they arise.

2.2 The main significance of the going concern concept is that the assets of the business should not be valued at their 'break-up' value, which is the amount that they would sell for if they were sold off piecemeal and the business were thus broken up

3 THE PRUDENCE CONCEPT

> **KEY TERM**
>
> The **prudence concept** states that, where alternative procedures or valuations are possible, the one selected should give the *most cautious* presentation of the business's financial position or results.

3.1 Assume that you were in business making washing machines. A machine costs £100 to make, but is sold for £150. Stocks of finished washing machines would be valued in the balance sheet at £100 each. This is one aspect of the prudence concept: to value the machines at £150 would be to anticipate making a profit before the profit had been **realised** (ie obtained in cash or the promise of cash, see below).

3.2 Another aspect of the prudence concept is that, where a **loss** is foreseen, it should be **anticipated** and accounted for immediately. If a business buys stock for £1,200 but due to a sudden slump in the market only £900 is likely to be received when the stock is sold, the prudence concept states that the stock should be valued at £900 and the £300 deducted as an expense from profit. It is not enough to wait until the stock is sold, and then recognise the £300 loss; **the loss should be recognised as soon as it is foreseen.**

3.3   A profit can be considered to be a **realised profit** when it is in the form of:

- Cash

- Another asset which has a reasonably certain cash value eg amounts owing from debtors, if it is reasonably certain that the debtors will eventually pay the debt.

3.4   **Revenue and profits** are not anticipated, but are included in the profit and loss account only when realised in the form of cash (or of other assets which are certain to be exchanged for cash in the near future). In addition, all known **expenses and losses** should be included in the profit and loss account whether the amount of these is known with certainty or a best estimate is used in the light of the information available.

3.5   EXAMPLE: PRUDENCE CONCEPT

A company begins trading on 1 January 20X0 and sells goods for £100,000 during the year to 31 December. At 31 December there are debts outstanding of £15,000. Of these, the company has now decided that £6,000 will never be paid.

The company should **write off the bad debts** of £6,000. Sales for 20X0 will be shown in the profit and loss account at their full value of £100,000, but the write off of bad debts would be an expense of £6,000. Because there is uncertainty that the sales will be realised, the prudence concept dictates that the £6,000 should not be included in the profit for the year.

4   THE ACCRUALS CONCEPT OR MATCHING CONCEPT

> **KEY TERM**
>
> The **accruals or matching concept** states that, in computing profit, revenue earned must be *matched* against the expenditure incurred in earning it.

4.1   EXAMPLE: ACCRUALS BASIS

Sally has a business importing and selling model ponies made out of pottery. In October 20X0, she makes the following purchases and sales.

Purchases			
Invoice date	*Number*	*Invoiced cost*	*Invoice paid*
		£	
7.10.X0	30	300	1.11.X0
Sales			
		£	
8.10.X0	6	90	1.11.X0
12.10.X0	9	135	1.11.X0
23.10.X0	15	225	1.12.X0

What is Sally's profit and loss account for October on both a cash basis and an accruals basis?

4.2 SOLUTION

	£
Cash basis	
Sales	-
Purchases	-
Profit/loss	-

	£
Accruals basis	
Sales £(90 + 135 + 225)	450
Purchases	300
Profit	150

4.3 If, Sally had only sold 25 ponies (£375), it would be wrong to charge her profit and loss account with the cost of 30 ponies (£300), as five ponies remain in stock (£50). If she sells them in November she is likely to make a profit on the sale. Only the purchase cost of 25 ponies (£250) should be matched with her sales revenue, leaving her with a profit of £125.

Her balance sheet would therefore look like this.

	£
Assets	
Stock (at cost, ie 5 × £10)	50
Debtors (25 × £15)	375
	425
Liabilities	
Creditors	300
	125
Proprietor's capital (profit for the period)	125

4.4 The accruals basis gives a **truer picture** than the cash basis. Sally receives no cash until November but her customers are legally bound to pay her and she is legally bound to pay for her purchases.

Returning to the original example where all the ponies are sold her balance sheet as at 31 October 20X0 would therefore show her assets and liabilities as follows.

	£
Assets: Debtors £(90 + 135 + 225)	450
Liabilities: Creditors	300
Net assets	150
Proprietor's capital	150

4.5 If Sally decided to give up selling ponies, then the **going concern concept** (see paragraph 2.1 above) would no longer apply and the value of the five ponies in the balance sheet would be on a '**break-up**' valuation rather than cost, ie the amount that would be obtained by selling the stock following break-up or liquidation of the business. Similarly, if the five unsold ponies were now unlikely to be sold at more than their cost of £10 each (say, because of damage or a fall in demand) then they should be recorded on the balance sheet at their **net realisable value** (ie the likely eventual sales price less any expenses incurred to make them saleable, eg paint) rather than cost. This shows the application of the **prudence concept**.

4.6 In this example, the concepts of going concern and matching are **linked**. Because the business is assumed to be a going concern it is possible to carry forward the cost of the unsold ponies as a charge against profits of the next period.

4.7 Under the accruals concept, revenues and costs are **accrued** (that is, recognised as they are earned or incurred, not as money is received or paid), matched with one another if they are related to each other, and shown in the profit and loss account of the period to which they relate.

4.8 Revenue and profits in the profit and loss account of the period are **matched** with associated costs and expenses by including them in the same accounting period. Businesses must take credit for sales and purchases when made, rather than when paid for, and they must also carry unsold stock forward in the balance sheet rather than deduct its cost from profit for the period.

Activity 4.1

Accounting concepts never conflict. True or false? Explain your answer.

---

5 THE CONSISTENCY CONCEPT

5.1 Accounting is not an exact science. There are areas in which **judgement** must be used to estimate the money values of items appearing in accounts. Certain procedures and principles have come to be recognised as good accounting practice, but within these limits there are often various acceptable methods of accounting for similar items.

> ### KEY TERM
>
> The **consistency concept** states that similar items should be accorded similar accounting treatment

5.2 In preparing accounts consistency should be observed in two respects.

- **Similar items** in a set of accounts should be given similar accounting treatment.

- The same treatment should be applied **from one period to another** in accounting for similar items. This allows comparisons to be made from one period to the next.

6 THE MATERIALITY CONCEPT

> ### KEY TERM
>
> Under the **materiality concept** only material items should appear in the financial statements. Items are **material** if their omission or misstatement would affect the impact of the financial statements on the reader.

6.1 An error which is too trivial to affect anyone's understanding of the accounts is **immaterial**. In preparing accounts it is important to ask the following questions.

(a) Do materiality considerations apply? (You will pay the **exact** amount of a purchase invoice, no matter how large it is. You would not **round up or down,** or approximate.)

(b) What is material and what is not? Time and money should not be wasted on **excessive detail.**

6.2 Determining whether an item is material is a very **subjective exercise**. There is no absolute measure of materiality. It is common to apply a convenient rule of thumb (eg those items with a value greater than 5% of net profit). But some items are regarded as **particularly sensitive** and even a very small misstatement would be seen as a material error.

6.3 Whether an item is judged as material or immaterial may affect its **treatment in the accounts**. For example, the profit and loss account will show the expenses incurred by a business grouped under suitable headings (heating and light, rent and rates etc); but in the case of minor expenses it may be appropriate to put them together under a 'sundry expenses' heading, because a more detailed breakdown would not be useful.

6.4 The **context** is also important in assessing whether or not an item is material.

(a) The financial statements shows sales of £2 million and stocks of £30,000, an error of £20,000 in the sales figure might not be regarded as material, whereas an error of £20,000 in the stock valuation probably would be. In other words, the total of which the erroneous item forms part must be considered.

(b) If a business has a bank loan of £50,000 and a £55,000 balance on bank deposit account, it might well be regarded as a material misstatement if these two amounts were netted off on the balance sheet as 'cash at bank £5,000'. Incorrect presentation may amount to material misstatement even if there is no monetary error.

Activity 4.2

You work for a multinational company and you are preparing two accounting documents.

(a) A statement for a customer, listing invoices and receipts, and detailing the amounts owed

(b) A report sent to the senior management of a division, who want a brief comparative summary of how well the firm is doing in the UK and in France

How would considerations of *materiality* influence your preparation of each document?

---

7 DEVELOPMENT OF ACCOUNTING STANDARDS

7.1 Up until 1970, the basic conventions used in preparing accounts had evolved over the century, the result of the 'collective experience' of practising accountants, and were not based on any theory of accounting. Conformity in reporting methods was not tackled until **accounting standards** were first introduced in the 1970s.

> **KEY TERM**
>
> An **accounting standard** is a rule or set of rules which prescribes the method by which accounts should be prepared and presented. These 'working regulations' are issued by a national or international body of the accountancy profession.

7.2 From 1970 until July 1990 accounting standards were created and issued by the **Accounting Standards Committee (ASC)**. The standards were called **Statements of Standard Accounting Practice (SSAPs)**.

7.3 On 1 August 1990 the ASC was disbanded. A new standard setting regime consisting of various bodies was set up.

Body	Format/role
Financial Reporting Council (FRC)	Created to cover a wide constituency of interests at a high level. It guides the ASB on policy and ensures that the standard-setting body is properly financed. The FRC also funds and oversees the Review Panel. It has about 25 members drawn from users, preparers and auditors of accounts.
Accounting Standards Board (ASB)	The ASB devises and issues standards on its own behalf (with a two-thirds majority). The standards produced by the ASB are called Financial Reporting Standards (FRSs): see below. The ASB adopted all the SSAPs in force as at 1 August 1990, but these are gradually being replaced by FRSs.
Urgent Issues Task Force (UITF)	An offshoot of the ASB whose function it is to tackle urgent matters not covered by existing standards, given the urgency, the normal standard setting process is not practicable.
Financial Reporting Review Panel	Reviews departures from accounting standards by large companies. It can take companies to court to force them to revise their accounts.

7.4 The structure of the standard-setting framework can be seen in the following diagram.

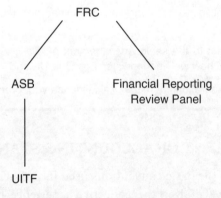

Activity 4.3

What are the aims of accounting standards and by whom are they issued?

8 RELEVANT ACCOUNTING STANDARDS

Legal status

8.1 In the UK, the Companies Act 1985 requires *companies* (ie not sole traders, partnerships or clubs) to include a note to the accounts stating that the accounts have been prepared **in accordance with applicable accounting standards** or, to give details of material departures from those standards, with reasons. The Review Panel and the Secretary of State for Trade and Industry have the power to apply to the court for revision of the accounts where non-compliance is not justified. **These provisions mean that for companies accounting standards have the force of law, even though accounting standards are not** *required* **by law.** For the entities with which you are concerned (sole traders, partnerships and clubs), accounting standards represent *best practice* and are assessable where relevant.

8.2 Below is the list of the UK accounting standards which you need to know about for Unit 5.

Number	Title	Chapter in this Text
FRS 15	Tangible fixed assets	5
FRS 18	Accounting policies	4
SSAP 5	Accounting for value added tax	6
SSAP 9	Stocks and long-term contracts	9
SSAP 13	Accounting for research and development	6

ASSESSMENT ALERT

You only need to be competent in dealing with SSAPs 5, 9 and 13 and FRSs 15 and 18. If you refer to a SSAP or FRS make sure you are using the correct one.

BPP
PUBLISHING

Key learning points

- In preparing financial statements, certain **concepts** are adopted as a framework. We have examined some of the particularly important concepts.

  - **Going concern**: the business will continue in the foreseeable future
  - **Prudence**: a cautious approach is advised
  - **Accruals**: revenues and costs should be matched in the same period
  - **Consistency**: like items should be treated in a like way
  - **Materiality**: in some cases, attention to detail can obscure the 'big picture'

- Accounting standards were developed to give **consistency** to financial reporting.

- Older accounting standards are called **SSAPs** (Statements of Standard Accounting Practice), but these have nearly all been replaced by **FRSs** (Financial Reporting Standards).

- Accounting standards are **reinforced** by the law (principally for companies), but they are **not required** by it. They are **best practice**.

Quick quiz

1   Where is most guidance given on how items should be treated in the accounts?

2   Whether an item is material or not in a set of accounts is entirely objective. True or false?

Answers to quick quiz _____

1   Accounting standards and company law.

2   False. Deciding whether an item is material or not is always a *subjective* exercise.

Part B
Recording capital acquisitions and disposals

5 Capital acquisition and disposal

This chapter contains

1   Fixed assets: the basics

2   Acquiring fixed assets

3   Recording capital acquisitions

4   The fixed assets register

5   Depreciation

6   Methods of depreciation

7   Recording depreciation in the accounts

8   Disposing of fixed assets

9   Reconciling physical assets, ledger accounts and register

Learning objectives

- Create and maintain a fixed asset register and general ledger accounts for fixed assets

- Enter relevant details relating to capital expenditure in the appropriate records

- Account for capital items sold, scrapped or otherwise retired from service

- Identify and record acquisition and disposal costs correctly in the appropriate records

- Show clearly that acquisitions and disposals have been properly authorised and funding methods agreed

- Understand funding by part exchange

- Understand the objectives of making a provision for depreciation

- Calculate and record depreciation charges and other adjustments in the appropriate records

- Calculate depreciation on straight line and reducing balance methods

- Calculate and record profit or loss on disposal in the appropriate records

- Agree records with the physical presence of capital items

BPP PUBLISHING

- Identify and resolve/refer to the appropriate person any lack of agreement between physical items and records
- Suggest improvements to the appropriate person as to how the organisation maintains its capital records
- Adhere to policies and procedures in maintaining capital records
- Appreciate the key issues relating to capital acquisition and disposal

Performance criteria

5.1.1 Relevant details relating to capital expenditure are correctly entered in the appropriate records

5.1.2 The organisation's records agree with the physical presence of capital items

5.1.3 All acquisition and disposal costs and revenues are correctly identified and recorded in the appropriate records

5.1.4 Depreciation charges and other necessary entries and adjustments are correctly calculated and recorded in the appropriate records

5.1.5 The records clearly show the prior authority for capital expenditure and disposal and indicate the approved method of funding and disposal

5.1.6 Profit and loss on disposal is correctly calculated and recorded in the appropriate records

5.1.7 The organisation's policies and procedures relating to the maintenance of capital records are adhered to

5.1.8 Lack of agreement between physical items and records are identified and either resolved or referred to the appropriate person

5.1.9 When possible, suggestions for improvements in the way the organisation maintains its capital records are made to the appropriate person

Range Statement

5.1.1 Methods of calculating depreciation: straight line; reducing balance

5.1.2 Records: asset register; ledger

Knowledge and understanding

Types and characteristics of different assets and key issues relating to the acquisition and disposal of capital assets

Methods of depreciation: straight line; reducing balance

Accounting treatment of capital items sold, scrapped or otherwise retired from service

Use of plant registers and similar subsidiary records

Methods of funding: part exchange deals

1   FIXED ASSETS: THE BASICS

KEY TERM

A **fixed asset** is acquired and retained in the business with a view to earning profits not merely for resale. It is normally used over more than one accounting period.

1.1   Here are some examples of fixed assets.

- Motor vehicles
- Plant and machinery
- Fixtures and fittings
- Land and buildings

1.2 Fixed assets are to be **distinguished from** stocks which we buy or make in order to sell. Stocks are **current assets**, along with cash and amounts owed to us by debtors.

Materiality

1.3 Many **small value assets**, although purchased for continuing use in the business, will not be recorded as assets but will instead be written off directly as an expense when purchased. An example would be a box of pencils or a set of file dividers. You would not bother to capitalise them and calculate depreciation on them at the year end!

1.4 Whether items are 'small enough' to be written off or 'large enough' to be capitalised is generally clear cut. However, what about **borderline items**, such as computer software?

1.5 The decision taken depends on whether the amount is **material**, that is whether it has a significant effect on the financial statements. Something that is material to a small organisation may not be material to a large one.

Self-constructed assets

1.6 Where a business **builds its own fixed asset** (eg a builder might build his own office), then all the costs involved in building the asset should be included in the recorded cost of the fixed asset. These costs will include raw materials, but also labour costs and related overhead costs. This treatment means that assets which are self-constructed are treated in a similar way as purchased fixed assets (where all such costs are included in the purchase price of the asset).

Tangible and intangible assets

1.7 To be a fixed asset, an item does not have to have a physical presence. It can be intangible.

> **KEY TERMS**
>
> - A **tangible** fixed asset is a physical asset. It has a real, 'solid' existence.
>
> - An **intangible** fixed asset is an asset which does not have a physical existence.

1.8 Intangible fixed assets represent payments by a business to acquire benefits of a long-term nature. If a business purchases some patent rights, or a database, or a concession from another business, or the right to use a trademark, the cost of the purchase can be accounted for as the purchase of an intangible fixed asset. These assets must then be depreciated over their economic life, as with other fixed assets (see Sections 5-7 below).

BPP
PUBLISHING

2 ACQUIRING FIXED ASSETS

2.1 The acquisition of a fixed asset is likely to be **material** to the business. This raises three important processes that need to be addressed before the business can actually acquire the asset.

- How is it going to be paid for or **funded**?
- How should the purchase be **authorised**?
- What are the **organisational implications** of acquiring the asset?

Funding the acquisition of fixed assets

2.2 If a business has only, say, £1,000 in the bank this should not prevent it from purchasing a fixed asset for, say, £10,000. Indeed, making such an acquisition may be the only way the business can increase its output, generating more profit and hence more cash. How, then, can a business find the funds to make a fixed asset purchase?

Funding method	Details
Cash from retained profits	Quite simple: spend the money in the bank
Borrowing	Approach the bank with a business plan setting out the benefits to be conferred by owning the fixed asset. Agree interest rate, period of loan and any security the bank may want.
Hire purchase (HP)	This is a credit agreement whereby regular payments, including interest, are paid to the lender for an agreed period of time; at the end of that time, the asset becomes the property of the business.
Leasing	This is also a credit agreement involving regular payments, but at the end of the agreement the asset does not become the property of the business.
Part exchange	Part of the cost of the asset is satisfied by transferring to the seller an asset owned by the business. The rest of the funds are provided by one of the methods above.

2.3 The method of funding to adopt is a management decision. What concerns us here is how we should account for the funding, as well as the purchase.

Step 1	Record the inflow of funds (where relevant)
Step 2	Record the outflow of funds and acquisition of the asset

2.4 EXAMPLE: ACCOUNTING FOR DIFFERENT FUNDING METHODS

Gubbins Co, a furniture wholesaler, needs new racking for its main distribution warehouse. The racking will cost £20,000. Set out the accounting entries for the acquisition by each of the five funding methods in paragraph 2.2.

2.5 SOLUTION

Cash from retained profits

			£	£
Step 1	No need to record anything – cash is already there.			
Step 2	DEBIT	Fixed assets (racking)	20,000	
	CREDIT	Cash		20,000

Borrowing

			£	£
Step 1	DEBIT	Cash	20,000	
	CREDIT	Loan creditor		20,000
Step 2	DEBIT	Fixed assets	20,000	
	CREDIT	Cash		20,000

Hire purchase

Although the asset does not fully become the business's property until the payments have all been made, it is recorded as a fixed asset on its **initial acquisition**. In a hire purchase transaction, the creditor for the loan is the seller of the fixed asset, so the business does not receive and then pay out cash and the entry is simply:

			£	£
Steps 1 and 2	DEBIT	Fixed assets	20,000	
	CREDIT	Hire purchase creditor		20,000

Leasing

The distinction between hire purchase and some of the different types of lease available is a fine one. For our purposes, a leased asset is a rented one – **ownership never passes to the business** and so no accounting entries recording acquisition are required. If the monthly rental of the asset is, say, £500, the monthly entries would be:

			£	£
Steps 1 and 2	DEBIT	Rental (leasing) expense	500	
	CREDIT	Cash		500

Part-exchange

If the old racking is worth £10,000, with the balance funded by borrowing from the bank, then the entries would be:

			£	£
Step 1	DEBIT	Cash	10,000	
	CREDIT	Loan creditor		10,000
Step 2	DEBIT	Fixed assets	20,000	
	CREDIT	Cash		10,000
		Disposals		10,000

See Section 8 of this Chapter for further details of the disposals account in relation to part exchange.

Authorisation of fixed asset acquisitions

2.6 Capital expenditure over a certain amount must normally be authorised by senior managers of a business and major projects will be noted in the minutes of management meetings. Generally, a document called a **capital expenditure authorisation form** (or some similar name) is used.

2.7 This form should show the **prior authority** for capital expenditure and indicate the **approved method of funding**, eg outright purchase, lease or part exchange. Below is an example of a capital expenditure authorisation form.

CAPITAL EXPENDITURE AUTHORISATION FORM

Business ....

Description of item and reason for purchase ....

....

....

Supplier ....

Cost ....

Was this the cheapest quote obtained (if not state reason)?...................................

....

....

Authorised by: ....

Counter-authorised (if over £1,000) by: ....

Purchase/lease/part exchange (state asset transferred) *......................................

Terms of lease...

....

PLEASE RETURN TO PENNY WISE, FINANCIAL CONTROLLER

* delete as applicable

2.8 Whilst all businesses differ, it would be unusual for capital expenditure *not* to require this sort of formal authorisation.

Organisational implications of fixed asset acquisition

2.9 Substantial expenditure on fixed assets is undertaken to increase profitability. The **organisational implications** of the purchase, and hence its ultimate success or otherwise can be complex and may have adverse effects on profitability if they are not properly managed. The following example illustrates this.

2.10 EXAMPLE: ACQUIRING A NEW PRINTING PRESS

Norman Bate has a number of basic printing presses which produce leaflets in black and white. He decides to buy a new press which can produce bound leaflets printed in two or four colours. What are the implications for his business?

Area	Effect	Comments
Liquidity	A cash purchase could seriously affect his cash flow	He should consider alternative methods, although the cost of interest on any amount borrowed may be very unattractive
Staffing	The new press may require two or three skilled operatives if it is to function effectively	He may wish to recruit fully trained operatives
Training	Existing operatives, especially where a one-colour press has been used in part exchange for the new press, may be trained in the ways of the new press	If existing employees are used it may be necessary to train them in advance of the new machine going in, making use of the manufacturer's training programme perhaps
Productivity	Depending on whether an old machine was part exchanged, Norman should see an increase in productivity **once the machine is up and running**	While the machine is settling in, productivity may actually decrease as operatives learn how to use it. Quite a lot of Norman's time will be spent on it too
Marketing	Existing customers should be informed of the development. New ones need to be found	Marketing expenditure will need to be incurred in order to make sure the machine is kept busy
Premises	New floorspace may be needed and new utilities (eg air conditioning, waste disposal) installed	If Norman has fully utilised all existing floorspace in his factory, he may need to move everything and get new premises
Running expenses	The machine may increase the use of electricity	Norman may now exceed the usage agreed with this current provider; he could look for new suppliers
Profitability	The machine *should* increase Norman's profits	The combination of the costs of the above factors may mean the machine is not profitable!

3 RECORDING CAPITAL ACQUISITIONS

Posting the ledger from the books of prime entry

3.1 When a fixed asset is acquired it is recorded first of all in the **books of prime entry**. These could be the **purchase day book** or the **cash book,** which could then be posted to the total creditors account or the cash account respectively in the general ledger.

BPP
PUBLISHING

Source	General ledger accounts	DR	CR
PDB	Fixed assets	20,000	
PDB	Total creditors		20,000
or			
CB	Fixed assets	20,000	
CB	Cash account		20,000

3.2 However, the book of prime entry in which credit purchases of fixed assets are usually first recorded is the **journal**. We discussed journals in Chapter 2. It is used to record those transactions which take place only infrequently. Purchases of fixed assets do not normally take place very often.

Example of journal entries for credit purchase of fixed assets

3.3 An example of journal entries relating to purchase of fixed assets on credit is shown below. (In this example there is an integrated purchase ledger, so the creditors' names appear on separate accounts in the nominal ledger.)

JOURNAL				Page 51
Date	Details	Folio Ref	£	£
12 June	Motor vehicles a/c Van Gogh Ltd Being purchase of delivery van reg. X298 PTO per invoice no. ED/142	NLM2 SLV6	14,500	14,500
13 June	Furniture a/c Sofa Miredo Being purchase of sofa for reception invoice no. LA/TI123	NLF1 BLS12	1,000	1,000

Activity 5.1

Post the journal to the relevant ledger accounts for the journal entries in paragraph 3.3.

3.4 The journal and the ledger accounts are not the only places where capital acquisitions are recorded. Because of the value and the long-term nature of fixed assets, they are also recorded in the **fixed asset register**.

4   THE FIXED ASSETS REGISTER

4.1   Capital transactions represent considerable sums spent by a business. There could be many **valuable fixed assets** kept in various departments or on factory floors. Some of these will be scrapped or sold and replaced by new ones. As significant investment capital is tied up in fixed assets, **tight control** of the details concerning each fixed asset is required. The journal is used as a book of prime entry to record the purchase and sale of fixed assets, but this is not sufficient to record and control what happens to them over time.

4.2   Nearly all but the smallest organisations keep a **fixed assets register**.

> **KEY TERM**
>
> A **fixed assets register** (or simply **asset register**) is a listing of all fixed assets owned by the organisation, broken down perhaps by department, location or asset type.

4.3   A fixed assets register is kept mainly for internal purposes. It is **not part of the double entry system** and does not record rights over or obligations towards third parties but shows an organisation's investment in capital equipment. A fixed asset register is also part of the **internal control system**. This is discussed further in Section 9 below. Fixed assets registers or ledgers are sometimes called **real accounts**, to distinguish them from impersonal accounts such as 'rent' in the general ledger and personal accounts such as 'A Detta' in the sales ledger. They tend to include very few transactions and for this reason they are separated from those accounts that are more heavily used.

Data kept in a fixed assets register

4.4   **Details** held about each fixed asset *might* include the following.

- The organisation's internal reference number (for physical identification purposes)

- Manufacturer's serial number (for maintenance purposes)

- Description of asset

- Location of asset

- Insurance details (sometimes)

- Department which 'owns' asset

4.5   However, the **most important details** from an accounting point of view will be as follows.

- Purchase date (for calculation of depreciation)

- Cost

- Depreciation method and estimated useful life (for calculation of depreciation - see Sections 5 to 7 below)

- Accumulated depreciation brought forward and carried forward

- Date of disposal

- Disposal proceeds

- Profit/loss on disposal

4.6 The **main events** giving rise to entries in a fixed asset register or 'inputs' in the case of a computerised one, would be the following.

- Purchase of an asset
- Sale of an asset
- Loss or destruction of an asset
- Transfer of assets between departments
- Revision of estimated useful life of an asset
- Scrapping of an asset

4.7 **Outputs** from a fixed assets register would be made:

- To enable **reconciliations** to be made to the general ledger fixed asset accounts

- To enable **depreciation charges** to be posted to the general ledger

- For physical verification/audit purposes.

Layout of fixed assets register

4.8 The layout of a fixed assets register and the detail included will depend on the organisation. Some may have an individual page for each type of fixed asset. Others may have columns with various headings and list the assets in an organised way, for example by department or by the type of asset it is. Below is a typical layout from a manual fixed assets register.

Date of purchase	Invoice number	Ref	Item	Cost	Accum'd dep'n b/d	Dep'n expense	Accum'd dep'n c/d	Date of disposal	Disposal proceeds	(Loss)/ gain

4.9 Most fixed assets registers will be **computerised**. Here is an extract from a fixed asset register showing one item as it might appear when the details are printed out.

FASSET HOLDINGS PLC

Asset Code: 938	Next depreciation: 539.36
A Description: publisher	1 × Seisha Laser printer YCA40809 office
B Date of purchase:	25/05/X4
C Cost:	1618.25
D Accumulated depreciation:	584.35
E Depreciation %:	33.33%
F Depreciation type:	straight line
G Date of disposal:	NOT SET
H Sale proceeds:	0.00
I Accumulated depreciation amount:	55Q O/EQPT DEP CHARGE
J Depreciation expense account:	34F DEPN O/EQPT
K Depreciation period:	standard
L Comments:	Electronic office
M Residual value:	0.00
N Cost account:	65C O/E ADDITIONS

4.10 Section summary

Before we go on to look at depreciation and disposal of fixed assets, let us summarise the key steps involved in **acquisition of fixed assets**.

Step 1	Decide on method of funding and consider organisational implications
Step 2	Check capital expenditure authorisation form
Step 3	Enter details into journal
Step 4	Post journal to ledger account
Step 5	Write up details in the fixed assets register

5 DEPRECIATION

Introduction

5.1 Most fixed assets **wear out over time**, the exception is freehold land. Machines, vehicles, fixtures and fittings and even buildings do not last forever.

5.2 When a business acquires a fixed asset, it will have some idea about how long its **useful life** will be, and might decide to do one of two things.

(a) It may use the fixed asset until it is **completely worn out**, useless and worthless.

(b) It may **sell off** the fixed asset at the end of its useful life either as a second-hand item or as scrap.

5.3 Since a fixed asset has a cost, and a limited useful life, and its value eventually declines, it follows that a charge should be made in the profit and loss account to

BPP PUBLISHING

reflect the use that is made of the asset by the business. This charge is called **depreciation**.

5.4 Suppose that a business buys a machine for £40,000. Its expected life is four years, and at the end of that time it is expected to be worthless. Since the fixed asset is used to make profits for four years, it would be reasonable to charge the cost of the asset over those four years (perhaps by charging £10,000 per annum) so that at the end of the four years the total cost of £40,000 would have been charged against profits.

5.5 One way of defining depreciation is as **a means of spreading the cost of a fixed asset over its useful life**, thereby **matching** the cost against the full period during which it earns profits for the business.

5.6 A better definition of depreciation is given below.

> ### KEY TERM
>
> **Depreciation** is a measurement of the wearing out, use or other reduction in the useful economic life of a fixed asset, whether arising from use, passage of time or obsolescence through technological or market changes. Depreciation should be allocated so that a fair proportion of cost or valuation of the asset is charged to each accounting period expected to benefit from its use.

5.7 This definition makes two important points.

(a) Depreciation is a measure of the **wearing out** of a fixed asset through use, time or obsolescence.

(b) Depreciation charges should be **spread fairly** over a fixed asset's life, and so allocated to the accounting periods expected to **benefit** from the asset's use.

The total charge for depreciation

5.8 The total amount to be charged over the life of a fixed asset (the **depreciable amount**) is usually its **cost less any expected 'residual' sales value** or disposal value at the end of the asset's life.

Cost	Expected life	Residual value	Total depreciation over expected life
£	Years	£	£
20,000	5	0	20,000
20,000	5	3,000	17,000
20,000	3	2,000	18,000

Depreciation in the accounts of a business

5.9 When a fixed asset is depreciated, two things must be accounted for, one in the **profit and loss account** and one in the **balance sheet**.

Financial statement	Item	As
Profit and loss account	Depreciation charge for period	An expense of the period
Balance sheet	Total accumulated depreciation (accumulated depreciation b/d plus this period's charge)	Deduction from cost of fixed asset, giving the asset's net book value (which is not the same as its market value)

5.10 Depreciation deducted from the cost of a fixed asset to arrive at its net book value will build up (or 'accumulate') over time, as more is charged in each successive accounting period. This **accumulated depreciation** is a 'provision' as it provides for the fall in value of the fixed asset. The term 'provision for depreciation' refers to the 'accumulated depreciation' of a fixed asset.

What is depreciation for?

5.11 There are frequent misconceptions about depreciation's **purpose**.

Depreciation is not a cash expense

5.12 Depreciation spreads the cost of a fixed asset (less its residual value) over the asset's life. The cash payment for the fixed asset will be made when, or soon after, the asset is purchased. Annual depreciation of the asset in subsequent years is not a cash expense; rather, it **allocates costs** under the matching concept to those later years for a cash payment that has occurred previously.

Depreciation is not a fund set aside for future replacement of fixed assets

5.13 The concept of depreciation as such a fund could not be applied, for instance, if the asset was **not replaced** or was replaced with a very **different asset**, at a different cost, due to technological advances. Depreciation, then, allocates the cost of the **existing asset** to future periods; it does not anticipate the purchase of fixed assets in the future.

Subjectivity and consistency

5.14 The way in which an asset is depreciated is a subjective matter. The business needs to make choices in **three areas**.

- Estimated useful life
- Residual value
- Method and rate of depreciation

Judgement based on experience of similar assets and known conditions should be used when determining all of these, but there are arbitrary elements.

5.15 Consequently, once the decisions on these three aspects have been made, the **consistency concept** demands that they continue to be applied, particularly in the case of the **method** of depreciation. New information or changes in the business's market may change the estimated useful life and the expected residual value. The depreciation method should only be changed, if it became clear that the existing method does not reflect the way the asset is being used up. A business cannot change the method every year just to give a more favourable depreciation figure in the accounts.

Activity 5.2

What does depreciation do and why is it necessary?

5.16 EXAMPLE: DEPRECIATION

A fixed asset costing £40,000 has an expected life of four years and an estimated residual value of nil. It might be depreciated by £10,000 per annum.

	Depreciation charge for the year (P & L a/c) (A) £	Accumulated depreciation at end of year (B) £	Cost of the asset (C) £	Net book value at end of year (C–B) £
At beginning of its life	-	-	40,000	40,000
Year 1	10,000	10,000	40,000	30,000
Year 2	10,000	20,000	40,000	20,000
Year 3	10,000	30,000	40,000	10,000
Year 4	10,000	40,000	40,000	0
	40,000			

In year 4, the full £40,000 of depreciation charges have been made in the profit and loss accounts of the four years. The net book value of the fixed asset is now nil. In theory, the business will no longer use the fixed asset, which would now need replacing.

6 METHODS OF DEPRECIATION

6.1 There are several methods of depreciation. Of these, two are most commonly used.

- The straight line method
- The reducing balance method

CENTRAL ASSESSMENT ALERT

You will be required to use one or both of these methods in your assessment.

The straight line method

6.2 This is the most common method. The total depreciable amount is charged in **equal instalments** to each accounting period over the expected useful life of the asset. In this way, the net book value of the fixed asset declines in a 'straight line' over time.

6.3 The **annual depreciation charge** is calculated as:

$$\frac{\text{Cost of asset less residual value}}{\text{Expected useful life of the asset}}$$

6.4 EXAMPLE: STRAIGHT LINE DEPRECIATION

Examples of straight line depreciation are as follows.

(a) A fixed asset costing £20,000 with an estimated life of ten years and no residual value would be depreciated at the rate of:

$$\frac{£20,000}{10 \text{ years}} = £2,000 \text{ per annum}$$

(b) A fixed asset costing £60,000 has an estimated life of five years and a residual value of £7,000. The annual depreciation charge using the straight line method would be calculated as follows.

$$\frac{£(60,000 - 7,000)}{5 \text{ years}} = £10,600 \text{ per annum}$$

The net book value of the fixed asset would reduce each year as follows.

	After 1 year £	After 2 years £	After 3 years £	After 4 years £	After 5 years £
Cost of the asset	60,000	60,000	60,000	60,000	60,000
Accumulated depreciation	10,600	21,200	31,800	42,400	53,000
Net book value	49,400	38,800	28,200	17,600	7,000*

* ie its estimated residual value.

6.5 Since the depreciation charge per annum is the same amount every year with the straight line method, it is often convenient to state that depreciation is charged at the rate of **x per cent per annum on the cost of the asset**. In the example in Paragraph 6.4(a) above, the depreciation charge per annum is 10% of cost (ie 10% of £20,000 = £2,000).

6.6 The straight line method of depreciation is a fair allocation of the total depreciable amount between the different accounting periods, provided that it is reasonable to assume that the business enjoys **equal benefits** from the use of the asset in every period throughout its life.

The reducing balance method

6.7 The reducing balance method of depreciation calculates the annual depreciation charge as a **fixed percentage of the net book value** of the asset, as at the end of the **previous** accounting period.

6.8 EXAMPLE: REDUCING BALANCE METHOD

A business purchases a fixed asset at a cost of £10,000. Its expected useful life is three years and its estimated residual value is £2,160. The business wishes to use the reducing balance method to depreciate the asset, and calculates that the rate of depreciation should be 40% of the reducing (net book) value of the asset. (The method of deciding that 40% is a suitable percentage is a problem of mathematics and is not described here.)

The total depreciable amount is £(10,000 – 2,160) = £7,840.

The depreciation charge per annum and the net book value of the asset as at the end of each year will be as follows.

	£	*Accumulated depreciation* £
Asset at cost	10,000	
Depreciation in year 1 (40%)	4,000	4,000
Net book value at end of year	6,000	
Depreciation in year 2		
(40% of reducing balance)	2,400	6,400 (4,000 + 2,400)
Net book value at end of year	3,600	
Depreciation in year 3 (40%)	1,440	7,840 (6,400 + 1,440)
Net book value at end of year	2,160	

6.9 With the reducing balance method, the annual charge for depreciation is **higher in the earlier years of the asset's life,** and lower in the later years. In the example above, the annual charges for years 1, 2 and 3 are £4,000, £2,400 and £1,440 respectively.

6.10 The reducing balance method might be used when it is considered fair to allocate a **greater proportion** of the total depreciable amount to the earlier years and a lower amount in the later years, on the assumption that the benefits obtained by the business from using the asset decline over time.

Activity 5.3

On 1 January 20X2 a business purchased a laser printer costing £1,800. The printer has an estimated life of 4 years after which it will have no residual value.

Required

Calculate the annual depreciation charges for 20X2, 20X3, 20X4 and 20X5 on the laser printer on the following bases.

(a) The straight line basis
(b) The reducing balance method at 60% per annum

Note. Your workings should be to the nearest £.

Which method of depreciation should be used?

6.11 A **different method** can be used for each type of asset, such as buildings, machinery, motor vehicles and so on. The method chosen must, however, **be fair in allocating the charges between different accounting periods,** and must be used **consistently.**

6.12 The following points need to be taken into consideration when selecting a method of depreciation.

(a) The method should **allocate costs in proportion to the benefits** (revenues or profits) earned during each accounting period by the asset. These profits almost certainly cannot be calculated exactly, but the business should be able to decide whether:

- The asset provides greater benefits in the earlier years of its life, in which case the reducing balance method would be suitable

- The asset provides equal benefits to each period throughout its life, in which case the straight line method would be suitable

(b)   The method used for any fixed asset should be the same as the method used for **similar assets** (consistency concept).

(c)   The method used should be one which is **easy to apply** in practice. There is no point in creating unnecessary complications.

6.13   The **straight line method is the most commonly used**. It is easy to use and it is generally fair to assume that all periods benefit equally from the use of a fixed asset during its useful life.

Assets acquired in the middle of an accounting period

6.14   A business will purchase fixed assets at any time during the course of an accounting period, and so it seems fair to charge depreciation in the period when the purchase occurs which reflects the **limited amount of use** the business has had from the asset in that period.

6.15   EXAMPLE: ASSETS ACQUIRED DURING AN ACCOUNTING PERIOD

A business with an accounting year which runs from 1 January to 31 December purchases a fixed asset on 1 April 20X0, costing £24,000. The expected life of the asset is four years, and its residual value is nil.

What should be the depreciation charge for 20X0?

6.16   SOLUTION

The annual depreciation charge will be $\dfrac{24,000}{4 \text{ years}}$ = £6,000 per annum.

Since the asset was acquired on 1 April 20X0, the business has only benefited from its use for nine months. It would therefore seem fair to charge nine months' depreciation in 20X0 as follows.

$^9/_{12} \times £6,000 = £4,500$

> **CENTRAL ASSESSMENT ALERT**
>
> If you are given a purchase date of a fixed asset which is in the middle of an accounting period, you should assume that depreciation should be calculated in this way, as a 'part-year' amount. However you should be aware that, in practice, many businesses ignore part-year depreciation, and charge a full year's depreciation in the year of purchase, regardless of the time of year the fixed assets were acquired, and then none in the year of disposal.

7   RECORDING DEPRECIATION IN THE ACCOUNTS

7.1   There are two basic aspects of the provision for depreciation to remember.

(a)   A **depreciation charge** is made in the profit and loss account of each accounting period for every depreciable fixed asset.

BPP
PUBLISHING

(b) The total **accumulated depreciation** on a fixed asset builds up as the asset gets older. Unlike a provision for doubtful debts, the total provision for depreciation is always getting larger, until the fixed asset is fully depreciated.

7.2 The ledger accounting period entries for the provision of depreciation are as follows (the journal should be the book of prime entry.)

> **Step 1** There is a **provision for depreciation account** for each separate category of fixed asset. The balance on the account is the **total accumulated depreciation**. This is always a **credit balance** brought down.
>
> **Step 2** The **depreciation charge** for an accounting period is accounted for as follows.
>
> DEBIT   Depreciation expense (in the P & L account)
> CREDIT   Provision for depreciation account
>
> **Step 3** The fixed asset accounts are **unaffected by depreciation**. Fixed assets are recorded in these accounts at cost.

In the **balance sheet** of the business, the total balance on the provision for depreciation account (ie accumulated depreciation) is set against the value of fixed asset accounts (ie fixed assets at cost) to derive the net book value of the fixed assets.

7.3 EXAMPLE: LEDGER ENTRIES FOR DEPRECIATION

Brian set up his own computer software business on 1 March 20X2. He purchased a computer system on credit from a manufacturer, at a cost of £16,000. The system has an expected life of three years and a residual value of £2,500.

Using the straight line method of depreciation, show the fixed asset account, provision for depreciation account and profit and loss account (extract) and balance sheet (extract) for each of the next three years, 28 February 20X3, 20X4 and 20X5.

7.4 SOLUTION

FIXED ASSET: COMPUTER EQUIPMENT

	Date		£	Date		£
(a)	1 Mar 20X2	Creditor	16,000	28 Feb 20X3	Balance c/d	16,000
(b)	1 Mar 20X3	Balance b/d	16,000	28 Feb 20X4	Balance c/d	16,000
(c)	1 Mar 20X4	Balance b/d	16,000	28 Feb 20X5	Balance c/d	16,000
(d)	1 Mar 20X5	Balance b/d	16,000			

In theory, the fixed asset has out lasted its expected useful life. However, until it is sold off or scrapped, the asset will appear in the balance sheet at cost, less accumulated depreciation, and it should remain in the ledger account for computer equipment until it is eventually disposed of.

The annual depreciation charge is $\dfrac{£(16,000 - 2,500)}{3 \text{ years}} = £4,500$

PROVISION FOR DEPRECIATION

	Date		£	Date		£
(a)	28 Feb 20X3	Balance c/d	4,500	28 Feb 20X3	Dep'n expense	4,500
(b)	28 Feb 20X4	Balance c/d	9,000	1 Mar 20X3	Balance b/d	4,500
				28 Feb 20X4	Dep'n expense	4,500
			9,000			9,000
(c)	28 Feb 20X5	Balance c/d	13,500	1 Mar 20X4	Balance b/d	9,000
				28 Feb 20X5	Dep'n expense	4,500
			13,500			13,500
				1 Mar 20X5	Balance b/d	13,500

After three years, the asset is fully depreciated to its residual value of £2,500. If it continues to be used by Brian, it will not be depreciated any further (unless its estimated residual value is reduced).

DEPRECIATION EXPENSE ACCOUNT (EXTRACT)

	Date		£
(a)	28 Feb 20X3	Provision for depreciation	4,500
(b)	28 Feb 20X4	Provision for depreciation	4,500
(c)	28 Feb 20X5	Provision for depreciation	4,500

BALANCE SHEET (EXTRACT) AS AT 28 FEBRUARY

	20X3	20X4	20X5
	£	£	£
Computer equipment at cost	16,000	16,000	16,000
Less accumulated depreciation	4,500	9,000	13,500
Net book value	11,500	7,000	2,500

7.5 EXAMPLE: JOURNAL ENTRIES FOR YEAR END DEPRECIATION TRANSFER

Depreciation on motor vehicles which cost £100,000 is to be calculated at 20% on cost for the year ended 30 September. The journal entries required are shown below.

JOURNAL

Page 142

Date	Details	Folio Ref	£	£
30 Sept	Motor vehicles depreciation a/c	NLD2	20,000	
	Motor vehicles provision for depreciation	NLP3		20,000
	Being year-end provision for depreciation			

Activity 5.4

Brian prospers in his computer software business, and before long he purchases a car for himself, and later for his chief assistant Bill. Relevant data is as follows.

	Date of purchase	Cost	Estimated life	Estimated residual value
Brian car	1 June 20X2	£20,000	3 years	£2,000
Bill car	1 June 20X3	£8,000	3 years	£2,000

The straight line method of depreciation is to be used.

Required

Prepare the motor vehicles account and provision for depreciation of motor vehicle account for the years to 28 February 20X3 and 20X4. (You should allow for the part-year's use of a car in computing the annual charge for depreciation.) Calculate the net book value of the motor vehicles as at 28 February 20X4.

8 DISPOSING OF FIXED ASSETS

8.1 Fixed assets are not purchased by a business with the intention of reselling them in the normal course of trade. However, they might be sold off at some stage during their life, either when their useful life is over, or before then. A business might decide to sell off a fixed asset long **before its useful life has ended**.

8.2 When fixed assets are disposed of, there will be a **profit or loss on disposal**. Because it is a capital item being sold, the **profit or loss** will be a **capital gain** or a **capital loss**. These gains or losses are reported in the profit and loss account of the business (and not as a trading profit in the trading account). They are referred to as 'profit **(or loss) on disposal of fixed assets**'.

CENTRAL ASSESSMENT ALERT

Questions on the disposal of fixed assets are likely to ask for ledger accounts to be prepared, showing the entries in the accounts to record the disposal. But before we look at the ledger accounting for disposing of assets, we should look at the principles behind calculating the profit (or loss) on disposal of assets.

The principles behind calculating the profit or loss on disposal

8.3 The profit or loss on the disposal of a fixed asset is the **difference** between:

- The **net book value** of the asset at the time of its sale

- Its **net sale price**, which is the price minus any costs of making the sale.

	£	£
Sales proceeds		X
Less: cost of making the sale		(X)
Net sale proceeds		X
Cost of fixed asset	X	
Less: accumulated depreciation	(X)	
Net book value		(X)
Profit/(loss) on disposal		X/(X)

A **profit** is made when the **net sale proceeds exceed the net book value,** and a **loss** is made when the **net sales proceeds are less than the net book value.** (There may be no proceeds, if the asset is scrapped, stolen or destroyed. In that case the net book value is the **loss** to the business.)

8.4 EXAMPLE: DISPOSAL OF A FIXED ASSET

A business purchased a fixed asset on 1 January 20X4 for £25,000. It had an estimated life of six years and an estimated residual value of £7,000. The asset was eventually sold after three years on 1 January 20X7 to another trader who paid £17,500 for it.

What was the profit or loss on disposal, assuming that the business uses the straight line method for depreciation?

8.5 SOLUTION

$$\text{Annual depreciation} = \frac{£(25,000 - 7,000)}{6 \text{ years}}$$

$$= £3,000 \text{ per annum}$$

	£
Cost of asset	25,000
Less accumulated depreciation (three years)	9,000
Net book value at date of disposal	16,000
Sale price	17,500
Profit on disposal	1,500

This profit will be shown in the profit and loss account where it will be an item of **other income** added to the gross profit brought down from the trading account.

Activity 5.5

A business purchased a machine on 1 July 20X4 at a cost of £35,000. The machine had an estimated residual value of £3,000 and a life of eight years. The machine was sold for £18,600 on 31 December 20X7, the last day of the accounting year. To make the sale, the business incurred dismantling costs and transportation costs to the buyer's premises. These amounted to £1,200.

The business uses the straight line method of depreciation. What was the profit or loss on disposal?

Accounting for the disposal of fixed assets

8.6 It is customary in ledger accounting to record the disposal of fixed assets in a **disposal of fixed assets account.**

> *Step 1* Calculate the profit or loss on disposal which is the difference between:
>
> (a) The **sale price** of the asset (if any)
> (b) The **net book value** of the asset at the time of sale

BPP
PUBLISHING

Step 2 The **relevant items** which must appear in the disposal of fixed assets account are as follows.

(a) The original value of the asset at cost (DR)
(b) The accumulated depreciation up to the date of sale (CR)
(c) The sale price of the asset (CR)

Step 3 The **ledger accounting entries** are therefore as follows.

(a) DEBIT Disposal of fixed asset account
  CREDIT Fixed asset account

  with the cost of the asset disposed of

(b) DEBIT Provision for depreciation account
  CREDIT Disposal of fixed asset account

  with the accumulated depreciation on the asset as at the date of sale

(c) DEBIT Debtor account or cash book
  CREDIT Disposal of fixed asset account

  with the sale price of the asset

The sale is therefore not recorded in a sales account, but in the disposal of fixed asset account.

Step 4 The balance on the disposal account is the **profit or loss on disposal** and the corresponding double entry is recorded in the **profit and loss account.**

DISPOSAL OF FIXED ASSETS

	£		£
Fixed asset account	100	Provision for depreciation account	50
Profit and loss account (profit)	15	Cash/debtor account	65
	115		115

8.7 EXAMPLE: LEDGER ENTRIES FOR THE DISPOSAL OF FIXED ASSETS

A business has £110,000 worth of machinery at cost. Its policy is to make a provision for depreciation at 20% per annum straight line. The total provision now stands at £70,000. The business now sells for £19,000 a machine which it purchased exactly two years ago for £30,000. Show the relevant ledger entries.

8.8 SOLUTION

PLANT AND MACHINERY ACCOUNT

	£		£
Balance b/d	110,000	Plant disposals account	30,000
		Balance c/d	80,000
	110,000		110,000
Balance b/d	80,000		

PLANT AND MACHINERY DEPRECIATION PROVISION

	£		£
Plant disposals (20% of		Balance b/d	70,000
£30,000 for 2 years)	12,000		
Balance c/d	58,000		
	70,000		70,000
		Balance b/d	58,000

PLANT DISPOSALS

	£		£
Plant and machinery account	30,000	Depreciation provision	12,000
P&L a/c (profit on sale)	1,000	Cash	19,000
	31,000		31,000

Check

	£
Asset at cost	30,000
Accumulated depreciation at time of sale	12,000
Net book value at time of sale	18,000
Sale price	19,000
Profit on sale	1,000

8.9 FURTHER EXAMPLE: LEDGER ENTRIES FOR THE DISPOSAL OF FIXED ASSETS

A business purchased two bolt-making machines on 1 January 20X5 at a cost of £15,000 each. Each had an estimated life of five years and a nil residual value. The straight line method of depreciation is used.

Owing to an unforeseen slump in demand for bolts, the business decided to reduce its output of bolts, and switch to making other products instead. On 31 March 20X7, one bolt-making machine was sold (on credit) to a buyer for £8,000. Later in the year, it was decided to abandon production of bolts altogether, and the second machine was sold on 1 December 20X7 for £2,500 cash.

Prepare the machinery account, provision for depreciation of machinery account and disposal of machinery account for the accounting year to 31 December 20X7.

8.10 SOLUTION

Workings

(1) At 1 January 20X7, accumulated depreciation on the machines will be:

$$2 \text{ machines} \times 2 \text{ years} \times \frac{£15,000}{5} = £12,000, \text{ or } £6,000 \text{ per machine}$$

(2) Monthly depreciation is $\frac{£3,000}{12} = £250$ per machine per month

(3) The machines are disposed of in 20X7.

    (i)   *On 31 March:* after three months of the year

        Depreciation for the year on the machine = 3 months × £250 = £750

    (ii) *On 1 December:* after 11 months of the year

        Depreciation for the year on the machine = 11 months × £250 = £2,750

MACHINERY ACCOUNT

Date		£	Date		£
20X7			20X7		
1 Jan	Balance b/d	30,000	31 Mar	Disposal of machinery account	15,000
			1 Dec	Disposal of machinery account	15,000
		30,000			30,000

PROVISION FOR DEPRECIATION OF MACHINERY

Date		£	Date		£
20X7			20X7		
31 Mar	Disposal of machinery account*	6,750	1 Jan	Balance b/f	12,000
1 Dec	Disposal of machinery account**	8,750	31 Dec	P & L account***	3,500
		15,500			15,500

*Depreciation at date of disposal = £6,000 + £750
**Depreciation at date of disposal = £6,000 + £2,750
***Depreciation charge for the year = £750 + £2,750

DISPOSAL OF MACHINERY

Date		£	Date		£
20X7			20X7		
31 Mar	Machinery account	15,000	31 Mar	Debtor account (sale price)	8,000
			31 Mar	Provision for depreciation	6,750
1 Dec	Machinery account	15,000	1 Dec	Cash (sale price)	2,500
			1 Dec	Provision for depreciation	8,750
			31 Dec	P & L account (loss on disposals)	4,000
		30,000			30,000

You should be able to calculate that there was a loss on the first disposal of £250, and on the second disposal a loss of £3,750, giving a total loss of £4,000.

Activity 5.6

The financial year of Holloway Ltd ended on 31 May 20X7.

At 1 June 20X6 the company owned motor vehicles costing £124,000 which had been depreciated by a total of £88,000.

On 1 August 20X6 Holloway plc sold motor vehicles, which had cost £54,000 and which had been depreciated by £49,000, for £3,900 and purchased new motor vehicles costing £71,000.

It is the policy of Holloway plc to depreciate its motor vehicles at 35% per annum using the reducing balance method. A full year's depreciation is charged on all motor vehicles in use at the end of each year. No depreciation is charged for the year on assets disposed of during that year.

Required

Show the following accounts as they would appear in the ledger of Holloway plc for the year ended 31 May 20X7 only.

(a) The motor vehicles account
(b) The provision for depreciation: motor vehicles account

(c)   The assets disposals account

Accounting for part exchange: purchase and sale together

8.11   Frequently a business will choose to fund part or all of a purchase by **part exchange**. It hands over an asset it already owns in exchange for a new asset, and pays for any balance separately. The **value** attributed to the part exchanged asset is agreed with the buyer. It almost certainly will *not* be the asset's net book value.

8.12   From an accounting point of view, part exchange simply means that **a purchase and a sale need to be accounted for together** as follows.

Step 1	Open up a fixed asset disposal account.
Step 2	Enter in the disposal account the transferred asset's cost and accumulated depreciation.

DEBIT   Fixed asset disposal
CREDIT   Fixed asset account
DEBIT   Accumulated depreciation
CREDIT   Fixed asset disposal

Step 3	Open up the new fixed asset's account.
Step 4	Enter in the new fixed asset account the part of the new fixed asset's cost which is settled by the agreed part exchange value.

DEBIT   Fixed asset account
CREDIT   Fixed asset disposal

Step 5	Enter in the fixed asset account the balance of the purchase price (if any).

DEBIT   Fixed asset account
CREDIT   Cash/Creditors

Step 6	Calculate the profit/loss on the disposal account and transfer to the profit and loss account.

8.13 EXAMPLE: LEDGER ENTRIES FOR PART EXCHANGE

Sam has a number of sales reps who all have cars, which are each replaced after a year. Carrie's car, an Astro, is due for renewal on 31 May 20X3 having been bought on 1 June 20X2 for £13,500. Sam negotiates a part exchange value for the Astro of £9,000 on 31 May 20X3, at which time its accumulated depreciation is £5,500. Carrie's new car, a Smartie, costs £14,200. The balance of this cost is to be paid in cash on 31 May 20X3.

Required

Prepare journals reflecting these transactions and enter up and balance the required ledger accounts.

8.14 SOLUTION

			£	£
Step 1	See below			
Step 2	DEBIT	Fixed asset disposal a/c – Astro	13,500	
	CREDIT	Fixed asset a/c – Astro		13,500
	DEBIT	Accumulated depreciation a/c – Astro	5,500	
	CREDIT	Fixed asset disposal a/c - Astro		5,500
Step 3	See below			
Step 4	DEBIT	Fixed asset a/c - Smartie	9,000	
	CREDIT	Fixed asset disposal a/c - Astro		9,000
Step 5	DEBIT	Fixed asset a/c - Smartie	5,200	
	CREDIT	Cash		5,200
Step 6	DEBIT	Fixed asset disposal a/c - Astro	1,000	
	CREDIT	Profit and loss a/c - profit on sale of Astro		1,000

FIXED ASSET DISPOSAL - ASTRO

		£			£
31/5/X3	Fixed asset	13,500	31/5/X3	Accumulated dep'n	5,500
	P&L - profit on			Fixed asset -	
	disposal	1,000		Smartie	9,000
		14,500			14,500

FIXED ASSET - ASTRO

		£			£
31/5/X3	Balance b/d	13,500	31/5/X3	Fixed asset disposal	13,500

ACCUMULATED DEPRECIATION - ASTRO

		£			£
31/5/X3	Fixed asset disposal	5,500	31/5/X3	Balance b/d	5,500

FIXED ASSET - SMARTIE

		£			£
31/5/X3	Fixed asset disposal - Astro	9,000	31/5/X3	Balance c/d	14,200
	Cash	5,200			
		14,200			14,200

CASH (EXTRACT)

		£			£
			31/5/X3	Fixed asset - Smartie	5,200

PROFIT AND LOSS (EXTRACT)

		£			£
			31/5/X3	Fixed asset disposal - profit on Astro	1,000

Activity 5.7

Jim is the owner of a taxi business and his financial year runs from 1 July to 30 June. On 1 July 20X8 he had two vehicles used by his drivers, one a Ford purchased on 10 January 20X6 for £10,000 and the other a Lada purchased on 12 August 20X6 for £8,000.

Jim replaced the Ford and traded it in for a Skoda costing £15,500. Jim took delivery of the car on 14 November 20X8. The garage accepted the Ford together with a cheque for £9,500 in payment.

Vehicles are depreciated at 10% per annum reducing balance method, with a full year's depreciation charged in the year of purchase and no depreciation charged in the year of disposal.

Task

(a)   Calculate the value on 1 July 20X8 of both the Ford and the Lada.

(b)   Draw up the motor vehicles account, the provision for depreciation: motor vehicles account and the motor vehicles disposal account as they would appear in the ledger for the year ended 30 June 20X9. Show clearly any transfers to or from the profit and loss account and any closing balances.

Authorisation of disposals

8.15   A **disposal** (ie sale or scrapping) of an asset over a certain amount must be authorised. Below is an asset disposal authorisation form. Note that the form contains a space for the reason for disposal. This will generally be that the asset has become obsolete or worn out but it could be that the asset was not present at the last physical count, in this case the 'sale proceeds' would be nil, or it could be that the asset has been part exchanged.

ASSET DISPOSAL
AUTHORISATION FORM

Business ....

Description and location of asset ....

....

....

Date of purchase ....

Date of disposal ....

Original cost ....

Accumulated depreciation ....

Net book value ....

Sale/scrap proceeds/part exchange value ....

Profit/loss to profit and loss account ....

Reason for disposal ....

....

Part exchanged for: ....

Authorised by: ....

Counter-authorised (if original cost over £1,000) by: ....

PLEASE RETURN TO PENNY WISE, FINANCIAL CONTROLLER

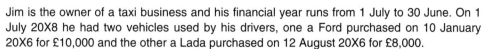

8.16 It is vital that the disposal of the asset should be recorded in the **asset register** as well as the ledger account, as we shall see in the next section.

9 RECONCILING PHYSICAL ASSETS, LEDGER ACCOUNTS AND REGISTER

9.1 It is very important that there are **controls over fixed assets**. The fixed assets register has already been mentioned. Two further points should be made in this context.

(a) The fixed assets register must **reconcile** with the **general ledger fixed asset account**.

(b) The fixed assets register must **reconcile** with the **physical presence** of capital items.

The fixed assets register and the general ledger

9.2 Generally, the fixed assets register is **not integrated** with the general ledger. In our example of a fixed assets register in Paragraph 4.8, the entry lists the general ledger accounts (cost account, accumulated depreciation account and depreciation expense account) to which the relevant amounts must be posted and also contains other details not required in those general ledger accounts. The fixed assets register is not part of the double entry and is there for **memorandum and control purposes**.

9.3 The fixed asset register must be **reconciled to the general ledger** to make sure that all additions, disposals and depreciation provisions and charges have been posted. The total of all the 'cost' figures in the fixed assets register for motor vehicles should equal the balance on the 'motor vehicles cost' account in the general ledger, the same goes for accumulated depreciation.

9.4 If discrepancies arise between the register and the general ledger, these must be **investigated**. It could be that there is a delay in sending the appropriate authorisation form where an asset has been disposed of.

The fixed assets register and the fixed assets

9.5 It is possible that the fixed assets register may not reconcile with the fixed assets actually present. This may be for the following reasons.

(a) An asset has been **stolen** and this has not been noticed or not recorded.

(b) A fixed asset may have become **obsolete or damaged** and needs to be written down but the appropriate entries have not been made.

(c) New assets have been **purchased** but are not yet recorded in the register because the register has not been kept up to date.

(d) **Errors** have been made in entering details in the register.

9.6 It is important therefore that the company:

(a) **Physically inspects** all the items in the fixed assets register

(b) Keeps the fixed assets register **up to date**.

9.7 The inspection will obviously vary between organisations. A large company might carry out a fixed asset inspection of 25% of assets by value each year, aiming to cover all categories every four years. A small business might be able to inspect all its fixed assets each day, although this 'inspection' will probably not be formally recorded.

Dealing with discrepancies

9.8 Some assets may require an adjustment in their **expected life** due to excessive wear and tear. Changes in estimations of the life of an asset must have the correct authorisation, and the information should be communicated to the accounts department who will need to make adjustments in the journal, the register and the ledger.

9.9 When discrepancies are discovered, the **appropriate action** must be taken. It may be possible to resolve the discrepancy by updating the fixed assets register and/or nominal ledger to reflect the new position. It may not be possible for the person who discovers the discrepancy to resolve it himself. For example, if a fixed asset has to be revalued downwards due to wear and tear or obsolescence, he may have to refer the matter to his superior who has more experience and judgement in such matters.

Computer-based asset management systems

9.10 Larger businesses can use computer-based asset management systems which work on **barcodes**, all assets have a barcode affixed on purchase and hand-held barcode readers can be used to check assets to the register automatically. This makes the management of assets much easier, but it is expensive to install. Barcodes do help to combat theft, however, and the subsequent savings can be substantial.

Activity 5.8

The following information has been taken from the ledger of Annette Ltd as at 31 May 20X7.

	£
Land	80,000
Buildings	160,000
Fixtures and fittings	176,000
Motor vehicles	90,000
Provisions for depreciation	
Land and buildings	32,000
Fixtures and fittings	88,000
Motor vehicles	54,000

The above information is before taking the following into account.

(a) During the year ended 31 May 20X7 motor vehicles which had cost £30,000 and which had a net book value of £6,000 were sold for £9,000.

(b) Depreciation has yet to be provided for as follows.

On buildings	2% straight line method
On fixtures and fittings	25% reducing balance method
On motor vehicles	20% straight line method

Note that no depreciation is charged on land.

Part B: Recording capital acquisitions and disposals

Required

Prepare in so far as the above information permits the following ledger accounts for the year ended 31 May 20X7.

(a)   Assets disposals
(b)   Provision for depreciation: land and buildings
(c)   Provision for depreciation: fixtures and fittings
(d)   Provision for depreciation: motor vehicles

Key learning points

- **Capital expenditure** results in the acquisition of fixed assets or an improvement in their earning capacity. **Revenue expenditure** is expenditure which is incurred for the purpose of the trade of the business or to maintain the existing earning capacity of fixed assets.

- Only **material items** should be capitalised.

- Three important matters must be considered before proceeding with the acquisition of a fixed asset:
  - ° **Funding** (retained profit, borrowing, HP, leasing, part exchange)
  - ° **Authorisation**
  - ° **Organisational implications** (liquidity, staffing, training, productivity, marketing, premises, running expenses, profitability)

- The book of prime entry from which postings are made relating to purchases, sales and depreciation of fixed assets is the **journal**.

- Most organisations keep a **fixed assets register**. This is a listing of all fixed assets owned by the organisation broken down perhaps by department, location or asset type. This must be kept up to date.

- Since a fixed asset has a cost and a limited useful life and its value eventually declines, it follows that a charge should be made in the trading, profit and loss account to reflect the use that is made of the asset by the business. This charge is called **depreciation**.

- The two most common methods of depreciation are:
  - ° The **straight line** method
  - ° The **reducing balance** method.

- The **accounting entries** to record depreciation are:

  DEBIT   Depreciation expense account (in the P & L)
  CREDIT   Provision for depreciation account

- The **profit or loss on disposal** of fixed assets is the difference between the sale proceeds of the asset (if any) and the net book value of the asset at the time of sale.

- Disposals must be properly **authorised**.

- **Discrepancies** between the fixed assets register and the actual fixed assets present and between the fixed assets register and the nominal ledger must be investigated and either resolved or referred to the appropriate person.

Quick quiz

1   Define a fixed asset.
2   Under which concept should small value assets not be capitalised?
3   The fixed asset register is part of the double entry system. True or false?
4   What does depreciation measure?
5   What is an asset's net book value?
6   Depreciation is a cash expense. True or false?
7   When would it be appropriate to use the reducing balance method of deprecation?
8   What considerations should apply when deciding which method of depreciation to use?

9   How is the profit or loss on the sale of a fixed asset calculated?

10   What types of checks should be made over fixed assets and the register?

Answers to quick quiz

1   A fixed asset is one which is bought and kept by a business with a view to earning profits and not merely turning into cash.

2   The materiality concept.

3   False. The fixed asset register is separate from the double entry system.

4   Depreciation measures the wearing out, consumption or other reduction in the economic life of a fixed asset.

5   Net book value is the value (usually cost) of the asset less accumulated depreciation to date.

6   False. Depreciation allocates costs to future periods under the matching concept.

7   When it is fair to allocate a greater proportion of depreciation in the early years of ownership and a lower amount towards the end.

8   (a)   Allocation of costs to benefits (matching)
     (b)   Method used for similar assets (consistency)
     (c)   Ease of application

9   The profit or loss is the difference between the sale price of the asset (if any) and the net book value of the asset at the time of sale.

10   The register should be reconciled with the physical assets and with the fixed asset accounts in the nominal ledger.

Part C
Recording income and expenditure; final accounts

6 Final accounts and the accounting system

This chapter contains

1   Introduction to final accounts

2   The accounting system

3   Classifying income and expenditure

4   SSAP 13 Accounting for research and development

Learning objectives

- Ensure that all relevant information is correctly identified and recorded

- Ensure that the organisation's policies, procedures, regulations and timescales for preparing final accounts are observed

- Identify ledgers as the key source of information

- Analyse income and expenditure

- Understand how the accounting systems of an organisation are affected by its structure, administrative systems and procedures, and transactions

- Understand the main requirements of SSAP 13 (R&D)

- Investigate business transactions with tact and courtesy

- Maintain the confidentiality of business transactions

Performance criteria

5.2.1 All income and expenditure is correctly identified and recorded in the appropriate records

5.2.3 The organisation's policies, regulations, procedures and timescales in relation to recording income and expenditure are observed

5.3.2 All relevant information is correctly identified and recorded

5.3.3 Investigations into business transactions are conducted with tact and courtesy

5.3.4 The organisation's policies, regulations, procedures and timescales relating to preparing final accounts are observed

Range

5.2.1 Records: day book; journal; ledger

5.3.1 Sources of information: ledger; bank reconciliation; creditors' reconciliation; debtors' reconciliation

Knowledge and understanding

Main requirements of relevant SSAPs

1 INTRODUCTION TO FINAL ACCOUNTS

Starting at the end

1.1 We are starting our examination of the collection and collation of information for the completion of final accounts at the end of the process: **the final accounts**. Keep in mind what we are trying to achieve as we proceed through each stage of the preparation process. Go back to Sections 7 and 11 of Chapter 3 and familiarise yourself again with the layout of the balance sheet and profit and loss accounts.

CENTRAL ASSESSMENT ALERT

You have already looked at basic accounting, including the accounting system, ledger accounting and the concept of double entry accounting. Here we extend this basic knowledge, building up your skills in recording transactions and in accounts preparation. This will enable you to tackle the accounting and practical exercises in the Central Assessment.

1.2 As well as final accounts, we will look at some of the **rules** which must be used when preparing accounts. These rules are contained in Financial Reporting Standards (FRSs) and Statements of Standard Accounting Practice (SSAPs) which directly affect the preparation of accounts.

Why prepare accounts?

1.3 There are many reasons for preparing accounts, those given below are the main ones.

(a) The managers of a business will want to know how well the business is doing, and whether it is making a profit. Regular **management accounts** (often monthly) will help the managers control and guide the business.

(b) In some businesses the accounts are used to calculate **important numbers**, such as the share of profit due to each partner or the bonus due to the directors.

(c) Accounts must be prepared as a basis for the calculation of the **tax due** on any profits of the business.

(d) All limited companies are **obliged by law** to prepare accounts (usually yearly) in specific formats laid out in the Companies Act 1985. These form part of the company report which must be sent to all shareholders and filed at Companies House with the Registrar of Companies. Charities are also obliged by law to file accounts.

1.4 Whatever the primary reason is for the preparation of accounts, generally **all items are recorded in the same way,** although the presentation of the information in the final accounts may differ depending on the organisation in question. This chapter is concerned with how items of **income and expenditure** are recorded and classified.

Activity 6.1

What are the main reasons for and purposes behind preparing accounts?

The need for confidentiality, tact and courtesy

1.5 It is important to keep in perspective the role of the accountant in the organisation. The business transacted by any organisation - buying and selling, hiring and firing, doing deals, having new ideas and developing them - is often done in a climate of **uncertainty**, and information to hand is **not always perfect**. Many managers are not financially orientated, the priorities of accountants - to collect and collate information for the preparation of final accounts - actively **conflict** with those of managers: to get business done.

1.6 Because of this, and because any accountant is expected to behave professionally, two very important aspects of behaviour must always be demonstrated.

(a) **Confidentiality.** Information handled by accountants must always be treated with respect, and not disclosed to anyone inside or outside the organisation without good cause and due authorisation. This is particularly the case with: wages and salaries, terms of trade with customers and suppliers, total sales and profit margins, payment histories, customer databases. The requirements of the Data Protection Act must also be adhered to (see Unit 20 *Information Technology*).

(b) **Tact and courtesy.** People outside the organisation will judge it in relation to what they know of the organisation's staff. Rudeness, lateness and failure to reply to correspondence are examples of **discourtesy**. It is also important to be tactful, especially on matters such as payment histories, though **honesty** is also important. With insiders, these qualities are also true; if you want that accruals list today, you are more likely to get it if you're tactful, polite and helpful!

2 THE ACCOUNTING SYSTEM

2.1 You should have a good working knowledge of not only the accounting system, but also double entry accounting and ledger accounting. We can summarise the accounting system in the diagram below like the one shown in Chapter 1, but this time the **fixed asset register**, which we learnt about in Chapter 5, is added.

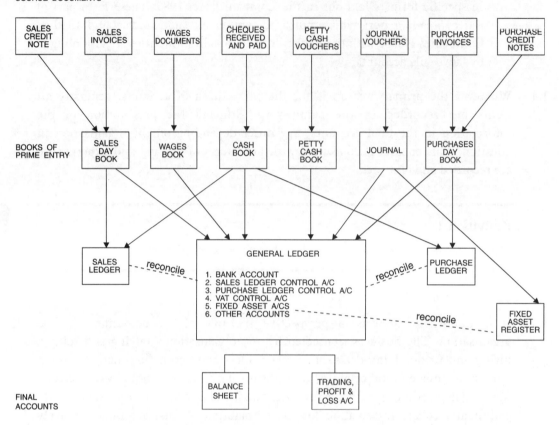

3 CLASSIFYING INCOME AND EXPENDITURE

3.1 In the profit and loss account we saw in Chapter 3, income and expenditure are classed under major headings, namely 'sales', 'cost of sales', 'distribution (and sales) expenses' and 'administrative expenses'. These headings group income and costs together in a convenient manner because they are deemed to be of the **same type** in some way. Although the distinction between different types of item is more arbitrary than between capital and revenue items, it is still important that **expense items are correctly recorded and classified**, both for management control purposes and to give a clear picture of the affairs of the business to the outside world.

3.2 In general, it will be the **policy of the organisation** which decides exactly how and where to record all items of income and expenditure.

Step 1 Accounts for **specific items** will be created within the accounting.

Step 2 The business will lay out guidelines which determine where **types** of income and expenditure should be posted. Transactions should be coded accordingly.

Step 3	Once items have been coded for posting, a person in authority (such as an accounts supervisor) should mark the item as **correctly coded**. Where it is uncertain how an item should be coded, then the **supervisor or a manager** should be consulted.
Step 4	A manager or supervisor will check posting summaries, or similar records, to ensure no **misposting** (posting to the wrong account) has taken place.

3.3 Sometimes it is necessary to split a single item into its different components for posting. Because of this the prime document used for posting is **stamped with a grid** on which the account numbers are marked; alternatively a 'posting slip' may be stuck on the document, showing the same information.

4 SSAP 13 ACCOUNTING FOR RESEARCH AND DEVELOPMENT

4.1 In your Foundation stage studies, and earlier in this Interactive Text, you have been concerned with making the following distinction:

Items	Dealt with by being:
Revenue	Expensed in the profit and loss account
Capital	Capitalised (included as an item) in the balance sheet and depreciated through the profit and loss account

In this section, we examine a similar problem in relation to **research and development (R & D) expenditure**.

4.2 In many businesses, especially those which produce food, or 'scientific' products such as medicines, or 'high technology' products, the expenditure on **research and development** is big. When R & D is a large item of cost, its accounting treatment may have a **material** impact on the profits of a business and its balance sheet valuation.

4.3 SSAP 13 defines research and development expenditure as falling into one or more of the following categories.

Category	Definition	Comment
Pure research	Original research to obtain **new scientific or** technical **knowledge** or understanding	There is no clear commercial benefit. Such research work does not have a practical application. This type of research may provide new knowledge which can subsequently be exploited
Applied research	Original research work which seeks to obtain new scientific or technical knowledge, but which has a **specific practical aim or application** (ie research on improvements in the effectiveness of medicines)	Applied research may develop from 'pioneering' pure research, but many businesses have full-time research teams working on applied research projects

BPP PUBLISHING

Category	Definition	Comment
Development	The use of existing scientific and technical knowledge to produce new (or substantially improved) products or systems, prior to starting commercial production operations	Many different parts of a business will be involved in the development stage, for instance, marketing and finance, as well as technical people.

4.4   The dividing line between each of these categories will often be **indistinct in practice,** and some expenditure might be classified as research or as development. It may be even more difficult to distinguish development costs from production costs. For example, if a prototype model of a new product is developed and then sold to a customer, the costs of the prototype will include both development and production expenditure.

4.5   SSAP 13 states that, although there may be practical difficulties in isolating research costs and development costs, there is a difference of principle in the method of accounting for each type of expenditure.

(a)   Expenditure on **pure and applied research** is usually a continuing operation which is necessary to ensure a business's survival. One accounting period does not gain more than any other from such work, and it is therefore appropriate that research costs should be written off as they are incurred (in the year of expenditure).

(b)   The **development** of new and improved products is different, because development expenditure is incurred with a particular commercial aim in view and in the reasonable expectation of earning profits or reducing costs. **In these circumstances it is appropriate that development costs should be capitalised and matched against the future revenues.**

ASSESSMENT ALERT

Do not skip this section on research and development. It came up in a central assessment and it may come up again.

Activity 6.2

Farahead plc spends a great deal on research and development each year. In the year to 30 June 20X4 it employed a number of scientists engaged in academic pure research projects in astrophysics and biochemistry, at a cost of £350,000. Two such projects proved interesting and in the six months from 1 January 20X4 they have been developed further so as to find a way of applying the discoveries made to a commercial objective. This has cost £150,000. On 1 April 20X4 another project, commercialised in this way some time ago, reached the stage where a product was developed which should be marketed successfully within six months. £200,000 has been spent on this phase.

All these costs are currently expensed through the research ledger account. Draft journal entries to reflect the accounting treatment required by SSAP 13. State reasons for the approach you have taken.

Key learning points

- **Final accounts** in most organisations include a balance sheet and a profit and loss account.

- **Management accounts** are produced to help the managers guide and control the business.

- Items of income and expenditure are recorded in the accounting system once they have been **classified** so as to determine **where** they are recorded.

- Classification of items, and the **coding** required, depends on the **policies and procedures of the organisation**.

- Items need to end up in particular **categories in the profit and loss account and balance sheet,** and this helps any organisation to determine where items are recorded so as to facilitate preparation of final accounts.

- Key **final account headings** are as follows.

P&L account	Balance sheet
Sales	Fixed assets
Cost of sales	Current assets
Selling & distribution expenses	Current liabilities
Administration expenses	Long-term liabilities
Finance expenses	Capital

- Often, general ledger codes are constructed so as to reflect the final account headings.

- SSAP 13 Accounting for research and development distinguishes between research costs and development costs. The latter may be capitalised and matched against future revenues.

Quick quiz

1   Why do we prepare accounts?

2   On what principle do final account headings group items of income or expense together?

3   How do you determine how items should be coded for posting?

4   What are the three main headings in the profit and loss account (*after* gross profit) to which items of expense are coded?

5   Is this always the case?

6   Following SSAP 13, what can happen to development costs in an organisation's final accounts?

Answers to quick quiz

1   Management accounts help the organisation's managers to control and guide it. Accounts help to calculate important numbers such as the profit share in a partnership and bonuses for managers in other businesses. Tax due is normally based on the business's accounts. And some organisations (companies and charities) are required to produce accounts by law.

2   On the basis that they are alike in some way.

3   By following the organisation's policies and procedures.

4   Selling and distribution expenses, administration expenses and finance expenses.

5   No - it depends on the organisation. For some businesses, this would be inappropriate.

6   The organisation may capitalise development costs in the balance sheet and depreciate them so as to match the expenditure with the income generated.

7 Control accounts and the correction of errors

This chapter contains

1   The operation of control accounts

2   The purpose of control accounts

3   Types of error in accounting

4   The correction of errors: journal entries

5   The correction of errors: suspense accounts

6   Other controls over business operations

7   Bank reconciliations

Learning objectives

- Prepare relevant accounts and reconciliations to allow for preparing final accounts

- Open and reconcile a suspense account

- Prepare creditors and debtors reconciliations, and bank reconciliations

- Use the transfer journal for correcting errors

- Identify and correct different types of error

Performance criteria

5.3.1 Relevant accounts and reconciliations are correctly prepared to allow the preparation of final accounts

5.3.6 The trial balance is accurately prepared and, where necessary, a suspense account is opened and reconciled

Range statement

5.2.1 Records: day book; journal; ledger

5.3.1 Sources of information: ledger; bank reconciliation; creditors' reconciliation; debtors' reconciliation

5.3.2 Discrepancies and unusual features: insufficient data has been provided; inconsistencies within the data

Knowledge and understanding

Identification and correction of different types of error

1 THE OPERATION OF CONTROL ACCOUNTS

1.1 **Typical entries** in the sales ledger and purchase ledger control accounts are listed below.

- Folio reference **Jnl** indicates that the transaction is first lodged in the journal before posting to the control account and other accounts indicated.

- References **SRDB** and **PRDB** are to sales returns and purchase returns day books.

SALES LEDGER (DEBTORS) CONTROL

	Folio	£		Folio	£
Opening debit balances	b/d	7,000	Opening credit balances	b/d	200
Sales	SDB	52,390	Cash received	CB	52,250
Dishonoured bills or	Jnl	1,000	Discounts allowed	CB	1,250
cheques			Returns inwards from		
Cash paid to clear credit			debtors	SRDB	800
balances	CB	110	Bad debts	Jnl	300
Closing credit balances	c/d	120	Closing debit balances	c/d	5,820
		60,620			60,620
Debit balances b/d		5,820	Credit balances b/d		120

Notes

1 Opening credit balances are unusual in the debtors control account. They represent debtors to whom the business owes money, probably as a result of the over payment of debts or for advance payments of debts for which no invoices have yet been sent.

2 Don't worry about bad debts here: they are covered in the next chapter. You only need to know that the double entry to record a bad debt written off is:

DEBIT Bad debt expense
CREDIT Sales ledger (debtors) control

PURCHASE LEDGER (CREDITORS) CONTROL

	Folio	£		Folio	£
Opening debit balance	b/d	70	Opening credit balances	b/d	8,300
Cash paid	CB	29,840	Purchases and other		
Discounts received	CB	30	expenses	PDB	31,000
Returns outwards to	PRDB		Cash received clearing		
suppliers		60	debit balances	CB	20
Closing credit balances	c/d	9,400	Closing debit balances	c/d	80
		39,400			39,400
Debit balances	b/d	80	Credit balances	b/d	9,400

Note. Opening debit balances in the creditors control account would represent suppliers who owe the business money, perhaps because debts have been overpaid or because debts have been prepaid before the supplier has sent an invoice.

1.2 **Posting** from the journal to the memorandum sales or bought ledgers and to the general ledger may be done as follows, where J Matthews has returned goods with a sales value of £100.

Journal entry	Folio	Dr £	Cr £
Sales	GL 401	100	
To debtors' control	GL 200		100
To J Matthews (memorandum)	SL 017	-	100
Return of electrical goods inwards			

Activity 7.1

At 1 September 20X7, the Earthminder Garden Business had no debtors at all. During September, the following transactions affecting credit sales and customers occurred.

(a) Sept 3   Invoiced H Duckworth for the sale on credit of plants: £170

(b) Sept 11   Invoiced T Carter for the sale on credit of garden tools: £260

(c) Sept 15   Invoiced J Matthews for the sale on credit of plants: £330

(d) Sept 10   Received payment from H Duckworth of £150, in settlement of his debt in full, having taken a permitted discount of £20 for payment within seven days

(e) Sept 18   Received a payment of £108 from T Carter in part settlement of £120 of his debt. A discount of £12 was allowed for payment within seven days of invoice

(f) Sept 28   Received a payment of £200 from J Matthews, who was unable to claim any discount

Account numbers are as follows.

SL 028   Personal account: H Duckworth
SL 105   Personal account: T Carter
SL 017   Personal account: J Matthews
GL 200   Debtors control account
GL 207   Discounts allowed
GL 401   Sales: plants
GL 402   Sales: garden tools
GL 100   Cash control account

Folio numbers beginning:

(a) SDB, refer to a page in the sales day book
(b) SL, refer to a particular account in the sales ledger
(c) GL, refer to a particular account in the general ledger
(d) CB, refer to a page in the cash book

Tasks

(a) Write up all the accounts listed above for the transactions which took place in September.

(b) Produce a trial balance as far as you are able.

Activity 7.2

A creditors control account contains the following entries:

	£
Bank	83,000
Credit purchases	86,700
Discounts received	4,130
Contra with debtors control account	5,200
Balance c/f at 31 December 20X7	13,700

There are no other entries in the account. What was the opening balance brought forward at 1 January 20X7?

Activity 7.3

The total of the balances in a business's sales ledger is £1,000 more than the debit balance on its debtors control account. Which one of the following errors could by itself account for the discrepancy?

A The sales day book has been undercast by £1,000

B Settlement discounts totalling £1,000 have been omitted from the general ledger

C One sales ledger account with a credit balance of £1,000 has been treated as a debit balance

D The cash receipts book has been undercast by £1,000

1.3 It may help you to see how the debtors ledger and debtors (control) account are used set out in **flowchart form**.

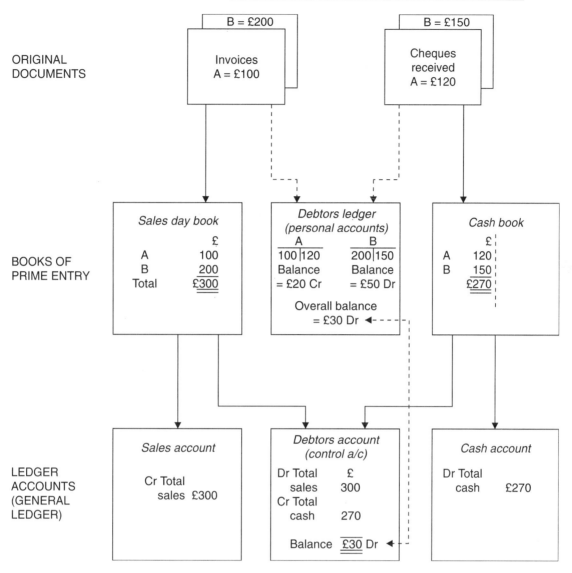

ORIGINAL
DOCUMENTS

BOOKS OF
PRIME ENTRY

LEDGER
ACCOUNTS
(GENERAL
LEDGER)

ASSESSMENT ALERT

Remember these important points.

*   The debtors ledger is not part of the double entry system (it is not used to post the ledger accounts).

*   Nevertheless, the total balance on the debtors ledger (ie all the personal account balances added up) should equal the balance on the debtors account (the debtors control account).

Activity 7.4

On examining the books of Archright Ltd, you ascertain that on 1 October 20X6 the debtors' ledger balances were £20,347 debit and £228 credit, and the creditors' ledger balances on the same date £18,024 credit and £319 debit.

For the year ended 30 September 20X7 the following particulars are available.

BPP PUBLISHING

		£
Sales		176,429
Purchases		108,726
Cash received from debtors		148,481
Cash paid to creditors		95,184
Discount received		2,798
Discount allowed		5,273
Returns inwards		3,180
Returns outwards		1,417
Bad debts written off		1,079
Cash received in respect of debit balances in creditors' ledger		319
Amount due from customer as shown by debtors' ledger, offset against amount due to the same firm as shown by creditors' ledger (settlement by contra)		949
Allowances to customers on goods damaged in transit		553

On 30 September 20X7 there were no credit balances in the debtors' ledger except those outstanding on 1 October 20X6, and no debit balances in the creditors' ledger.

You are required to write up the following accounts recording the above transactions bringing down the balances as on 30 September 20X7:

(a) Debtors control account
(b) Creditors control account

---

2 THE PURPOSE OF CONTROL ACCOUNTS

Reasons for having control accounts

2.1 There are various reasons for having control accounts; here is a comprehensive list.

Accuracy check

2.2 Control accounts provide a **check on the accuracy of entries made in the personal accounts** in the sales ledger and purchase ledger. It is very easy to make a mistake in posting entries, because there might be hundreds of entries to make. Figures might get transposed. Some entries might be omitted altogether, so that an invoice or a payment transaction does not appear in a personal account as it should. Compare:

(a) The total balance on the debtors control account with the total of individual balances on the personal accounts in the sales ledger

(b) The total balance on the creditors control account with the total of individual balances on the personal accounts in the purchase ledger

It is then possible to identify the fact that errors have been made.

Discovering errors

2.3 The control accounts can assist in the **location of errors,** where postings to the control accounts are made daily, weekly, or even monthly. If a clerk fails to record an invoice or a payment in a personal account, or makes a transposition error, it would be a formidable task to locate the error or errors at the end of a year, given the large number of transactions during the year. By using the control account, a comparison with the individual balances in the sales or purchase ledger can be made for every week or day of the month, and the error found much more quickly than if control accounts did not exist.

Internal check

2.4 Where there is a separation of clerical (bookkeeping) duties, the control account provides an **internal check**. The person posting entries to the control accounts will act as a check on a different person whose job it is to post entries to the sales and purchase ledger accounts.

Provides a total balance

2.5 To provide debtors' and creditors' balances more quickly for producing a trial balance or balance sheet. A single balance on a control account is **extracted more simply and quickly** than many individual balances in the sales or purchase ledger. The number of accounts in the double entry bookkeeping system can be kept down to a manageable size, since the personal accounts are memorandum accounts only and the control accounts instead provide the accounts required for a double entry system.

2.6 Particularly in **computerised systems**, it may be feasible to use sales and purchase ledgers without the need for operating separate control accounts. In such a system, the sales or purchase ledger printouts constitute the list of individual balances as well as providing a total balance which represents the control account balance.

CENTRAL ASSESSMENT ALERT

You may be asked to explain the purpose of control accounts. However, the most likely type of question is a **control account reconciliation**. This is covered below.

Balancing and agreeing control accounts with sales and purchase ledgers

2.7 The control accounts should be **balanced regularly** (at least monthly), and the balance on the account agreed with the sum of the individual debtors' or creditors' balances extracted from the sales or purchase ledgers respectively. More often than not the balance on the control account does not agree with the sum of balances extracted, for one or more of the following reasons.

(a) An **incorrect amount** may be **posted** to the control account because of a miscast of the total in the book of prime entry (ie adding up incorrectly the total value of invoices or payments). The general ledger debit and credit postings will then balance, but the control account balance will not agree with the sum of individual balances extracted from the (memorandum) sales ledger or purchase ledger. A journal entry must then be made in the general ledger to correct the control account and the corresponding sales or expense account.

(b) A **transposition** error may occur in posting an individual's balance from the book of prime entry to the memorandum ledger, eg the sale to J Matthews of £330 might be posted to his account as £303. This means that the sum of balances extracted from the memorandum ledger must be corrected. No accounting entry would be required to do this, except to alter the figure in J Matthews's account. (*Note*. It is easy to spot a possible transposition error, as the total error is always divisible by 9.)

(c) A transaction may be recorded in the control account and not in the memorandum ledger, or vice versa. This requires an entry in the ledger that has been **missed out** which means a double posting if the control account has to be corrected, and a single posting if it is the individual's balance in the memorandum ledger that is at fault.

(d) The sum of balances extracted from the memorandum ledger may be **incorrectly extracted** or **miscast**. This would mean correcting the total of the balances.

2.8 Reconciling the control account balance with the sum of the balances extracted from the (memorandum) sales ledger or purchase ledger should be done in two stages.

Step 1 Balance the accounts in the memorandum ledger, checking for errors. Correct the total of the balances extracted from the memorandum ledger.

	£	£
Sales ledger total		
Original total extracted		15,320
Add difference arising from transposition error (£95 written as £59)		36
		15,356
Less		
Credit balance of £60 extracted as a debit balance (£60 × 2)	120	
Overcast of list of balances	90	
		210
		15,146

Step 2 Bring down the balance before adjustments on the control account, and adjust or post the account with correcting entries.

DEBTORS CONTROL

	£		£
Balance before adjustments	15,091	Petty cash: posting omitted	10
		Returns inwards: individual posting omitted from control account	35
Undercast of total invoices issued in sales day book	100	Balance c/d (now in agreement with the corrected total of individual balances)	15,146
	15,191		15,191
Balance b/d	15,146		

Activity 7.5

Jackoran & Co sells goods on credit to most of its customers. In order to control its debtor collection system, the company maintains a sales ledger control account. In preparing the accounts for the year to 31 October 20X7 the accountant discovers that the total of all the personal accounts in the sales ledger amounts to £12,802, whereas the balance on the sales ledger control account is £12,550.

Upon investigating the matter, the following errors were discovered.

(a) Sales for the week ending 27 March 20X7 amounting to £850 had been omitted from the control account.

(b) A debtor's account balance of £300 had not been included in the list of balances.

(c) Cash received of £750 had been entered in a personal account as £570.

(d) Discounts allowed totalling £100 had not been entered in the control account.

(e) A personal account balance had been undercast by £200

(f) A contra item of £400 with the purchase ledger had not been entered in the control account.

(g) A bad debt of £500 had not been entered in the control account.

(h) Cash received of £250 had been debited to a personal account.

(i) Discounts received of £50 had been debited to Kenton's sales ledger account.

(j) Returns inwards valued at £200 had not been included in the control account.

(k) Cash received of £80 had been credited to a personal account as £8.

(l) A cheque for £300 received from a customer had been dishonoured by the bank, but no adjustment had been made in the control account.

Tasks

(a) Prepare a corrected sales ledger control account, bringing down the amended balance as at 1 November 20X7.

(b) Prepare a statement showing the adjustments that are necessary to the list of personal account balances so that it reconciles with the amended sales ledger control account balance.

3   TYPES OF ERROR IN ACCOUNTING

3.1   You have already learned about errors which arise in the context of the cash book or the sales and purchase ledgers and debtors and creditors control account. Here we deal with errors that may be corrected by means of the **journal** or a **suspense account**.

3.2   It is not possible to draw up a complete list of all the errors which might be made by bookkeepers and accountants. If you tried, it is likely someone would commit a completely new error that you had not thought of. However, it is possible to describe five **types of error** which cover most of the errors which might occur. They are as follows (you may remember some of these from an earlier section).

- Errors of **transposition**
- Errors of **omission**
- Errors of **principle**
- Errors of **commission**
- **Compensating** errors

3.3   Once an error has been detected, it needs to be put right.

(a) If the correction **involves a double entry** in the ledger accounts, then it is done by using a **journal entry** in the journal.

(b) When the error **breaks the rule of double entry,** then it is corrected by the use of a **suspense account** as well as a journal entry.

Errors of transposition

> **KEY TERM**
>
> **Transposition** is when two digits are accidentally recorded the wrong way round.

BPP PUBLISHING

3.4 Suppose that a sale is recorded in the sales account as £11,279, but it has been incorrectly recorded in the total debtors account as £11,729. The error is the transposition of the 7 and the 2. The consequence is that total debits will not be equal to total credits. You can often detect a transposition error by checking whether the difference between debits and credits can be divided exactly by 9. For example, £11,729 – £11,279 = £450; £450 ÷ 9 = 50. (This only works, if transposition is the *only* problem!)

Errors of omission

> **KEY TERM**
>
> An **error of omission** means failing to record a transaction at all, or making a debit or credit entry, but not the corresponding double entry.

3.5 Here are two examples.

  (a) If a business receives an invoice from a supplier for £1,350, the transaction might be omitted from the books entirely. As a result, both the total debits and the total credits of the business will be out by £1,350.

  (b) If a business receives an invoice from a supplier for £820, the purchase ledger control account might be credited, but the debit entry in the purchases account might be omitted. In this case, the total credits would not equal total debits (because total debits are £820 less than they ought to be).

Errors of principle

> **KEY TERM**
>
> An **error of principle** involves making a double entry in the belief that the transaction is being entered in the correct accounts, but subsequently finding out that the accounting entry breaks the 'rules' of an accounting principle or concept.

3.6 A typical example of such an error is to treat certain revenue expenditure incorrectly as capital expenditure.

  (a) For example, repairs to a machine costing £300 should be treated as revenue expenditure, and debited to a repairs account. If, the repair costs are added to the cost of the fixed asset (capital expenditure) an error of principle would have occurred. Although total debits equal total credits, the repairs account is £300 less than it should be and the cost of the fixed asset is £300 greater than it should be.

  (b) Similarly, suppose that a proprietor sometimes takes cash for his personal use and during a certain year these drawings amount to £1,400. The bookkeeper reduces cash sales by £1,400 so that the cash book could be made to balance. This would be an error of principle, and the result of it would be that the drawings account is understated by £1,400, and so is the total value of sales in the sales account.

Errors of commission

> **KEY TERM**
>
> **Errors of commission** are where the bookkeeper makes a mistake in carrying out his or her task of recording transactions in the accounts.

3.7 Here are two common errors of commission.

(a) **Putting a debit entry or a credit entry in the wrong account**. If telephone expenses of £342 are debited to the electricity expenses account, an error of commission has occurred. Although total debits and total credits balance, telephone expenses are understated by £342 and electricity expenses are overstated by £342.

(b) **Errors of casting (adding up)**. Suppose that the total daily credit sales in the sales day book of a business should add up to £79,925, but are incorrectly added up as £79,325. The total sales in the sales day book are then used to credit total sales and debit total debtors in the ledger accounts, so that total debits and total credits are still equal, although incorrect.

Compensating errors

> **KEY TERM**
>
> **Compensating errors** are, coincidentally, equal and opposite to one another.

3.8 Two transposition errors of £360 might occur in extracting ledger balances, one on each side of the double entry. In the administration expenses account, £3,158 is written instead of £3,518, while in the sundry income account, £6,483 is written instead of £6,843. The debits and the credits would be £360 too low, and the mistake would not be apparent when the trial balance is cast. Consequently, compensating errors hide the fact that there are errors in the trial balance.

4   THE CORRECTION OF ERRORS: JOURNAL ENTRIES

4.1 Some errors can be corrected by **journal entries**. The format of a journal entry is:

Date	Folio	Debit	Credit
		£	£
Account to be debited		X	
Account to be credited			X
(Narrative to explain the transaction)			

> **ASSESSMENT ALERT**
>
> As already indicated, you are likely to be asked in a central or devolved assessment to present answers in the form of journal entries.

4.2 The journal requires a debit and an equal credit entry for each 'transaction' - ie for each correction. This means that if total debits equal total credits before a journal entry is made then they will still be equal after the journal entry is made. This would be the case if, for example, the original error was a debit wrongly posted as a credit or *vice versa*.

4.3 Similarly, if total debits and total credits are unequal before a journal entry is made, then they will still be unequal (by the same amount) after it is made.

4.4 Suppose £200 is misposted to the gas account instead of to the business rates account. A trial balance is drawn up, and total debits are £100,000 and total credits are £100,000. A journal entry is made to correct the misposting error as follows.

1.5.1997

| DEBIT | Business rates account | £200 | |
| CREDIT | Gas account | | £200 |

To correct a misposting of £200 between the gas account and the rates account.

4.5 After the journal has been posted, total debits will still be £100,000 and total credits will be £100,000. Total debits and totals credits are still equal.

4.6 Now suppose that, because of an error which has not yet been detected, total debits were originally £100,000 but total credits were £99,520. If the same correcting journal is put through, total debits will remain £100,000 and total credits will remain £99,520. Total debits were different by £480 *before* the journal, and they are still different by £480 *after* the journal.

4.7 This means that journals can only be used to correct errors which require both a credit and (an equal) debit adjustment.

4.8 EXAMPLE: JOURNAL ENTRIES

Listed below are five errors which were discussed in Section 3 of this chapter. Write out the journal entries which would correct these errors.

(a) A business receives an invoice for £1,350 from a supplier which was omitted from the books entirely.

(b) Repairs worth £300 were incorrectly debited to the fixed asset (machinery) account instead of the repairs account.

(c) The bookkeeper of a business reduces cash sales by £1,400 because he was not sure what the £1,400 represented. In fact, it was drawings.

(d) Telephone expenses of £342 are incorrectly debited to the electricity account.

(e) A page in the sales day book has been added up to £79,325 instead of £79,925.

4.9 SOLUTION

| (a) | DEBIT | Purchases | £1,350 | |
| | CREDIT | Creditors | | £1,350 |

A transaction previously omitted.

| (b) | DEBIT | Repairs account | £300 | |
| | CREDIT | Fixed asset (machinery) a/c | | £300 |

The correction of an error of principle: repairs costs incorrectly added to fixed asset costs

(c) DEBIT   Drawings   £1,400
      CREDIT   Sales   £1,400

An error of principle, in which sales were reduced to compensate for cash drawings not accounted for.

(d) DEBIT   Telephone expenses   £342
      CREDIT   Electricity expenses   £342

Correction of an error of commission; telephone expenses wrongly charged to the electricity account

(e) DEBIT   Debtors   £600
      CREDIT   Sales   £600

The correction of a casting error in the sales day book
(£79,925 – £79,325 = £600)

CENTRAL ASSESSMENT ALERT

A question might ask you to 'journalise' a transaction (ie write it out in the form of a journal entry), even though the transaction is perfectly normal and nothing to do with an error. This is the assessor's way of finding out whether you know your debits and credits. For example:

Question: A business sells £1,300 of goods on credit. Journalise the transaction.

Answer:

DEBIT   Debtors   £1,300
CREDIT   Sales   £1,300

Goods to the value of £1,300 sold on credit

No error has occurred here, just a normal credit sale. By asking you to put it in the form of a journal, the assessor can see that you understand the double entry accounting involved.

---

5   THE CORRECTION OF ERRORS: SUSPENSE ACCOUNTS

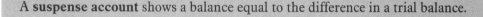

KEY TERM

A **suspense account** shows a balance equal to the difference in a trial balance.

5.1   A suspense account is a **temporary** account which can be opened for a number of reasons. The most common reasons are as follows.

(a) A trial balance is drawn up which **does not balance** (ie total debits do not equal total credits).

(b) The bookkeeper knows where to post the credit side of a transaction, but **does not know where to post the debit (or vice versa)**. A cash payment might be made and must obviously be credited to cash. But the bookkeeper may not know what the payment is for, and so will not know which account to debit.

5.2   In both these cases, the procedure is as follows:

Step 1	A temporary suspense account is opened up.
Step 2	Identify the problem and decide how to resolve it.
Step 3	Post the correcting entries using the journal.

Use of suspense account: when the trial balance does not balance

5.3 Say an error occurs which results in an **imbalance** between total debits and total credits in the ledger accounts. Suppose an accountant draws up a trial balance and finds that, for some reason total debits exceed total credits by £207.

Step 1	He knows that there is an error somewhere, but for the time being he opens a suspense account and enters a credit of £207 in it. This serves two purposes.
	(a) The accountant will not forget that there is an error to be sorted out.
	(b) Now that there is a credit of £207 in the suspense account, the trial balance balances.
Step 2	He finds that he had accidentally failed to make a credit of £207 to purchases.
Step 3	The journal entry would be:

DEBIT	Suspense a/c	£207	
CREDIT	Purchases		£207

To close off suspense a/c and correct error

5.4 When an error results in total debits not being equal to total credits, the first step an accountant makes is to open up a **suspense account**. Three more examples are given below.

5.5 EXAMPLE: TRANSPOSITION ERROR

The bookkeeper of Remico made a transposition error when entering an amount for sales in the sales account. Instead of entering the correct amount of £49,287.90 he entered £49,827.90, transposing the 2 and 8. The debtors were posted correctly, and so when total debits and credits on the ledger accounts were compared, it was found that credits exceeded debits by £(49,827.90 – 49,287.90) = £540.

5.6 SOLUTION

The initial step is to equalise the total debits and credits by posting a debit of £540 to a suspense account. When the cause of the error is discovered, the double entry to correct it should be logged in the journal as:

DEBIT	Sales	£540	
CREDIT	Suspense a/c		£540

To close off suspense a/c and correct transposition error

5.7 EXAMPLE: ERROR OF OMISSION

When Reckless Records paid the monthly salary cheques to its office staff, the payment of £21,372 was correctly entered in the cash account, but the bookkeeper omitted to debit the office salaries account. So the total debit and credit balances on the ledger accounts were not equal, and credits exceeded debits by £21,372 in the trial balance.

5.8 SOLUTION

The initial step in correcting the situation is to debit £21,372 to a suspense account, to equalise the total debits and total credits.

When the cause of the error is discovered, the double entry to correct it should be logged in the journal as:

DEBIT	Office salaries account	£21,372	
CREDIT	Suspense account		£21,372

To close off suspense account and correct error of omission

5.9 EXAMPLE: ERROR OF COMMISSION

A bookkeeper might make a mistake by entering what should be a debit entry as a credit, or vice versa. Suppose that a credit customer pays £1,220 of the £1,500 he owes to Polypaint Ltd, but Polypaint's bookkeeper has debited £1,220 on the debtors account in the nominal ledger by mistake instead of crediting the payment received.

5.10 SOLUTION

The total debit balances in Polypaint's ledger accounts now exceed the total credits by $2 \times £1,220 = £2,440$. The initial step would be to make a credit entry of £2,440 in a suspense account. When the cause of the error is discovered, it should be corrected as follows.

DEBIT	Suspense account	£2,440	
CREDIT	Debtors		£2,440

To close off suspense account and correct error of commission

In the debtors account in the general ledger, the correction would appear as follows.

DEBTORS ACCOUNT

	£		£
Balance b/d	1,500	Suspense account: error corrected	2,440
Payment incorrectly debited	1,220	Balance c/d	280
	2,720		2,720

Use of suspense account: not knowing where to post a transaction

5.11 The second use of suspense accounts is when a bookkeeper **does not know in which account to post one side of a transaction**. Until this is sorted out, the entry can be recorded in a suspense account. An example is when cash is received through the post from a source which cannot be determined. Another example is to credit proceeds on disposal of fixed assets to the suspense account instead of working out the profit or loss on disposal.

5.12 EXAMPLE: NOT KNOWING WHERE TO POST A TRANSACTION

Conway received a cheque in the post for £350. The name on the cheque is B Down, but the staff have no idea who this is, nor why he should be sending £350. The bookkeeper opens a suspense account, so that the double entry for the transaction is:

DEBIT	Cash	£350	
CREDIT	Suspense account		£350

It transpires that the cheque was for a debt owed by Bob's Boutique and paid out of the proprietor's personal bank account. The suspense account can now be cleared.

DEBIT	Suspense account	£350	
CREDIT	Debtors		£350

Activity 7.6

You are assisting the accountant of Ranchurch Ltd in preparing the accounts for the year ended 31 December 20X7. You draw up a trial balance and you notice that the credit side is greater than the debit side by £5,607.82. You enter this difference in a suspense account.

On investigation, the following errors and omissions are found to have occurred.

(a) An invoice for £1,327.40 for general insurance has been posted to cash but not to the ledger account.

(b) A customer went into liquidation just before the year end, owing Ranchurch £428.52. The amount was taken off debtors but the corresponding entry to expense the bad debt has not been made.

(c) A cheque paid for purchases has been posted to the purchases account as £5,296.38, when the cheque was made out for £5,926.38.

(d) A van was purchased during the year for £1,610.95, but this amount was credited to the motor vehicles account.

Tasks

(a) Show the journal required to clear the suspense account.
(b) Show the suspense account in ledger account form.

Suspense accounts might contain several items

5.13 If more than one error or unidentifiable posting to a ledger account arises during an accounting period, they will all be **merged together** in the same suspense account. Indeed, until the causes of the errors are discovered, the bookkeepers are unlikely to know exactly how many errors there are.

CENTRAL ASSESSMENT ALERT

You may be faced with a balance on a suspense account, together with enough information to make the necessary corrections, leaving a nil balance on the suspense account and correct balances on various other accounts. In practice, of course, finding these errors is far from easy!

Suspense accounts are temporary

5.14 A suspense account can only be **temporary**. Postings to a suspense account are only made when the bookkeeper doesn't know yet what to do, or when an error has occurred. Mysteries must be solved, and errors must be corrected. Under no circumstances should there still be a suspense account when it comes to preparing the balance sheet. The suspense account **must be cleared** and all the correcting entries made before the final accounts are drawn up.

6   OTHER CONTROLS OVER BUSINESS OPERATIONS

6.1 The use of control accounts and the use of suspense accounts are two ways in which businesses monitor the accurate operation of the accounting system. You should already be aware of these procedures individually, but we will mention them again briefly. All these procedures must be carried out with **sufficient frequency and regularity.**

Bank reconciliation

6.2 A bank reconciliation compares the balance of the cash in the business's records to the balance held by the bank. Differences between the balance on the bank statement and the balance in the cash book will be errors or timing differences, and they must be **identified and satisfactorily explained.**

Petty cash count/reconciliation

6.3 Petty cash should be reconciled regularly and any **discrepancies cleared or authorised** for write off. This will usually take place when the imprest is topped up. An organisation should do unannounced spot checks on petty cash as a check on the honesty of the petty cashier.

Reconciliation of purchase ledger accounts to supplier statements

6.4 Reconciliation of any part of a business's records to a **third party's records** is a useful check on the accuracy of the accounting system. As with bank reconciliations, this is a way of checking that your own records *and* those of the supplier (or bank) are correct.

Clearance of wages and other control accounts

6.5 All other types of control accounts should be checked regularly and **cleared** of all items which are not valid. There should be no 'unknowns' left in a control account balance.

VAT/sales tax reconciliation

6.6 The need for regular checks on the VAT or sales tax accounts is all the greater because the tax authorities may impose **severe penalties** for errors made.

Internal audit

6.7 Organisations may have an internal audit department. Internal auditors, as part of their work, **check controls and procedures** (including those above). They also carry out any other work required to ensure the accounting system is operating properly and accurately.

Reconciliation of fixed assets to the register

6.8 Fixed assets should be checked by sight, to check that they actually exist, and that they have not been **stolen or damaged**. Checks should also be made from the register to the physical assets to ensure that 'ghost' assets are not kept on the register. We looked at this in detail in Chapter 5.

CENTRAL ASSESSMENT ALERT

Section 1 of the Central Assessment will contain one or more of the following important accounting exercises: **make sure you can do them.**

Task	Covered in Chapter
Prepare trial balance	2
Identify and correct errors	7
Create and then clear suspense accounts	7
Reconcile debtors' or creditors' control a/c	7
Prepare bank reconciliation	7 (below)

7 BANK RECONCILIATIONS

CENTRAL ASSESSMENT ALERT

If you completed Foundation stage you will have covered bank reconciliations. Do **not** omit this section however; the standards at Intermediate Stage make explicit the fact that you must demonstrate competence in preparing bank reconciliations in this Unit. If you started at Intermediate, follow this section **very** carefully; it is a topic ripe for Central Assessment.

KEY TERM

A **bank reconciliation** is a comparison of a bank statement with the cash book. Differences between the balance on the bank statement and the balance in the cash book will be errors or timing differences, and they should be identified and satisfactorily explained.

The bank statement

7.1 It is a common practice for a business to issue a monthly statement to each credit customer, itemising:

(a) The **balance** he owed on his account at the **beginning** of the month.
(b) **New debts** incurred by the customer during the month.
(c) **Payments** made by him during the month.
(d) The **balance** he owes on his account at the **end** of the month.

In the same way, a bank statement is sent by a bank to its short-term debtors and creditors - ie customers with bank overdrafts and customers with money in their account - itemising the opening balance on the account, receipts into the account and payments from the account during the period, and the balance at the end of the period.

7.2 Remember that if a customer has money in his account, the bank owes him that money. The customer is therefore a **creditor** of the bank (hence the phrase 'to be in credit'). So, if a business has £8,000 cash in the bank, it will have a debit balance in its own cash book, but the bank statement, if it reconciles exactly with the cash book, will state that there is a credit balance of £8,000. (**The bank's records are a 'mirror image' of the customer's own records, with debits and credits reversed.**)

Why is a bank reconciliation necessary?

7.3 A bank reconciliation is needed to identify and account for the differences between the cash book and the bank statement.

Cause of difference	Comments
Error	Errors in calculation, or recording income and payments, are more likely to have been made by you than by the bank, but it is conceivable that the bank has made a mistake too.
Bank charges or bank interest	The bank might deduct charges for interest on an overdraft or for its services, which you are not informed about until you receive the bank statement.
Timing differences	There might be some cheques that you have received and paid into the bank, but which have not yet been 'cleared' and added to your account (**outstanding lodgements**). So although your own records show that some cash has been added to your account, it has not yet been acknowledged by the bank - although it will be in a very short time when the cheque is eventually cleared.
	Similarly, you might have made some payments by cheque, and reduced the balance in your account accordingly in the cash book, but the person who receives the cheque might not bank it for a while (**unpresented cheques**). Even when it is banked, it takes a day or two for the banks to process it and for the money to be deducted from your account.

What to look for when doing a bank reconciliation

7.4 The cash book and bank statement will rarely agree at a given date. If you are doing a bank reconciliation, you have to look for the following items.

(a) **Corrections and adjustments to the cash book:**

- Payments made to or from the bank account by **standing order**, which have not yet been entered in the cash book.

- **Dividends received** (on investments held by the business), paid direct into the bank account but not yet entered in the cash book.

- **Bank interest and bank charges**, not yet entered in the cash book.

(b) **Items reconciling the correct cash book balance to the bank statement:**

- Cheques drawn (ie paid) by the business and credited in the cash book, which have not yet been presented to the bank, or 'cleared', and so do not yet appear on the bank statement (**unpresented cheques**).

- Cheques received, paid into the bank and debited in the cash book, but which have not been cleared and entered in the account by the bank, and so do not appear on the bank statement (**outstanding lodgements**).

7.5 EXAMPLE: BANK RECONCILIATION

At 30 September 20X6, the balance in the cash book of Wordsworth Ltd was £805.15 debit. A bank statement on 30 September 20X6 showed Wordsworth Ltd to be in credit by £1,112.30.

On investigation of the difference between the two sums, it was established that:

(a) The cash book had been undercast by £90.00 on the debit side.
(b) Cheques paid in not yet credited by the bank amounted to £208.20.
(c) Cheques drawn not yet presented to the bank amounted to £425.35.

Required

(a) Show the correction to the cash book.

(b) Prepare a statement reconciling the balance per bank statement to the balance per cash book.

7.6 SOLUTION

(a)		£
Cash book balance brought forward		805.15
Add		
Correction of undercast		90.00
Corrected balance		895.15

(b)	£	£
Balance per bank statement		1,112.30
Add		
Cheques paid in, recorded in the cash book, but not yet credited to the account by the bank	208.20	
Less		
Cheques paid by the company but not yet presented to the company's bank for settlement	425.35	
		(217.15)
Balance per cash book		895.15

Activity 7.7

On 31 January 20X8 a business's cash book showed a credit balance of £150 on its current account which did not agree with the bank statement balance. In performing the reconciliation the following points come to light.

	£
Not recorded in the cash book	
Bank charges	36
Transfer from deposit account to current account	500
Not recorded on the bank statement	
Unpresented cheques	116
Outstanding lodgements	630

It was also discovered that the bank had debited the business account with a cheque for £400 in error. What was the original balance on the bank statement?

Activity 7.8

A business's bank statement shows £715 direct debits and £353 investment income not recorded in the cash book. The bank statement does not show a customer's cheque for £875 entered in the cash book on the last day of the accounting period. If the cash book shows a credit balance of £610 what balance appears on the bank statement?

7.7 EXAMPLE: MORE COMPLICATED BANK RECONCILIATION

On 30 June 20X0, Cook's cash book showed that he had an overdraft of £300 on his current account at the bank. A bank statement as at the end of June 20X0 showed that Cook was in credit with the bank by £65.

On checking the cash book with the bank statement you find the following.

(a) Cheques drawn, amounting to £500, had been entered in the cash book but had not been presented.

(b) Cheques received, amounting to £400, had been entered in the cash book, but had not been credited by the bank.

(c) On instructions from Cook the bank had transferred interest received on his deposit account amounting to £60 to his current account, recording the transfer on 5 July 20X0. This amount had been credited in the cash book as on 30 June 20X0.

(d) Bank charges of £35 shown in the bank statement had not been entered in the cash book.

(e) The payments side of the cash book had been undercast by £10.

(f) Dividends received amounting to £200 had been paid direct to the bank and not entered in the cash book.

(g) A cheque for £50 drawn on deposit account had been shown in the cash book as drawn on current account.

(h) A cheque issued to Jones for £25 was replaced when out of date. It was entered again in the cash book, no other entry being made. Both cheques were included in the total of unpresented cheques shown above.

Tasks

(a) Indicate the appropriate adjustments in the cash book.

(b) Prepare a statement reconciling the amended balance with that shown in the bank statement.

7.8 SOLUTION

(a) The errors to correct are given in notes (c) (e) (f) (g) and (h) of the problem. Bank charges (note (d)) also call for an adjustment.

	Adjustments in cash book	
	Debit	*Credit*
	(ie add to	*(ie deduct from*
	cash balance)	*cash balance)*
	£	£
Item		
(c) Cash book incorrectly *credited* with interest on 30 June		
It should have been *debited* with the receipt	60	
(c) Debit cash book (current a/c) with transfer of interest from deposit a/c (note 1)	60	
(d) Bank charges		35
(e) Undercast on payments (credit) side of cash book		10
(f) Dividends received should be debited in the cash book	200	
(g) Cheque drawn on deposit account, not current account.		
Add cash back to current account	50	
(h) Cheque paid to Jones is out of date and so cancelled.		
Cash book should now be debited, since previous credit entry is no longer valid (note 2)	25	
	395	45

	£	£
Cash book: balance on current account as at 30 June 20X0		(300)
Adjustments and corrections:		
Debit entries (adding to cash)	395	
Credit entries (reducing cash balance)	(45)	
Net adjustments		350
Corrected balance in the cash book		50

Notes

1   Item (c) is rather complicated. The instruction to transfer interest from the deposit to the current account was presumably given to the bank on or before 30 June 20X0. The correct entry is to debit the current account (and credit the deposit account) the correction in the cash book should be to debit the current account with 2 × £60 = £120 - ie to cancel out the incorrect credit entry in the cash book and then to make the correct debit entry. The bank does not record the transfer until 5 July, and so it does not appear in the bank statement.

2   Item (h). Two cheques have been paid to Jones, but one is now cancelled. Since the cash book is credited whenever a cheque is paid, it should be debited whenever a cheque is cancelled. The amount of cheques paid but not yet presented should be reduced by the amount of the cancelled cheque.

(b)   BANK RECONCILIATION STATEMENT AT 30 JUNE 20X0

	£	£
Balance per bank statement		65
Add: outstanding lodgements		
(ie cheques paid in but not yet credited)	400	
deposit interest not yet credited	60	
		460
		525
Less: unpresented cheques	500	
less cheque to Jones cancelled	25	
		475
Balance per corrected cash book		50

Tutorial note. You might be interested to see the adjustments to the cash book in part (a) of the problem presented in ledger account format, as follows (corrections would be made via the journal).

CASH BOOK

20X0		£	20X0		£
Jun 30	Bank interest - reversal of incorrect entry	60	Jun 30	Balance brought down	300
	Bank interest account	60		Bank charges	35
	Dividends paid direct to bank	200		Correction of undercast	10
	Cheque drawn on deposit account written back	50		Balance carried down	50
	Cheque issued to Jones cancelled	25			
		395			395

7.9   In preparing a bank reconciliation it is good practice to begin with the balance shown by the **bank statement** and end with the balance shown by the **cash book**. It is this corrected cash book balance which will appear in the balance sheet as 'cash at bank'. But assessments sometimes ask for the reverse order: as always, **read the question carefully**.

Activity 7.9

From the information given below relating to Sanderson & Co you are required:

(a)   To correct the cash at bank account of Sanderson as at 31 October 20X2

(b)   To prepare a statement reconciling the correct balance in the cash at bank account (as shown in (a) above) with the balance at 31 October 20X2 that is shown on the bank statement from Z Bank plc

CASH AT BANK ACCOUNT

20X2 October		£	20X2 October		£
1	Balance b/d	274	1	Wages	3,146
8	Q Manufacturing	3,443	1	Petty Cash	55
8	R Cement	1,146	8	Wages	3,106
11	S Limited	638	8	Petty Cash	39
11	T & Sons	512	15	Wages	3,029
11	U & Co	4,174	15	Petty Cash	78
15	V plc	1,426	22	A & Sons	929
15	W Electrical	887	22	B Limited	134
22	X and Associates	1,202	22	C & Company	77
26	Y Limited	2,875	22	D & E	263
26	Z Limited	982	22	F Limited	1,782
29	ABC plc	1,003	22	G Associates	230
29	DEE Corporation	722	22	Wages	3,217
29	GHI Limited	2,461	22	Petty Cash	91
31	Balance c/d	14	25	H & Partners	26
			26	J Sons & Co Ltd	868
			26	K & Co	107
			26	L, M & N	666
			28	O Limited	112
			29	Wages	3,191
			29	Petty Cash	52
			29	P & Sons	561
		21,759			21,759

Z BANK PLC - STATEMENT OF ACCOUNT WITH SANDERSON

20X2 October		Payments £	Receipts £		Balance £
1					1,135
1	cheque	55			
1	cheque	3,146			
1	cheque	421		O/D	2,487
2	cheque	73			
2	cheque	155		O/D	2,715
6	cheque	212		O/D	2,927
8	sundry credit		4,589		
8	cheque	3,106			
8	cheque	39		O/D	1,483
11	sundry credit		5,324		3,841
15	sundry credit		2,313		
15	cheque	78			
15	cheque	3,029			3,047
22	sundry credit		1,202		
22	cheque	3,217			
22	cheque	91			941
25	cheque	1,782			
25	cheque	134		O/D	975
26	cheque	929			
26	sundry credit		3,857		
26	cheque	230			1,723
27	cheque	263			
27	cheque	77			1,383
29	sundry credit		4,186		
29	cheque	52			
29	cheque	3,191			
29	cheque	26			
29	dividends on investments		2,728		
29	cheque	666			4,362
31	bank charges	936			3,426

Key learning points

- The two most important **control accounts** are those for **debtors** and **creditors**. They are part of the double entry system.

- Cash books and day books are totalled periodically (say once a month) and the appropriate totals are posted to the control accounts.

- The individual entries in cash and day books will have been entered one by one in the appropriate personal accounts contained in the sales ledger and purchase ledger. These personal accounts are not part of the double entry system: they are memorandum only.

- At suitable intervals the balances on personal accounts are extracted from the ledgers, listed and totalled. The total of the outstanding balances can then be reconciled to the balance on the appropriate control account and any errors located and corrected.

- There are five **types of error**.
  - Errors of transposition
  - Errors of omission
  - Errors of principle
  - Errors of commission
  - Compensating errors

- Errors which leave total debits and total credits on the ledger accounts in balance can be corrected by using **journal entries**. Otherwise, a suspense account has to be opened first (and a journal entry used later to record the correction of the error, clearing the suspense account in the process).

- **Suspense accounts**, as well as being used to correct some errors, are also opened when it is not known immediately where to post an amount. When the mystery is solved, the suspense account is closed and the amount correctly posted using a journal entry.

- **Suspense accounts are only temporary**. None should exist when it comes to drawing up the financial statements at the end of the accounting period.

- In theory, the entries appearing on a business's **bank statement** should be exactly the same as those in the business **cash book**. The balance shown by the bank statement as on a particular date should be the same as the cash book balance at the same date.

- It is common (and a **very important financial control**) to check this at regular intervals, say weekly or monthly. Invariably it will be found that the picture shown by the bank statement differs from that shown by the cash book. There are three reasons for this.
  - **Errors**
  - **Omissions**
  - **Timing differences**

- **Appropriate adjustments** must be made: errors must be corrected; omissions from the cash book must be made good. The balance in the cash book will then be correct and up to date.

- Any remaining difference between the **cash book balance** and the **statement balance** should then be explained as the result of identifiable **timing differences**.

Quick quiz

1   What is a control account?

2   Is a write off of bad debts a debit or a credit in the sales ledger control account?

3   What are the main reasons for having control accounts?

4   What type of errors will cause the control account not to agree with the list of balances?

5   What are the five main types of error which might occur in accounting?

6   What are the two common errors of commission?

7   What is a suspense account?

8   Suspense accounts are temporary. True or false?

9   What kinds of check should be made on petty cash?

10 What can cause differences between the balances on the cash book and on the bank statement?

11 What two items generally appear on a bank reconciliation?

Answers to quick quiz

1   A control account is an account in the nominal ledger in which a record is kept of the total value of a number of similar but individual items

2   A credit: it reduces the debit balance on the control account.

3   (a)   A check on the accuracy of the personal ledger
    (b)   Assist in the location of errors
    (c)   An internal check
    (d)   Provides a total balance for the trial balance

4   (a)   Miscasting (adding up) of the book of prime entry
    (b)   A transposition error in posting to the memorandum ledger
    (c)   A transaction missed out of the control account or in the memorandum account
    (d)   The balances are incorrectly extracted from the memorandum ledger, or miscast

5   Errors of transposition, omission, principle, commission and compensating errors.

6   (a)   Putting a debit entry or a credit entry in the wrong account
    (b)   Errors of casting (adding up)

7   A suspense account is an account showing a balance equal to the difference in a trial balance.

8   True. Suspense accounts must be cleared before the final accounts are drawn up.

9   Petty cash should be reconciled regularly, and spot counts should also be carried out.

10 Errors. Bank charges and interest. Timing differences.

11 Outstanding lodgements and unpresented cheques.

8 Accruals, prepayments and bad/ doubtful debts

This chapter contains

1 The matching concept

2 Accruals

3 Prepayments

4 Bad and doubtful debts

5 Obtaining information

Learning objectives

- Identify and adjust for accrued and prepaid income and expenditure
- Provide the correct accounting treatment for accruals and prepayments
- Make and adjust provisions
- Understand the objectives of making provisions

Performance criteria

5.2.2 Relevant accrued and prepaid income and expenditure is correctly identified and adjustments are made

Range

5.2.1 Records: day book; journal; ledger

ASSESSMENT ALERT

We have now covered collecting and collating information which appears in the trial balance, including the identification and correction of errors. In this and the next chapter we shall look at some information which does not appear in the trial balance and yet which is vital for preparing final accounts – accruals, prepayments and other provisions, and stock. We will then look at how to fill in the gaps where available information is less than perfect, before looking at the results of all this work – the final accounts of sole traders, clubs and partnerships, and manufacturing accounts. Finally in Section D, we shall learn how to tackle the final step before actually preparing accounts – the Extended Trial Balance.

1 THE MATCHING CONCEPT

1.1 When income and expenditure is recorded, it is usually because an invoice has been received or an invoice has been issued, and the expense or income must therefore be recognised. The same applies when purchases or sales are made for cash. We know that the income or expenditure relates to the **time it is recorded**.

1.2 At the end of the accounting period, some bills may not have been received, although it is known that the expense has been incurred. The **liability** will therefore not be recorded until the following period. Similarly, an invoice may have been received and paid during the year, but it may cover **part of the following year**. In these cases, there is a problem as **the amounts do not relate wholly to the period in which they are recorded**.

1.3 As we saw in Chapter 4, the **accruals concept** states that income and expenditure should be matched to each other and recognised as they are earned or incurred, not when money is received or paid.

KEY TERMS

- **Accruals,** or accrued expenses, are expenses which are charged against the profits of a particular period, even though they have not yet been paid, because they were incurred in that period.

- **Prepayments** are payments which have been made in one accounting period, but should not be wholly or partly charged against profit until a later period, because they relate to that later period.

1.4 EXAMPLE: ACCRUAL

Cleverley started in business as a paper plate and cup manufacturer on 1 January 20X2, making up accounts to 31 December 20X2. Electricity bills received were as follows.

	20X2	*20X3*	*20X4*
	£	£	£
31 January	-	6,491.52	6,753.24
30 April	5,279.47	5,400.93	6,192.82
31 July	4,663.80	4,700.94	5,007.62
31 October	4,117.28	4,620.00	5,156.40

What should the electricity charge be for the year ended 31 December 20X2?

1.5 SOLUTION

The three invoices received during 20X2 totalled £14,060.55, but this is not the full charge for the year: the November and December electricity charge was not invoiced until the end of January. To show the correct charge for the year, it is necessary to **accrue** the charge for November and December based on January's bill. The charge for 20X2 is:

	£
Paid in year	14,060.55
Accrual ($^2/_3 \times$ £6,491.52)	4,327.68
	18,388.23

The double entry for the accrual (using the **journal**) will be:

DEBIT	Electricity account	£4,327.68	
CREDIT	Accruals (liability)		£4,327.68

1.6 EXAMPLE: PREPAYMENT

A business opens on 1 January 20X4 in a shop which is on a 20 year lease. The rent is £20,000 per year and is payable quarterly in advance. Payments were made on what are known as the 'quarter-days' (except the first payment) as follows.

	£
1 January 20X4	5,000.00
25 March 20X4	5,000.00
24 June 20X4	5,000.00
29 September 20X4	5,000.00
25 December 20X4	5,000.00

What will the rental charge be for the year ended 31 December 20X4?

1.7 SOLUTION

The total amount paid in the year is £25,000. The yearly rental, however, is only £20,000. The last payment was almost entirely a prepayment (give or take a few days) as it is payment in advance for the first three months of 20X5. The charge for 20X4 is therefore:

	£
Paid in year	25,000.00
Prepayment	(5,000.00)
	20,000.00

The double entry for this prepayment is:

DEBIT	Prepayments (asset)	£5,000.00	
CREDIT	Rent account		£5,000.00

Double entry for accruals and prepayments

1.8 You can see from the double entry shown for both these examples that the other side of the entry is taken to an asset or a liability account.

- **Prepayments** are included in **debtors** in current assets in the balance sheet. They arc **assets** as they represent money that has been paid out in advance of the expense being incurred.

- **Accruals** are included in **creditors** in **current liabilities** as they represent liabilities which have been incurred but not yet invoiced.

1.9

Transaction	DR	CR	Description
Accrual	Expense	Liability	Expense incurred in period, not recorded
Prepayment	Asset	(Reduction in) expense	Expense recorded in period, not incurred until next period

Reversing accruals and prepayments in subsequent periods

1.10 In each of the above examples, as with all prepayments and accruals, the double entry will be **reversed** in the following period, otherwise the organisation will charge itself twice for the same expense (accruals) *or* will never charge itself (prepayments). It may help to see the accounts in question.

ELECTRICITY ACCOUNT

20X2		£	20X2		£
30.4	Cash	5,279.47	31.12	P & L account	18,388.23
31.7	Cash	4,663.80			
31.10	Cash	4,117.28			
31.12	Balance c/d (accrual)	4,327.68			
		18,388.23			18,388.23
20X3			20X3		
31.1	Cash	6,491.52	1.1	Balance b/d	4,327.68
30.4	Cash	5,400.93	31.12	P&L account	21,387.87
31.7	Cash	4,700.94			
31.10	Cash	4,620.00			
31.12	Balance c/d (accrual)	4,502.16			
		25,715.55			25,715.55

The P&L charge and accrual for 20X3 can be checked as follows.

Invoice paid		*Proportion charged in 20X3*	£
31.1.X3	6,491.52	1/3	2,163.84
30.4.X3	5,400.94	all	5,400.93
31.7.X3	4,700.94	all	4,700.94
31.10.X3	4,620.00	all	4,620.00
31.1.X4	6,753.24	2/3	4,502.16
P&L charge in 20X3			21,387.87

1.11 It should be clear to you here that the £5,000 rent prepaid in 20X2 will be added to by the payments in 20X3, and then reduced at the end of 20X3 in the same way.

RENT ACCOUNT

20X2		£	20X2		£
1.1	Cash	5,000.00	31.12	P & L account	20,000.00
25.3	Cash	5,000.00	31.12	Balance c/d	
24.6	Cash	5,000.00		(prepayment)	5,000.00
29.9	Cash	5,000.00			
25.12	Cash	5,000.00			
		25,000.00			25,000.00
20X3			20X3		
1.1	Balance b/d	5,000.00			

2 ACCRUALS

2.1 The following are some of the **practical procedures** you might be required to carry out to identify and record accruals.

> **Step 1** Review the **accruals listing for the previous year** and consider whether similar conditions exist for each of the relevant accounts. This list may be used as the basis of the current year's accruals listing. Check that accruals and prepayments have been reversed (for instance, if an invoice has not been debited all year to an account on which an accrual is brought down then there is something wrong which needs investigating).

> **Step 2** Review every income and expenditure account. Examine the transactions passing through the accounts and identify any accounts where fewer invoices have been received than expected (eg only three quarterly telephone bills).

> **Step 3** Review all invoices received after the year end to identify any amounts which relate to the year in question (eg an electricity bill received one month after the year end which covers a whole quarter).

> **Step 4** Collate and compare all the information found and **calculate the relevant accruals**. Compare the final list with the previous year's accruals to check for any omissions.

Accruals listing from previous year

2.2 Many businesses run on a **similar basis from year to year**. The same transactions recur year on year. For the accountant seeking to identify all accruals, this regularity gives an ideal starting point as the previous year's accruals calculated for the previous year will give a strong indication of those required for the current year.

2.3 As an example of a **complete accruals listing,** consider this.

Accruals Listing Year ended 31 December 20X6		£
A/C No.	*Name*	
P001	Purchases	32,148.42
E002	Electricity	927.28
T004	Telephone	1,427.19
G011	Gas	2,119.40
I001	Bank interest	1,307.07
S007	Salaries	10,172.29
W001	Wages	9,428.56
E012	Mileage allowance	322.27
E013	Salesmen's expenses	584.71
C100	**TOTAL**	58,437.19

Note. The figure for purchases represents goods received into stock where no invoice has yet been received. We will look at stock accruals in more detail in Chapter 9.

2.4 The types of expenditure shown in this listing are usually **regular** in nature and accruals would be expected to arise again on these accounts in the following year.

Review expense accounts

2.5 Reviewing **expense accounts** will often reveal the need for an accrual where an invoice relating to the current year is not received until after the year end. This is often the case with utilities (electricity, gas) as payments are usually made quarterly and the end of a quarter may not coincide with the year end of the business. For example, you might examine the electricity account for the year ended 31 December 20X7.

ACCOUNT NAME	E0002 ELECTRICITY	ENQUIRY DATE 0202X8	
		Amount £	*Balance* £
0101X7	Balance	(927.28)	(927.28)
2802X7	Invoice	2,781.84	1,854.56
3005X7	Invoice	2,417.38	4,271.94
3008X7	Invoice	2,559.61	6,831.55
3011X7	Invoice	3,172.31	10,003.86

Although four quarterly invoices have been received during the year, the last one does not include December's charge for electricity and so an accrual is necessary.

2.6 It is **not sufficient to carry forward the same accrual** year on year as consumption may change, as it has here, with the charge increasing towards the year end.

Review post year end invoices

2.7 The first two steps in paragraph 2.1 may fail to highlight some expenses which should be accrued, perhaps because they are unusual or unexpected. To avoid missing such expenses, all **invoices received after the year end should be checked**, to ensure that they do not relate to the previous period. This exercise should be continued for a reasonable amount of time after the year end, although within the bounds of practicality, eg up until the date the accounts are finalised by the auditors.

2.8 EXAMPLE: REVIEW OF POST YEAR-END INVOICES

Suppose you carried out this exercise while preparing accounts for the year ended 31 December 20X7 and found the two invoices shown here (among others).

WORKBASE OFFICE SUPPLIES LTD			Invoice No.	7012
63 Conduit street Liverpool L1 6NN			Order No.	1137
			Account No.	R001
Telephone: 0151-432 2222 Fax: 0151-432 2210			Date/Tax point	31 January 20X8
VAT Reg No. 924 4614 29				

Rabbit Fast Food Franchises Ltd
62 Hellon Avenue
Bournley
L24 6BS

Product code	Description	Quantity	Unit price £ p	Total amount £ p
P11110	Photocopier rental 1.11.X7 - 31.1.X8	N/A	450.00	450.00

Comments:	NET TOTAL	450.00
Your photocopier is due for a service on 31 May 20X8	VAT @ 17.5%	78.75
	TOTAL	528.75

Registered office: 63 Conduit Street, Liverpool L1 6NN   Registered No: 822 4742

```
┌──────────────────────────────────────────────────────────────┐
│  ERGONOME  LTD                        SALES  INVOICE          │
│  Fonda House, 12 Angriman Street                              │
│  Pleading, Lincs                                              │
│  TO:    Rabbit Fast Food              Invoice No:      8742    │
│         Franchises Ltd                                        │
│         62 Hellon Avenue              Account No.      DEF 2   │
│         Bownley                                               │
│         L24 6BS                       Date/Tax pt:   28.02.X8  │
│  F.A.O   Purchase Ledger                                      │
│                                                  Price        │
│                                                  £     p      │
│                                                               │
│    Answering service 1 daytime               2,000 . 00       │
│    1.12.20X7 - 28.2.20X8                                      │
│                                                               │
│    Night answering service                     500 . 00       │
│    1.12.20X7 - 28.2.20X8                                      │
│                                                               │
│                                               2,500 . 00       │
│            VAT at 17.5%                         437 . 50       │
│                                                               │
│                                               2,937 . 50       │
│  VAT Reg: 3 495 0721                                          │
└──────────────────────────────────────────────────────────────┘
```

2.9 SOLUTION

Both the photocopier and the answering service were used for the first time this year and therefore no accrual would have been anticipated based on the previous year's figures. As you can see, however, these invoices relate in part to the year ended 31 December 20X7.

Calculating accruals

2.10 Once the need for an accrual has been identified, you must calculate the correct amount of the accrual. Two different circumstances may arise here, generally relating to the **timing** of the accruals calculation. *Note*. Be careful not to include VAT in calculations; VAT does not appear in the profit and loss account and so an accrual is not necessary.

(a) Invoice received **after** the year end but **before** the preparation of the accounts, giving an **actual** charge for a given period. In this case, the only calculation made will be that required to **apportion** the charge to the period in question. For example, from the invoice given above from Workbase Office Supplies Ltd, it can be seen that the amount of the charge relating to 20X7 is:

$$\frac{2 \text{ months}}{3 \text{ months}} \times £450.00 = £300.00 \qquad \left(\text{or } \frac{61 \text{ days}}{92 \text{ days}} \times £450.00 = £298.37\right)$$

(b) Invoice **not** received by the time the accounts are prepared. In such cases, it is necessary to **estimate** the accrual based on current or expected consumption. For example, when we looked at the electricity account in Paragraph 2.5 above, we might have decided that consumption in December has been the same as in the previous three months. We would therefore calculate the accrual as:

$$\frac{1 \text{ month}}{3 \text{ months}} \times £3,172.31 = £1,057.44$$

2.11 The method used to estimate or calculate the accrual, should be a **reasonable** approximation to the actual charge and it should be applied **consistently** from year to year.

Activity 8.1

An electricity accrual of £375 was treated as a prepayment in preparing the profit and loss account.

What was the resulting effect on the profit of the company?

---

3   PREPAYMENTS

3.1 Many of the principles discussed in relation to identifying and calculating accruals apply to identifying and calculating **prepayments**. The major practical difference is that invoices have been received and paid during the year in the case of prepayments. As the information is already within the accounting system at the year end, no post year end review of invoices is necessary, but the following steps should be carried out.

> *Step 1*   **Review the list of prepayments from the previous year end**. Regular payments such as those for rent, business rates or water rates, which are normally paid in advance, should show up.
>
> *Step 2*   **Review all expense accounts** for the year to identify any prepaid expenses. During the year, it is often helpful to make a note when any invoice is paid which partly relates to the next accounting period. This procedure could easily be incorporated into the preparation of monthly management accounts.
>
> *Step 3*   **Calculate and list all the prepayments.** Compare the list with that of the previous year and check that there are no omissions.

Prepayments listing from previous year

3.2 The **listing** below gives an idea of the type of expenses which might be prepaid. It will give you a starting point from which to work.

Prepayments Listing Year ended 31 December 20X7		£
A/C No.	Name	
U004	Unified business rate	11,407.18
W001	Water rates	1,773.21
R003	Rent	6,400.00
T004	Telephone	101.72
I001	Insurance - building	3,211.96
I002	Insurance - general	1,195.20
P010	Plant hire	429.50
D100	TOTAL	24,518.77

Review expense accounts

3.3 All the expense accounts should be reviewed, to check whether any contain prepaid expenses. The types of **regular payment** shown above are often paid in advance, but so are many **one-off expenses**, which may be harder to spot.

Calculation of prepayments

3.4 Prepayments are usually easy to calculate, as the expenses can be apportioned on a **time basis**.

3.5 EXAMPLE: CALCULATING PREPAYMENTS

Suppose that £22,472.58 was paid for business rates on 1 April 20X8 for the year to 31 March 20X9. The business, which is preparing accounts to 31 December 20X8, has prepaid for the three months in 20X9 and so the prepayment is calculated as:

$^3/_{12} \times £22,472.58 = £5,618.15$

As a further example an insurance bill for £9,473.80 was paid on 1 August 20X8 for the year ended 31 July 20X9. Seven months worth of the bill relates to 20X9, and so the prepayment is:

$^7/_{12} \times £9,473.80 = £5,526.38$

3.6 You may have noticed that, in both the accruals and prepayments listing, there is an amount under the heading of **telephone**. You can see why a **prepayment *and* an accrual** might arise by looking at the telephone bill below.

Assuming that no further bill has been received, at 31 December 20X7 the following calculations will be made.

Prepayment: rental for January and February 20X8 $= \frac{2}{3} \times £56.84 = £37.89$

Accrual: call charges for December 20X7 $= \frac{1}{3} \times £262.50 = £87.50$

Payments received in advance: deferred income

3.7 This is a convenient point to mention the treatment of payments received by a business **in advance**. This arises often with **clubs** which receive subscriptions in advance (see Chapter 11).

3.8 A payment received in advance is the opposite of a prepayment. It is, in effect, **deferred income**. It is treated as a **liability** in the accounts of the current period and as **income** in the accounting period to which it relates.

Transaction	DR	CR	Description
Payment in advance	Income	Liability	Income recorded in period, not earned

We shall see more about this in Chapter 11 on club accounts, and more about the accounting entries for accruals and prepayments in Chapter 12.

Activity 8.2

As at 1 January 20X5 Hedges & Co have accruals of £240 and prepayments of £500 on its administration costs account. Cash has been paid out during the year of £32,095.50, and as at 31 December 20X5 there are accruals of £530 and prepayments of £825. How much will be shown for administration costs for the year?

Activity 8.3

The Print Shop rents a photocopier from a supplier for which it makes quarterly payments as follows:

(a) Three months rental in advance
(b) A further charge of 2 pence per copy made during the quarter just ended

The rental agreement began on 1 August 20X6 and the first six quarterly bills were as follows.

Bills dated and received	Rental	Costs of copies taken	Total
	£	£	£
1 August 20X6	2,100	0	2,100
1 November 20X6	2,100	1,500	3,600
1 February 20X7	2,100	1,400	3,500
1 May 20X7	2,100	1,800	3,900
1 August 20X7	2,700	1,650	4,350
1 November 20X7	2,700	1,950	4,650

The bills are paid promptly, as soon as they are received.

(a) Calculate the charge for photocopying expenses for the year to 31 August 20X6 and the amount of prepayments and/or accrued charges as at that date.

(b) Calculate the charge for photocopying expenses for the following year to 31 August 20X7, and the amount of prepayments and/or accrued charges as at that date.

Activity 8.4

This extract from the cash book of Morgan Associates was taken at 31 December 20X2, which is the accounting year end of Morgan.

CASH BOOK: PAYMENTS

Date	Details	Total	Purchases	Premises costs	Admin
		£	£	£	£
20X2					
24/11	Kincaid District Council	450.00		450.00	
25/11	Upright Insurance Co	600.00			600.00
26/11	SurePatents	5,000.00	5,000.00		
27/11	Westheat Fuels plc	480.00		480.00	
		6,530.00	5,000.00	930.00	600.00

You are given the following further information.

(a) The payment to Kincaid District Council comprises a payment in advance of three months business rates.

(b) The payment to Upright Insurance Company is the full annual premium for contents insurance from 1 December 20X2.

(c) The payment to SurePatents is the royalty due on a product made under a patent held by Morgan Associates for sales from 1 Jul 20X2 to 30 September 20X2 of

£100,000.00. Sales under the terms of the patent to 31 December 20X2 were £120,000.00.

(d) The payment to Westheat Fuels plc is a service charge for the three months to 28 February 20X3 of £150.00, plus charges for fuel used in the three months to 30 November 20X2 of £330.00. The same monthly usage is estimated to have occurred in December.

Draft journal entries to record any relevant accruals and prepayments that need to be reflected in the accounts of Morgan Associates.

4 BAD AND DOUBTFUL DEBTS

4.1 For some debts on the ledger, there may be little or no prospect of the business being paid, usually for one of the following reasons.

- The customer has gone **bankrupt.**

- The customer has gone **out of business.**

- **Dishonesty** may be involved.

- Customers in another country might be prevented from paying by the unexpected introduction of **foreign exchange control** restrictions by their country's government during the credit period.

4.2 For one reason or another, therefore, a business might decide to give up expecting payment and to **write the debt off as a 'lost cause'.**

> ### KEY TERM
>
> A **bad debt** is a specific debt which is not expected to be repaid.

Bad debts written off: ledger accounting entries

4.3 For bad debts written off, there is a **bad debts expense account** in the general ledger. The double-entry accounting is fairly straightforward. When it is decided that a particular debt will not be paid, the customer is no longer called an outstanding debtor, and becomes a bad debt. We therefore:

DEBIT	Bad debts expense account
CREDIT	Total debtors account
(CREDIT	Individual account in the sales ledger)

A **write off of any bad debt will need the authorisation of senior management.**

4.4 EXAMPLE: BAD DEBTS WRITTEN OFF

At 1 October 20X7 a business had total outstanding debts of £8,600. During the year to 30 September 20X8:

(a) Credit sales amounted to £44,000

(b) Payments from various debtors amounted to £49,000

(c) Two debts, for £180 and £420 (both excluding VAT) were declared bad. These are to be written off

We need to prepare the total debtors account and the bad debts expense account for the year.

4.5 SOLUTION

TOTAL DEBTORS ACCOUNT

Date	Details	£	Date	Details	£
1.10.X7	Balance b/d	8,600		Cash	49,000
	Sales for the year	44,000	30.9.X8	Bad debts	180
			30.9.X8	Bad debts	420
			30.9.X8	Balance c/d	3,000
		52,600			52,600
	Balance b/d	3,000			

BAD DEBTS EXPENSE

Date	Details	£	Date	Details	£
30.9.X8	Debtors	180	30.9.X8	P&L account	600
30.9.X8	Debtors	420			
		600			600

4.6 In the sales ledger, personal accounts of the customers whose debts are bad will be **taken off the ledger**. The business should then take steps to ensure that it does not sell goods to those customers again.

VAT bad debt relief

4.7 A business can claim relief from VAT on bad debts which:

(a) Are **at least six months old** (from the time of supply)

(b) Which have been **written off** in the accounts of the business

4.8 **VAT bad debt relief** is accounted for as follows:

DEBIT	VAT account	17.5	
	Bad debts expense	100.0	
CREDIT	Total debtors		117.5

4.9 EXAMPLE: VAT BAD DEBT RELIEF

If both the debts written off in Paragraph 4.5 had included VAT, the accounts would be as follows:

TOTAL DEBTORS ACCOUNT - no change

BAD DEBTS EXPENSE

Date	Details	£	Date	Details	£
30.9.X8	Debtors	153.19	30.9.X8	P&L account	510.64
30.9.X8	Debtors	357.45			
		510.64			510.64

VAT ACCOUNT (part)

Date	Details	£	Date	Details	£
30.9.X8	Debtors	26.81			
30.9.X8	Debtors	62.55			

Bad debts written off and subsequently paid

4.10 If a bad debt is unexpectedly paid after it has been written off, then the accounting treatment is described as 'writing back' the debt. How this is done depends on **when** the payment is made.

(a) If the payment is received **before** the end of the period in which the debt was written off, simply reverse the entry for the write off.

DEBIT   Debtors control account
CREDIT   Bad debts expenses account

and then record the receipt in the normal way.

DEBIT   Bank account
CREDIT   Debtors control account

(b) If the payment is received **after** the end of the period in which the debt was written off, then it can be treated as above or sometimes is treated as sundry income in the profit and loss account.

DEBIT   Cash
CREDIT   Sundry income

Provision for doubtful debts

4.11 A provision for doubtful debts is completely different from a bad debt written off. A business might know from past experience that, say, 2% of debtors' balances are unlikely to be collected. It would then be considered prudent to make a **general provision of 2% of total debtor balances**. It may be that no particular customers are regarded as suspect and so it is not possible to write off any individual customer balances as bad debts.

> **KEY TERM**
>
> A **general provision for doubtful debts** is a general estimate of the percentage of debts which are not expected to be repaid. It does *not* relate to specific debts.

Setting up a provision for doubtful debts

4.12 The procedure is to leave the total debtors account completely untouched, but to **open up a provision account** by the following entries:

DEBIT   Doubtful debts expense account (P&L)
CREDIT   Provision for doubtful debts (balance sheet)

When preparing a balance sheet, the credit balance on the provision account is deducted from the total debit balances in the debtors ledger.

Adjusting the amount of the provision in subsequent years

4.13 In **subsequent years**, adjustments may be needed to the amount of the provision. The procedure to be followed then is as follows.

Step 1   Calculate the new provision required.

Step 2   Compare it with the existing balance on the provision account (ie the balance b/d from the previous accounting period).

Step 3   Calculate the increase or decrease required.

(a)   If a **higher** provision is required now (either because the total of debtors has increased, or because the percentage of total debtors which are doubtful has increased, or both):

DEBIT   Doubtful debts expense account
CREDIT   Provision for doubtful debts

with the amount of the increase.

(b)   If a **lower** provision is needed now than before (either because the total of debtors has decreased, or because the percentage of total debtors which are doubtful has decreased, or both):

DEBIT   Provision for doubtful debts
CREDIT   Doubtful debts expense account

with the amount of the decrease (leaving the expense account with a credit balance).

4.14   The provision for doubtful debts in the balance sheet must not be used to debit the expense of an actual bad debt. The expense of setting up the provision, plus the expense of actual bad debts written off, must be shown in the profit and loss account.

4.15 EXAMPLE: PROVISION FOR DOUBTFUL DEBTS

Alex has total debtors' balances outstanding at 31 December 20X7 of £28,000. He believes that about 1% of these balances will not be paid and wishes to make an appropriate provision. Before now, he has not made any provision for doubtful debts.

On 31 December 20X8 his debtors' balances amount to £40,000. His experience during the year has convinced him that a provision of 5% should be made.

What accounting entries should Alex make on 31 December 20X7 and 31 December 20X8, and what figures for debtors will appear in his balance sheets as at those dates?

4.16 SOLUTION

At 31 December 20X7

Provision required   = 1% × £28,000
                       = £280

Alex will make the following entries.

DEBIT   Doubtful debts expense account   £280
CREDIT   Provision for doubtful debts   £280

In the balance sheet debtors will appear as follows under current assets.

	£
Sales ledger balances	28,000
Less provision for doubtful debts	280
	27,720

At 31 December 20X8

Following the procedure described above, Alex will calculate as follows.

		£
Provision required now (5% × £40,000)		2,000
Existing provision		(280)
Additional provision required		1,720

DEBIT	Doubtful debts expense account	£1,720	
CREDIT	Provision for doubtful debts		£1,720

The provision account will by now appear as follows.

PROVISION FOR DOUBTFUL DEBTS

Date	Details	£	Date	Details	£
20X7			20X7		
31 Dec	Balance c/d	280	31 Dec	Doubtful debts account	280
20X8			20X8		
			1 Jan	Balance b/d	280
31 Dec	Balance c/d	2,000	31 Dec	Doubtful debts account	1,720
		2,000			2,000
			20X9		
			1 Jan	Balance b/d	2,000

For the balance sheet, debtors will be valued as follows.

	£
Sales ledger balances	40,000
Less provision for doubtful debts	2,000
	38,000

Doubtful debts and VAT

4.17 Because it is a **general** provision, the **provision for doubtful debts has no effect whatsoever on VAT.**

4.18 Section summary

Transaction	DR	CR
Write off bad debts*	Bad debts expense	Total debtors
Write back bad debt paid in period*	Total debtors	Bad debts expense
Write back bad debt paid in next period*	Cash	Sundry income
Set up general provision	Doubtful debts expense	Provision for doubtful debts
Increase in general provision	Doubtful debts expense	Provision for doubtful debts
Reduce general provision	Provision for doubtful debts	Doubtful debts expense *or* sundry income
* Can include VAT		

Activity 8.5

Johnsons Kitchens Ltd has just been informed that one of its main customers, The House Building Company, has gone into liquidation. The liquidator expects only 40% of the debts of the company to be paid. As at 31 August 20X7 the sales ledger account for The House Building Company stood at £32,703.25. Draft a journal to record the necessary write off of the bad debt. (Ignore VAT.)

Activity 8.6

Simon Fawcett owns and runs the Real Coffee and Tea Shop. He began trading on 1 January 20X5, selling coffee, tea and related products to customers, most of whom make use of a credit facility that Simon offers. (Customers are allowed to purchase up to £50 of goods on credit but must repay a certain proportion of their outstanding debt every month.)

This credit system gives rise to a large number of bad debts, and the figures for debtors, bad debts and required provisions for the first three years of trading for Simon Fawcett are as follows.

Year to 31 December 20X5
Bad debts written off	£2,000
Debts owed by customers as at 31 December 20X5	£10,000
Provision for doubtful debts	2½% of outstanding debtors

Year to 31 December 20X6
Bad debts written off	£2,500
Debts owed by customers as at 31 December 20X6	£13,000
Provision for doubtful debts	2½% of outstanding debtors

Year to 31 December 20X7
Bad debts written off	£2,750
Debts owed by customers as at 31 December 20X7	£7,500
Provision for doubtful debts	3% of outstanding debtors

Task

For each of these three years, prepare the bad debt expense account and provision for doubtful debts account. State the value of debtors appearing in the balance sheet as at 31 December.

Activity 8.7

Following on from Activity 8.5, no more transactions have affected the account of The House Building Company since August, so the balance stands at £13,081.30. Johnsons Kitchens Ltd has now been informed by the liquidator of The House Building Company that half of this debt will be paid immediately. The remaining half will not be paid.. During its review of the situation, the company has decided to set up a doubtful debt provision of 2% of debtors, which at 31 December stood at £206,983.00, including The House Building Company debt.

Draft a journal to record the necessary transactions in the accounts of Johnson's Kitchens Ltd.

5 OBTAINING INFORMATION

5.1 So far we have assumed that you will be performing the task of identifying and calculating prepayments and accruals. In larger organisations, you may find that the **managers of individual divisions** or companies will be asked to supply such information at the period end. The information is then collated in the central accounts department.

5.2 Where such delegation takes place, it is important that the managers know exactly what **information** is needed and what, if any, **supporting documentation** is required. Good **communications** need to be maintained between the division managers and the central accounting staff. (This should of course apply at all times, not just at the year end when such accounting information is required.)

5.3 One way to ensure that correct and complete accruals and prepayments information is sent by the managers is to send them a **checklist or listing sheet** which lays out all the information they should consider. An example of such a checklist is given below. It would be usual to request copies of all **supporting documentation** for the divisional accruals and prepayments as an aid to the central accounting function, and also to provide information for the company auditors. (The auditors will want to check all the figures in the accounts, including the accruals and prepayments.)

ACCRUALS/PREPAYMENTS CHECKLIST

                                               ✓

1. Stock accruals: all purchases made pre-year end, goods received but no invoice. ☐

   ENCLOSE COPY GRNS

2. All relevant expense accounts

   (a) last bills before the year end; and/or ☐

   (b) bills just after the year end; and ☐

   (c) list any others ☐

   ENCLOSE COPY INVOICES

3. All expense prepayments: last bills before year end ☐

   ENCLOSE COPY INVOICES

4. Full listing. Cross reference to supporting documents and any calculations or explanations.

5.4   There are other important matters to bear in mind.

- Managers should be **warned** well in advance in writing about the information they are required to supply.

- Details of **how to complete the exercise** should be supplied to them in writing and they should be encouraged to contact the central accounts department with queries.

- All communications should be **polite and tactful**.

Key learning points

- **Accrued expenses** are expenses which relate to an accounting period but have not yet been paid for. They are a **charge against the profit** for the period and they are shown in the balance sheet as at the end of the period as a **current liability**. They are reversed in the subsequent period.

- **Prepayments** are expenses which have already been paid but relate to a future accounting period. They are not **charged against the profit** of the current period, and they are shown in the balance sheet at the end of the period as a **current asset**. They are reversed in the subsequent period.

- Some debts may need to be written off as **bad debts** because there is no real prospect of them being paid.

- Alternatively or additionally, a **provision for doubtful debts** may be created. Rather than affecting individual customer balances, a provision for doubtful debts recognises the fact that ordinarily a certain proportion of all debts are unlikely to be collected. It is therefore prudent to make such a **general provision** when calculating the overall profit or loss of the business.

Quick quiz

1   If a business has paid rates of £1,000 for the year to 31 March 20X8, what is the prepayment in the accounts for the year to 31 December 20X7?

2   Define an accrual.

3   What happens to the double entry made for accruals and prepayments in the following period?

4   What is the double entry to write off a bad debt?

5   What is the double entry for a bad debt subsequently received after the period end?

6   How do you account for VAT on bad debts?

7   If you have a provision for doubtful debts you can use it to debit the expense of writing a bad debt off. True or false?

Answers to quick quiz

1    $^3/_{12} \times £1,000 = £250$

2   An accrual is an expense which is charged against the profits of a particular period, even though it has not yet been paid off, because it was incurred in that period.

3   The entries are reversed.

4   DEBIT   Bad debts expense account
     CREDIT   Total debtors account

5   DEBIT   Cash
     CREDIT   Sundry income

6   DEBIT   VAT account   17.5
                 Bad debts expense   100.0

     CREDIT   Total debtors   117.5

7   False. The provision for doubtful debts is a general one whereas writing off a bad debt is an actual expense of the period and must be expensed in the P&L.

9 Cost of goods sold and the treatment of stocks

This chapter contains

1   Cost of goods sold

2   Accounting for opening and closing stocks

3   Stocktaking and stock accruals

4   Valuing stocks

5   Finding the historic cost

6   Stock valuations and profit

Learning objectives

- Determine the correct valuation of closing stock

- Apply the main requirements of SSAP 9

- Apply the basic principles of stock valuation: cost or NRV; what is included in cost

Performance criteria

5.4.4 An agreed valuation of closing stock is correctly entered on the extended trial balance

Knowledge and understanding

Basic principles of stock valuation: cost or NRV; what is included in cost

BPP PUBLISHING

1 COST OF GOODS SOLD

1.1 There is one last important area we need to examine which has a direct bearing on the items in the accounts: **stocks**. The valuation of stock is important as it directly affects:

- **Gross profit** in the profit and loss account, as we will see in Section 4 of this chapter

- **Current assets** in the balance sheet

Best practice stock valuation rules are embodied in SSAP 9 *Stocks and long-term contracts*. (Long-term contracts are *not* assessed in Unit 5.)

What is stock?

1.2 We should start by giving the **SSAP 9 definition** of stock.

KEY TERM

SSAP 9 defines **stocks and work in progress** as:

- Goods or other assets purchased for resale

- Consumable stores

- Raw materials and components purchased for incorporation into products for sale

- Products and services in intermediate stages of completion

- Long-term contract balances

- Finished goods

1.3 In this chapter, we will only consider **goods or other assets purchased for resale,** or **raw materials for components bought from suppliers,** unless otherwise stated. We will consider some of the other items in Chapter 11 on manufacturing accounts, but the rest are beyond the scope of the Unit 5 standards.

1.4 In Chapter 3, we defined **profit** as **the value of sales less the cost of sales and expenses**. This definition might seem simple enough; but, it is not always clear how much the cost of sales or expenses are. A variety of difficulties can arise in measuring them. This chapter describes some of these problems and their solutions.

Unsold goods in stock at the end of an accounting period

1.5 Goods might be unsold at the accounting period end and so still be held in stock at the end of the period. When those goods were bought the accounting entry would have been:

DEBIT Purchases
CREDIT Creditors/cash

But the purchase cost of these goods should *not* be included in purchases and hence in the cost of sales of the period since they were not sold. **Their cost should**

be removed from the period of purchase and included in the period of sale. Accounting for stocks is thus an example of the **matching concept**.

1.6 EXAMPLE: CLOSING STOCK

James Terry, trading as the Raincoat Store, ends his financial year on 30 June each year. On 1 July 20X6 he had no goods in stock. During the year to 30 June 20X7 he purchased 6,000 raincoats costing £36,000 from raincoat wholesalers and suppliers. He resold the raincoats for £10 each, and sales for the year amounted to £45,000 (4,500 raincoats). At 30 June there were 1,500 unsold raincoats left in stock, valued at £6 each.

What was James Terry's gross profit for the year?

1.7 SOLUTION

James Terry purchased 6,000 raincoats, but only sold 4,500. Purchase costs of £36,000 and sales of £45,000 do not represent the same quantity of goods.

The gross profit for the year should be calculated by '**matching**' the sales value of the 4,500 raincoats sold with the cost of those 4,500 raincoats. The cost of sales in this example is therefore the cost of purchases minus the cost of goods in stock at the year end.

	£	£
Sales (4,500 units)		45,000
Purchases (6,000 units)	36,000	
Less closing stock (1,500 units @ £6)	9,000	
Cost of sales (4,500 units)		27,000
Gross profit		18,000

1.8 EXAMPLE CONTINUED: OPENING AND CLOSING STOCK

Suppose that during the course of the year to 30 June 20X8, James Terry purchased 8,000 raincoats at a total cost of £55,500. During the year he sold 8,500 raincoats for £95,000. At 30 June 20X8 he had 1,000 raincoats left in stock, which had cost £7 each.

What was his gross profit for the year?

1.9 SOLUTION

In the accounting year to 30 June 20X8, he purchased 8,000 raincoats to add to the 1,500 he already had in stock at the start of the year. He sold 8,500, leaving 1,000 raincoats in stock at the year end valued at £7 each. Once again, gross profit should be calculated by matching the value of 8,500 units of sales with the cost of those 8,500 units.

The cost of sales is the value of the 1,500 raincoats in stock at the beginning of the year, plus the cost of the 8,000 raincoats purchased, less the value of the 1,000 raincoats in stock at the year end.

	£	£
Sales (8,500 units)		95,000
Opening stock (1,500 units) *	9,000	
Add purchases (8,000 units)	55,500	
	64,500	
Less closing stock (1,000 units)	7,000	
Cost of sales (8,500 units)		57,500
Gross profit		37,500

*Taken from the closing stock value of the previous accounting year, see Paragraph 1.7.

The cost of goods sold

1.10   The cost of goods sold is thus found by applying the following formula.

> **FORMULA TO LEARN**
>
> | | £ |
> |---|---|
> | Opening stock value | X |
> | Add cost of purchases (or, in the case of a manufacturing company, the cost of production) | X |
> | | X |
> | Less closing stock value | (X) |
> | Equals cost of goods sold | X |

In other words, to **match 'sales' and the 'cost of goods sold'**, it is necessary to adjust the cost of goods purchased or manufactured to allow for increases or reduction in stock levels during the period. This matching of revenue and costs is required by SSAP 9.

Activity 9.1

On 1 January 20X7, Freddie's Health Food Store had goods in stock valued at £10,000. During 20X7 its proprietor, who ran the shop, purchased supplies costing £70,000. Sales for the year to 31 December 20X7 amounted to £120,000. The cost of goods in stock at 31 December 20X7 was £22,000.

Calculate the gross profit for the year.

The cost of carriage inwards and outwards

> **KEY TERM**
>
> **Carriage** refers to the cost of transporting purchased goods from the supplier to the premises of the business which has bought them. Someone has to pay for these delivery costs: sometimes the supplier pays, and sometimes the purchaser pays.
>
> - When the purchaser pays, the cost to the purchaser is **carriage inwards**.
>
> - When the supplier pays, the cost to the supplier is known as **carriage outwards**.

Cost	Included in	Shown in	Of
Carriage inwards	Cost of purchases	Trading account	Purchaser
Carriage outwards	Selling and distribution expense	P & L account	Supplier

1.11 EXAMPLE: CARRIAGE INWARDS AND CARRIAGE OUTWARDS

Janice, trading as Sven Interiors, imports and resells Scandinavian furniture. She must pay for the costs of delivering the furniture from her supplier in Sweden to her shop in Wales. She resells the furniture to other traders throughout the country, paying the costs of carriage for the consignments from her business premises to her customers.

Furniture stock was valued at £35,000 on 1 July 20X7. During the year to 30 June 20X8 she purchased more furniture at a cost of £180,000. Carriage inwards amounted to £5,000. Sales for the year were £330,000. Other business expenses amounted to £72,000 excluding carriage outwards costs of £7,200. Janice took drawings of £36,000 from the business during the year. Goods in stock at the year end were valued at £44,200.

Prepare the trading, profit and loss account of Sven Interiors for the year ended 30 June 20X8.

1.12 SOLUTION

SVEN INTERIORS
TRADING, PROFIT AND LOSS ACCOUNT
FOR THE YEAR ENDED 30 JUNE 20X8

	£	£
Sales		330,000
Opening stock	35,000	
Purchases	180,000	
Carriage inwards	5,000	
	220,000	
Less closing stock	44,200	
Cost of goods sold		175,800
Gross profit		154,200
Carriage outwards	7,200	
Other expenses	72,000	
		79,200
Net profit (transferred to balance sheet)		75,000

Activity 9.2

The following amounts appear in the books of Dearden Ltd at the end of the financial year.

	£
Opening stock	5,700
Closing stock	8,540
Carriage outwards	6,220
Purchases	75,280
Returns inwards	5,540
Carriage inwards	3,680

Calculate the figure for cost of sales for the trading account.

Goods written off or written down

1.13 A trader might be **unable to sell** all the goods that he purchases, because a number of things might happen to the goods before they can be sold. They might:

- Be **lost or stolen**

- Be **damaged**, and so become worthless. Damaged goods might be thrown away

- Become **obsolete or out of fashion**. These might have to be thrown away, or possibly sold off at a very low price in a clearance sale

1.14 When goods are lost, stolen or thrown away as worthless, the business will **make a loss** on those goods because their 'sales value' will be nil.

Similarly, when goods lose value because they have become obsolete or out of fashion, the business will make a loss if their clearance sales value is less than their cost. For example, if goods which originally cost £1,000 are now obsolete and could only be sold for £400, the business would suffer a loss of £600.

1.15 If, at the end of an accounting period, a business has goods in stock which are valueless or worth less than their original cost, the stocks' value should be **written down** to:

- **Nothing** if they are valueless
- Or their **net realisable value** if this is **less than their original cost**

The loss is reported as soon as it is foreseen, even if the goods have not yet been thrown away or sold off at a cheap price. This is an application of the **prudence concept**.

KEY TERM

Net realisable value of stock is the selling price (which may be less than original cost) less any costs still to be incurred in getting the stock ready to sell, and selling it.

1.16 The costs of stock written off or written down should not usually cause any problems in calculating the gross profit of a business, because the cost of goods sold will include the cost of stocks written off or written down, as the following example shows. (We shall look at the double entry for all aspects of stock a little later.)

1.17 EXAMPLE: STOCKS WRITTEN OFF AND WRITTEN DOWN

Sarah, trading as Serina Fashions, ends her financial year on 31 December. At 1 January 20X7 she had goods in stock valued at £21,500. During the year to 31 December 20X7, she purchased goods costing £73,000. Fashion goods which cost £4,300 were still held in stock at 31 December 20X7, and Sarah believes that these could only now be sold at a sale price of £800. The goods held in stock at 31 December 20X7 (including the fashion goods) had an original purchase cost of £18,700. The year's sales were £132,500.

Calculate the gross profit of Serina Fashions for the year ended 31 December 20X7.

1.18 SOLUTION

The initial calculation of closing stock values is as follows.

STOCK COUNT	At cost £	Revalued amount £	Amount written down £
Fashion goods	4,300	800	3,500
Other goods	14,400	14,400	-
	18,700	15,200	3,500

SERINA FASHIONS
TRADING ACCOUNT FOR THE YEAR ENDED 31 DECEMBER 20X7

	£	£
Sales		132,500
Value of opening stock	21,500	
Purchases	73,000	
	94,500	
Less closing stock	15,200	
Cost of goods sold		79,300
Gross profit		53,200

1.19 You should see that the write off of £3,500 is **automatic** because the closing stock deducted from cost of sales is £3,500 less than it would have been if valued at cost; cost of sales is therefore £3,500 higher than it would have been without the write down of stock.

Activity 9.3

Jackson Ltd's draft balance sheet includes a closing stock figure of £28,850. On further investigation the following facts are discovered.

(a) One stock sheet has been over-added by £212 and another under-added by £74.

(b) Goods included at their cost of £460 had deteriorated. They could still be sold at their normal selling price (£800) once repair work costing £270 was complete.

(c) Goods costing £430 sent to customers on a sale or return basis had been included in stock at their selling price of £665.

Calculate the revised stock figure.

2 ACCOUNTING FOR OPENING AND CLOSING STOCKS

2.1 In order to calculate gross profit it is necessary to work out the cost of goods sold, and to calculate the cost of goods sold it is necessary to have values for the **opening stock** and **closing stock**. Therefore, the trading part of a profit and loss account includes the following.

> **FORMULA TO LEARN**
>
> | | £ |
> | --- | --- |
> | Opening stock | X |
> | Plus purchases | X |
> | Less closing stock | (X) |
> | Equals cost of goods sold | X |

2.2 However, just writing down this formula hides three problems.

(a) How do you manage to get a precise **count of stock** in hand at any one time?

(b) Even once it has been counted, how do you **value the stock**?

(c) How does the **double entry accounting** for stock work?

Let us look at (c) first.

Ledger accounting for stocks

2.3 We saw in Chapter 3 that **purchases** are introduced to the trading account by means of the double entry:

DEBIT	Trading account	£X	
CREDIT	Purchases account		£X

2.4 But what about opening and closing stocks? How are their values accounted for in the double entry bookkeeping system? The answer is that a **stock account** must be kept. **This stock account is only ever used at the end of an accounting period, when the business counts up and values the stock in hand, in a stocktake.**

(a) When a stocktake is made, the business will have a value for its **closing stock**, and the double entry is:

DEBIT	Stock account (closing stock value)	£X	
CREDIT	Trading account		£X

Rather than show the closing stock as a 'plus' value in the trading account (say by adding it to sales) it is usual to show it as a 'minus' figure in arriving at cost of sales. This is illustrated in Paragraph 2.1 above. **The debit balance on stock account represents an asset, which will be shown as part of current assets in the balance sheet.**

(b) Closing stock at the end of one period becomes **opening stock** at the start of the next period. The stock account remains unchanged until the end of the next period, when the value of opening stock is taken to the trading account.

DEBIT	Trading account	£X	
CREDIT	Stock account (value of opening stock)		£X

The debit in the trading account would then have increased the cost of sales, ie opening stock is added to purchases in calculating cost of sales.

2.5 EXAMPLE: LEDGER ACCOUNTING FOR STOCK

The Swiss Chocolate Co began trading on 1 January 20X1 and has the following figures available for the year to 31 December 20X1 and 20X2.

	20X1	20X2
	£	£
Purchases	21,000	32,000
Closing stock	7,000	10,500
Sales	30,000	45,000

Prepare the ledger accounts required to produce a trading account for both 20X1 and 20X2.

2.6 SOLUTION

PURCHASES

		£			£
20X1	Cash/creditors	21,000	31/12/X1	Trading a/c	21,000
20X2	Cash/creditors	32,000	31/12/X2	Trading a/c	32,000

STOCK

		£			£
31/12/X1	Trading a/c (closing stock)	7,000	31/12/X1	Balance c/d	7,000
			31/12/X2	Trading a/c (opening stock)	7,000
1/1/X2	Balance b/d	7,000			
31/12/X2	Trading a/c (closing stock)	10,500	31/12/X2	Balance c/d (B/S)	10,500
		17,500			17,500
1/1/X3	Balance b/d	10,500			

SALES

		£			£
31/12/X1	Trading a/c	30,000	20X1	Cash/debtors	30,000
31/12/X2	Trading a/c	45,000	20X2	Cash/debtors	45,000

TRADING ACCOUNT

		£			£
31/12/X1	Purchases	21,000	31/12/X1	Sales	30,000
	Gross profit (P & L)	16,000		Stock (closing stock)	7,000
		37,000			37,000
31/12/X2	Purchases	32,000	31/12/X2	Sales	45,000
	Stock (opening stock)	7,000		Stock (closing stock)	10,500
	Gross profit (P & L)	16,500			
		55,500			55,500

SWISS CHOCOLATE CO
TRADING ACCOUNTS YEAR ENDED 31 DECEMBER

		20X1		*20X2*	
		£	£	£	£
Sales			30,000		45,000
Less	Cost of sales				
	Opening stock	-		7,000	
	Purchases	21,000		32,000	
		21,000		39,000	
Less:	Closing stock	(7,000)		(10,500)	
			14,000		28,500
Gross profit			16,000		16,500

ASSESSMENT ALERT

Make sure you are completely happy with these entries, before you go any further. Stocks are important in most organisations and you are likely to encounter them in your assessment, particularly in Section 2 of the Central Assessment where manufacturing accounts and incomplete data questions are set. You will almost certainly have to make stock entries in any extended trial balance question in Section 1 of your Central Assessment, as we will see in Chapter 12.

Activity 9.4

A business is established with capital of £4,000 and this amount is paid into a business bank account by the proprietor. During the first year's trading, the following transactions occurred.

	£
Purchases of goods for resale, on credit	8,200
Payments to trade creditors	7,100
Sales, all on credit	8,000
Payments from debtors	6,000
Fixed assets purchased for cash	2,900
Other expenses, all paid in cash	1,600

The bank has provided an overdraft facility of up to £6,000. All 'other expenses' relate to the current year.

Closing stocks of goods are valued at £3,500. (Because this is the first year of the business, there are no opening stocks.)

Prepare the ledger accounts and a trading, profit and loss account for the year. Ignore depreciation and drawings.

2.7 How do we establish the value of stocks on hand? The first step must be to establish **how much stock** is held by 'taking stock' in a **stocktake**.

3 STOCKTAKING AND STOCK ACCRUALS

3.1 Business trading is a continuous activity, but accounting statements must be drawn up at a particular date. In preparing a balance sheet it is necessary to 'freeze' the activity of a business so as to determine its assets and liabilities at a given moment. This includes establishing the **quantities of stocks** on hand.

3.2 A business buys stocks continually during its trading operations and either sells the goods onwards to customers or incorporates them as raw materials in manufactured products. This **constant movement of stocks** makes it difficult to establish what exactly is held at any precise moment.

3.3 In simple cases, when a business holds easily counted and relatively small amounts of stock, quantities of stocks on hand at the balance sheet date can be determined by **physically counting** them in a stocktake.

3.4 Trading activity may cause a problem in that stock movements will not necessarily cease during the time that the physical stocktake is in progress. Two possible solutions are:

(a) To **close down the business** while the count takes place

(b) To keep detailed **records of stock movements** during the course of the stocktake

3.5 **Closing down the business** for the stocktake (say over a weekend or at Christmas) is easier than trying to keep detailed records of stock movements during a stocktake. Most businesses prefer this method unless they keep detailed records of stock movements anyway.

3.6 In more complex cases, where a business holds large quantities of varied stock, an alternative approach is to maintain **continuous stock records**. This means that a card is kept for every item of stock, showing receipts and issues from the stores, and a running total. (Alternatively, the records may be computerised - quite likely in a large company.) A few stock items are counted each day to make sure their record cards are correct. This is called a 'continuous' stocktake because it is spread out over the year rather than completed in one stocktake at a designated time.

Stock accruals

3.7 In Chapter 8 we looked at accruals and mentioned **purchase accruals** (sometimes called **stock accruals**). These arise where goods have been received before the year end and included in stock, but no invoice has yet been received. Without an invoice, it will not have been possible to record the liability to the supplier. It is therefore necessary to determine those items of stock which have not been recorded as a liability.

3.8 Stock items for which no liability has been recorded can be identified and valued as follows.

Step 1 Match all invoices and Goods Received Notes (GRNs) received in the last month of the year.

Step 2 List all unmatched GRNs.

Step 3 The stock on the GRNs must be costed at its purchase price. Delivery notes (which should be kept with the GRNs) received from suppliers will sometimes show the prices of the items of stock delivered. Where this is not the case, it will be necessary to price the stock using current order forms or pricing lists.

3.9 The **double entry** once stock accruals are identified is:

DEBIT   Purchases (accrual c/d)
CREDIT   Stock accruals (liability)

3.10 What **value** should the business place on these stocks? SSAP 9 *Stocks and long-term contracts* contains the rules governing the valuation of stock.

4 VALUING STOCKS

4.1 There are several methods which, in theory, might be used for stock valuation .

(a) Stocks might be valued at their expected **selling price**.

(b) Stocks might be valued at their expected selling price, less any costs still to be incurred in getting them ready for sale and then selling them. This amount is referred to as the **net realisable value (NRV)** of the stocks.

(c) Stocks might be valued at their **historic cost** (the cost at which they were originally bought).

(d) Stocks might be valued at the amount it would cost to replace them. This is referred to as the **current replacement cost** of stocks. This method is not used in the type of accounts dealt with in this Interactive Text, and so is not considered further.

Use of selling price

4.2 The use of **selling prices** in stock valuation is ruled out because this would create a profit before the stock has been sold. This contradicts the accounting concept of **prudence**.

4.3 Suppose a trader buys two items of stock, each costing £150. He can sell them for £200 each, but in the accounting period he only sells one of them. The other is closing stock in hand.

4.4 Since only one item has been sold, profit ought to be £50. But if closing stock is (incorrectly) valued at selling price, profit would be £100 as profit would be taken on the closing stock as well.

	£	£
Sales		200
Opening stock	-	
Purchases (2 × 150)	300	
	300	
Less closing stock (at selling price)	200	
Cost of sale		100
Profit		100

Use of net realisable value

4.5 Contradicting the **prudence** concept *usually* applies as an objection to the use of **net realisable value (NRV)** in stock valuation. Say that an item purchased for £100 requires £5 of further expenditure in getting it ready for sale (for example £5 of processing costs and distribution costs). If its expected selling price is £140, its NRV is £(140 – 5) = £135. To value it at £135 in the balance sheet would still be to anticipate a profit of £35.

Use of historic cost

4.6 **Historic cost** is the normal basis of stock valuation. The only times when historic cost is *not* used is in the exceptional cases when the prudence concept requires a lower value to be used (normally net realisable value).

4.7 Staying with the example in Paragraph 4.5, suppose that the market for this product slumps and the item's expected selling price is only £90. The item's NRV is then £(90 − 5) = £85 and the business has in effect made a loss of £15 (£100 − £85). **The prudence concept requires that losses should be recognised as soon as they are foreseen**. This can be achieved by valuing the stock item in the balance sheet at its NRV of £85.

4.8 This suggests that the rule to follow is that stocks should be valued at cost, or if lower, net realisable value. SSAP 9 *Stocks and long-term contracts* states this.

> **RULE TO LEARN**
>
> **Stock should be valued at the lower of cost and net realisable value.**

Applying the basic valuation rule

4.9 Even if a business has many stock items, comparison of cost and NRV should be carried out for **each item separately**. It is not sufficient to compare the total cost of all stock items with the total NRV. This is an example of the accounting principle mentioned in Chapter 4: the **separate valuation principle**. An example will show why.

4.10 **EXAMPLE: SEPARATE VALUATION**

Suppose a business has four items of stock on hand at the end of its accounting period. Their costs and NRVs are as follows.

Stock item	Cost	NRV	Lower of cost/NRV
	£	£	£
1	27	32	27
2	14	8	8
3	43	55	43
4	29	40	29
	113	135	107

4.11 **SOLUTION**

It would be **incorrect** to compare total costs (£113) with total NRV (£135) and to state stocks at £113 in the balance sheet. The company can foresee a loss of £6 on item 2 and this should be recognised. If the four items are taken together in total the loss on item 2 is hidden by the anticipated profits on the other items. By performing the cost/NRV comparison for each item separately, the prudent valuation of £107 can be derived. This is the value which should appear in the balance sheet.

4.12 For a business with large amounts of stock this procedure may be impracticable. In this case it is acceptable to **group similar items** into categories and perform the comparison of cost and NRV category by category, rather than item by item.

Activity 9.5

Dean Ltd's stock includes three items for which the following details are available.

	Supplier's list price £	Net realisable value £
Product A	3,600	5,100
Product B	2,900	2,800
Product C	4,200	4,100
	10,700	12,000

The company receives a 2½% trade discount from its suppliers and it also takes advantage of a 2% discount for prompt payment.

Calculate the total value of products A, B and C which should be shown in stock in the balance sheet.

4.13 So have we now solved the problem of how a business should value its stocks? It seems that all the business has to do is to choose the lower of cost and net realisable value. This is fine, but **for a given item of stock, what *was* the historic cost?**

5 FINDING THE HISTORIC COST

5.1 Stock may be **raw materials** or components bought from suppliers, **finished goods** which have been made by the business but not yet sold, or work in the process of production, but only part-completed (**work in progress** or WIP). It will simplify matters, if we consider the historic cost of purchased raw materials and components, which ought to be their purchase price.

5.2 A business may be **continually purchasing** consignments of a particular component. As each consignment is received from suppliers they are stored in the appropriate bin, shelf or pallet, where they will be mixed with existing stocks. When components are issued to production the nearest components to hand, which may have arrived in the latest consignment or in an earlier consignments will be taken. Our concern is to devise a pricing technique, a rule of thumb which we can use to attribute a cost to each of the components issued from stores.

5.3 There are several techniques which are used in practice.

KEY TERMS

- **FIFO (first in, first out).** We assume components are used in the order in which they are received from suppliers. The components issued are deemed to have formed part of the oldest consignment still unused and are costed accordingly.

- **LIFO (last in, first out).** This involves the opposite assumption, that components issued to production originally formed part of the most recent delivery, while older consignments lie in the bin undisturbed.

- **Average cost.** As purchase prices change with each new consignment, the average price of components in the bin is constantly changed. Each component in the bin at any moment is assumed to have been purchased at the average price of all components in the bin at that moment.

5.4 Any or all of these methods might provide a suitable basis for valuing stocks. Note that if you are preparing **financial accounts** you would normally expect to use FIFO or average costs for the balance sheet valuation of stock. SSAP 9 specifically discourages the use of LIFO costs. Nevertheless, you should know about all of the methods so that you can discuss the differences between them. Remember that terms such as LIFO and FIFO refer to **pricing techniques** only. The actual components can be used in any order.

5.5 EXAMPLE: PRICING METHODS

To illustrate the various pricing methods, the following transactions will be used in each case.

TRANSACTIONS DURING MAY 20X7

	Quantity Units	Unit cost £	Total cost £	Market value per unit on date of transactions £
Opening balance 1 May	100	2.00	200	
Receipts 3 May	400	2.10	840	2.11
Issues 4 May	200			2.11
Receipts 9 May	300	2.12	636	2.15
Issues 11 May	400			2.20
Receipts 18 May	100	2.40	240	2.35
Issues 20 May	100			2.35
Closing balance 31 May	200			2.38
			1,916	

Receipts mean goods are received into stores and **issues** represent goods leaving stores.

The problem is to put a valuation on:

(a) The issues of materials
(b) The closing stock

How would issues and closing stock be valued using:

(a) FIFO?
(b) LIFO?

PUBLISHING

(c)   Average cost?

5.6   SOLUTION: FIFO (FIRST IN, FIRST OUT)

FIFO assumes materials are **issued from stock in the order in which they were delivered into stock,** ie issues are priced at the cost of the earliest delivery remaining in stock.

The cost of issues and closing stock value in the example, using FIFO would be as follows (note that o/s stands for opening stock).

Date of issue	Quantity	Value issued	Cost of issues	
	Units	£	£	£
4 May	200	100 o/s at £2	200	
		100 at £2.10	210	
				410
11 May	400	300 at £2.10	630	
		100 at £2.12	212	
				842
20 May	100	100 at £2.12		212
				1,464
Closing stock value	200	100 at £2.12	212	
		100 at £2.40	240	
				452
				1,916

Note that the cost of materials issued plus the value of closing stock equals the cost of purchases plus the value of opening stock (£1,916).

5.7   SOLUTION: LIFO (LAST IN, FIRST OUT)

LIFO assumes materials are **issued from stock in the reverse order to which they were delivered,** ie most recent deliveries are issued before earlier ones, and are priced accordingly.

The following table shows a method of calculating the cost of issues and the closing stock value under the LIFO method.

		Opening stock in units	Purchases in units 3 May	9 May	18 May
Issues		100	400	300	100
4 May			(200)		
11 May			(100)	(300)	
20 May					(100)
Closing stock		100	100	-	-
				£	£
Issues	4 May	200 @ £2.10			420
	11 May	300 @ £2.12		636	
		100 @ £2.10		210	
					846
	20 May	100 @ £2.40			240
Cost of materials					1,506
issued		100 @ £2.00		200	
Closing stock					
valuation:		100 @ £2.10		210	
					410
					1,916

Again, note that the cost of materials issued plus the value of closing stock equals the cost of purchases plus the value of opening stock (£1,916).

5.8 SOLUTION: AVERAGE COST

There are various ways in which average costs may be used in pricing stock issues. The most common (cumulative weighted average pricing) is illustrated below.

The **cumulative weighted average pricing method** calculates a weighted average price for all units in stock. Issues are priced at this average cost, and the balance of stock remaining would have the same unit valuation.

A new weighted average price is calculated whenever a new delivery of materials into store is received. This is the key feature of cumulative weighted average costing.

In our example, issue costs and closing stock values would be as follows.

Date	Received Units	Issued Units	Balance Units	Total stock value £	Unit cost £	Price of issue £
Opening stock			100	200	2.00	
3 May	400			840	2.10	
			500	1,040	2.08 *	
4 May		200		(416)	2.08 **	416
			300	624	2.08	
9 May	300			636	2.12	
			600	1,260	2.10 *	
11 May		400		(840)	2.10 **	840
			200	420	2.10	
18 May	100			240	2.40	
			300	660	2.20 *	
20 May		100		(220)	2.20 **	220
						1,476
Closing stock value			200	440	2.20	440
						1,916

* A new unit cost of stock is calculated whenever a new receipt of materials occurs.

** Whenever stocks are issued, the unit value of the items issued is the current weighted average cost per unit at the time of the issue.

For this method too, the cost of materials issued plus the value of closing stock equals the cost of purchases plus the value of opening stock (£1,916).

Activity 9.6

Hudson Ltd specialises in retailing one product. The firm purchases its stock from a regional wholesaler and sells through a catalogue. Details of Hudson Ltd's purchases and sales for the three month period 1 January to 31 March 20X7 are as follows.

Purchases

Date	Quantity in units	Price per unit £
14 January	280	24
30 January	160	24
15 February	300	25
3 March	150	26
29 March	240	26

Sales

Date	Quantity in units	Price per unit £
22 January	170	60
4 February	140	60
18 February	90	63
26 February	70	64
4 March	110	64
19 March	200	66
30 March	80	66

Note: Hudson Ltd had no stock in hand at 1 January 20X7.

Record the company's stock movements for the period 1 January to 31 March by applying:

(a)   FIFO principles
(b)   LIFO principles

6   STOCK VALUATIONS AND PROFIT

6.1   In the previous descriptions of FIFO, LIFO and average costing, the example used raw materials as an illustration. Each method of valuation produced different costs both of closing stocks and also of material issues. Since raw material costs affect the cost of production, and the cost of production works through eventually into the cost of sales, it follows that different methods of stock valuation will provide different profit figures. An example may help to illustrate this point.

6.2   EXAMPLE: STOCK VALUATIONS AND PROFIT

On 1 November 20X7 a company held 300 units of finished goods item No 9639 in stock. These were valued at £12 each. During November 20X7 three batches of finished goods were received into store from the production department as follows.

Date	Units received	Production cost per unit
10 November	400	£12.50
20 November	400	£14
25 November	400	£15

Goods sold out of stock during November were as follows.

Date	Units sold	Sale price per unit
14 November	500	£20
21 November	500	£20
28 November	100	£20

What was the profit from selling stock item 9639 in November 20X7, applying the following principles of stock valuation:

(a) FIFO?
(b) LIFO?

(c) Average cost?

Ignore administration, sales and distribution costs.

6.3 SOLUTION

(a) *FIFO*

		Issue cost *Total* £	*Closing* *stock* £
Date	*Issue costs*		
14 November	300 units × £12 plus		
	200 units × £12.50	6,100	
21 November	200 units × £12.50 plus		
	300 units × £14	6,700	
28 November	100 units × £14	1,400	
Closing stock	400 units × £15		6,000
		14,200	6,000

(b) *LIFO*

14 November	400 units × £12.50 plus		
	100 units × £12	6,200	
21 November	400 units × £14 plus		
	100 units × £12	6,800	
28 November	100 units × £15	1,500	
Closing stock	300 units × £15 plus		
	100 units × £12		5,700
		14,500	5,700

(c) *Average cost*

			Unit cost £	*Balance* *in stock* £	*Total cost* *of issues* £	*Closing* *stock* £
1 November	Opening stock	300	12.000	3,600		
10 November		400	12.500	5,000		
		700	12.286	8,600		
14 November		500	12.286	6,143	6,143	
		200	12.286	2,457		
20 November		400	14.000	5,600		
		600	13.428	8,057		
21 November		500	13.428	6,714	6,714	
		100	13.428	1,343		
25 November		400	15.000	6,000		
		500	14.686	7,343		
28 November		100	14.686	1,469	1,469	
30 November		400	14.686	5,874	14,326	5,874

(d) *Summary*

	FIFO £	*LIFO* £	*Weighted* *average* £
Profit:			
Opening stock	3,600	3,600	3,600
Cost of production	16,600	16,600	16,600
	20,200	20,200	20,200
Closing stock	6,000	5,700	5,874
Cost of sales	14,200	14,500	14,326
Sales (1,100 × £20)	22,000	22,000	22,000
Profit	7,800	7,500	7,674

6.4 **Different stock valuations have produced different cost of sales figures, and therefore different profits.** In our example opening stock values are the same, therefore the difference in the amount of profit under each method is the same as the difference in the valuations of closing stock.

6.5 The profit differences are only **temporary**. In our example, the opening stock in December 20X7 will be £6,000, £5,700 or £5,874, depending on the stock valuation used. Different opening stock values will affect the cost of sales and profits in December, so that in the long run inequalities in costs of sales each month will even themselves out.

ASSESSMENT ALERT

If you have to work out the closing stock value using one of the above rules you must set out your schedule neatly and clearly.

Activity 9.7

Assume that during the annual physical stock count, the closing stock figure shown in the business had been wrongly undercast by £1,000 and that error had been undetected.

Indicate what the effect would be:

(a) On this year's profit?
(b) On next year's profit?

Activity 9.8

Included in a flower shop's stock are some rose bushes. At the beginning of November 20X8 there were 40 rose bushes in stock, each costing £6. Stock movements during the month of November 20X8 were as follows:

Purchases 5/11/20X8   40 at £6.5
Sales 12/11/20X8   50
Sales 15/11/20X8   10
Purchases 23/11/20X8   30 at £6

Each rose bush is sold for £11. Stock is valued on a FIFO basis.

Calculate the value of the following.

(a) Sales of rose bushes for November 20X8
(b) Closing stock of rose bushes on 30 November 20X8
(c) Cost of goods sold of rose bushes for November 20X8

Activity 9.9

A firm has the following transactions with its product R.

Year 1

Opening stock: nil
Buys 10 units at £300 per unit
Buys 12 units at £250 per unit
Sells 8 units at £400 per unit
Buys 6 units at £200 per unit
Sells 12 units at £400 per unit

Year 2

Buys 10 units at £200 per unit
Sells 5 units at £400 per unit
Buys 12 units at £150 per unit
Sells 25 units at £400 per unit

Calculate on an item by item basis for both year 1 and year 2:

(a) The closing stock
(b) The sales
(c) The cost of sales
(d) The gross profit

Using, separately, the LIFO and the FIFO methods of stock valuation.

Key learning points

- The **cost of goods** sold is calculated by applying the formula:

	£
Opening stock value	X
Add cost of purchases or production	X
	X
Less closing stock value	(X)
Equals cost of goods sold	X

- A **stock ledger account** is kept which is only ever used at the end of an accounting period, when the business counts up and values stock in hand.

- The quantity of stocks held at the year end is established by means of a physical count of stock in an annual **stocktaking exercise,** or by a 'continuous' stocktake.

- The value of these stocks is then calculated, taking the **lower of cost and net realisable value** for each separate item or group of stock items.

  - **NRV** is the selling price less all costs to completion and less selling costs.
  - **Cost** comprises purchase costs and costs of conversion.

- In order to value the stocks, a pricing method must be adopted. The possibilities include **FIFO, LIFO and average costs**.

- The value of closing stocks is accounted for in the nominal ledger by debiting a stock account and crediting the trading account at the end of an accounting period. The stock will therefore always have a debit balance at the end of a period, and this balance will be shown in the balance sheet as a **current asset** for stocks.

- **Opening stocks** brought forward in the stock account are transferred to the **trading account,** and so at the end of the accounting year, the balance on the stock account ceases to be the opening stock value b/d, and becomes instead the closing stock value c/d.

Quick quiz

1 How is the cost of goods sold calculated?
2 Distinguish between carriage inwards and carriage outwards.
3 How is carriage inwards treated in the trading, profit and loss account?
4 Give three reasons why goods purchased might have to be written off.
5 When is a stock account used?
6 How is closing stock incorporated in final accounts?
7 What is 'continuous' stocktaking?
8 Define net realisable value.
9 Why is stock not valued at expected selling price?
10 Give three methods of pricing a stock item at historic cost.

Answers to quick quiz

1 Cost of goods sold = opening stock value *plus* purchases (or cost of production) *less* closing stock value.

2 (a) Carriage inwards is cost to the purchaser
  (b) Carriage outwards is cost to the seller

3   Carriage inwards is treated as an addition to the cost of sales when calculating gross profit.

4   Goods might be lost or stolen; damaged; or obsolete or out of fashion.

5   A stock account is only used at the end of the accounting period.

6   DEBIT   Stock account (balance sheet)
     CREDIT   Trading account

7   Continuous stocktaking is where permanent records are kept of stock movements and random counts carried out as a check, spread out over the year.

8   NRV is the expected selling price of stocks less any costs still to be incurred in getting them ready for sale and then selling them.

9   Valuation at selling price would create a profit for the business before the stock was sold.

10   First in, first out; last in, first out; average cost.

BPP
PUBLISHING

10 Incomplete records

This chapter contains

1   Preparing accounts from incomplete records

2   The opening balance sheet

3   Credit sales and debtors

4   Purchases and trade creditors

5   Purchases, stocks and cost of sales

6   The cash book

7   Accruals and prepayments

8   Drawings

9   Incomplete records in your central assessment

Learning objectives

- Identify and resolve situations where data is incomplete

- Identify and resolve situations where there are discrepancies, inconsistencies and/or unusual factors

- Implement different methods of restructuring accounts from incomplete evidence

Performance criteria

5.2.4 Incomplete data is identified and either resolved or referred to the appropriate person

5.3.5 Discrepancies and unusual features are identified and either resolved or referred to the appropriate person

Range statement

5.2.1 Records: day book; journal; ledger

5.3.2 Discrepancies and unusual features: insufficient data has been provided; inconsistencies within the data

Knowledge and understanding

Methods of restructuring accounts from incomplete evidence

BPP PUBLISHING

1 PREPARING ACCOUNTS FROM INCOMPLETE RECORDS

1.1 Incomplete records problems occur when a business does not have a full set of accounting records. The problems can arise for two reasons.

    (a) The proprietor of the business does not keep a full set of accounts, ie it has **limited accounting records.**

    (b) Some of the business accounts are **accidentally lost or destroyed.**

1.2 The challenge is to **prepare a set of year-end accounts** for the business; a trading, profit and loss account, and a balance sheet. Since there is not a full set of accounts, preparing the final accounts is not a simple matter of closing off accounts and transferring balances to the trading, profit and loss account, or showing outstanding balances in the balance sheet. Preparing the final accounts can involve some or all of the following tasks.

    (a) Establishing the cost of **purchases and other expenses**
    (b) Establishing the total amount of **sales**
    (c) Establishing the year end **creditors, accruals, debtors and prepayments**

1.3 Questions may go a stage further, by introducing a fire or burglary, say, which leaves the owner of the business uncertain about how much **stock has been destroyed or stolen.**

1.4 To understand what incomplete records are about, it will be useful now to look at what exactly might be incomplete. We shall consider the following items in turn.

- The opening balance sheet
- Credit sales and debtors
- Purchases and trade creditors
- Purchases, stocks and the cost of sales
- Stolen goods or goods destroyed
- The cash book
- Accruals and prepayments
- Drawings (for a sole trader)

CENTRAL ASSESSMENT ALERT

There is likely to be a strong element of incomplete records in Section 2 of your Central Assessment. Each question will use a variety of the techniques and procedures discussed below.

2 THE OPENING BALANCE SHEET

2.1 In practice there should not be any missing item in the opening balance sheet of the business, because it should be available from the preparation of the previous year's final accounts. However, a central assessment problem might provide information about the assets and liabilities of the business at the beginning of the period under review, but then leave the balancing figure unspecified. This **balancing figure** represents the opening balance of the proprietor's business capital.

2.2 EXAMPLE: OPENING BALANCE SHEET

For example, a business has the following assets and liabilities as at 1 January 20X7.

	£
Fixtures and fittings at cost	7,000
Provision for depreciation, fixtures and fittings	4,000
Motor vehicles at cost	12,000
Provision for depreciation, motor vehicles	6,800
Stock in trade	4,500
Trade debtors	5,200
Cash at bank and in hand	1,230
Trade creditors	3,700
Prepayment	450
Accrued rent	2,000

Prepare a balance sheet for the business inserting a balancing figure for proprietor's capital.

2.3 SOLUTION

The balance sheet of the business can be prepared and the balancing figure is the proprietor's capital.

	£	£
Fixtures and fittings at cost	7,000	
Less accumulated depreciation	4,000	
		3,000
Motor vehicles at cost	12,000	
Less accumulated depreciation	6,800	
		5,200
		8,200
Current assets		
Stock in trade	4,500	
Trade debtors	5,200	
Prepayment	450	
Cash	1,230	
	11,380	
Current liabilities		
Trade creditors	3,700	
Accrual	2,000	
	5,700	
Net current assets		5,680
		13,880
Capital		
Proprietor's capital as at 1.1.X7 (balancing figure)		13,880

2.4 The opening balance sheet should now provide some of the information needed to prepare the final accounts for the current period.

3 CREDIT SALES AND DEBTORS

3.1 If a business does not keep a record of its **sales on credit**, the value of these sales can be derived from the opening balance of trade debtors, the closing balance of trade debtors, and the payments received from trade debtors during the period.

Credit sales are calculated as follows.

> **FORMULA TO LEARN**
>
> | | £ |
> |---|---|
> | Payments received from trade debtors | X |
> | *Plus* closing balance of trade debtors (since these represent sales in the current period for which cash payment has not yet been received) | X |
> | *Less* opening balance of trade debtors (unless these become bad debts, they will pay what they owe in the current period for sales in a previous period) | (X) |
> | Credit sales during the period | X |

3.2 Suppose that a business had trade debtors of £1,750 on 1 April 20X7 and £3,140 on 31 March 20X8. If payments received in the cash book from trade debtors during the year to 31 March 20X8 were £28,490, and if there are no bad debts, then credit sales for the period would be as follows.

	£
Cash received from debtors	28,490
Plus closing debtors	3,140
Less opening debtors	(1,750)
Credit sales during the period	29,880

3.3 If there are **bad debts** during the period, the value of sales will be **increased** by the amount of bad debts written off, no matter whether they relate to opening debtors or credit sales during the current period. In the above example, if there were bad debts of £120 written off then credit sales would be £30,000.

3.4 This calculation could be made in a ledger account, with credit sales being the balancing figure to complete the account.

DEBTORS

	£		£
Opening balance b/d	1,750	Cash received	28,490
Credit sales (balancing figure)	30,000	Bad debts written off	120
		Closing balance c/d	3,140
	31,750		31,750

3.5 The same interrelationship between credit sales, cash from debtors, and opening and closing debtors balances can be used to derive a missing figure for cash from debtors, or opening or closing debtors, given the values for the three other items.

Activity 10.1

We know for Synergie & Partners that opening debtors are £6,700, closing debtors are £3,200 and credit sales for the period are £69,400. What cash has been received from debtors in the period?

3.6 There is an alternative way of presenting the same calculation.

	£
Opening balance of debtors	X
Plus credit sales during the period	X
Total money owed to the business	X
Less closing balance of debtors	(X)
Equals cash received during the period	X

Control account

3.7 Control account reconciliations were covered in Chapter 7. It is possible that you will be asked to **reconcile control accounts** in an incomplete records question. Note the complications which might arise in a sales ledger control account, they might include the following.

SALES LEDGER CONTROL ACCOUNT

	£		£
Opening debit balances	X	Opening credit balances (if any)	X
Sales	X	Cash received	X
Dishonoured bills or cheques	X	Discounts allowed	X
Cash paid to clear credit balances	X	Returns inwards	X
Bad debts recovered	X	Bad debts	X
Closing credit balances	X	Cash from bad debts recovered	X
		Contra with P/L control a/c	X
		Allowances on goods damaged	X
		Closing debit balances	X
	$\overline{\underline{X}}$		$\overline{\underline{X}}$

Activity 10.2

A debtors control account contains the following entries:

	£
Balance b/d 1 January	42,800
Bank	204,000
Discounts allowed	16,250
Credit sales	240,200

Assuming there are no other entries into the account, what is the closing balance at 31 December?

---

4 PURCHASES AND TRADE CREDITORS

4.1 A similar relationship exists between **purchases** during a period, the opening and closing balances for trade creditors, and amounts paid to trade creditors during the period.

To calculate an unknown amount for purchases, the amount would be derived as follows.

FORMULA TO LEARN

	£
Payments to trade creditors during the period	X
Plus closing balance of trade creditors (since these represent purchases in the current period for which payment has not yet been made)	X
Less opening balance of trade creditors (these debts, paid in the current period, relate to purchases in a previous period)	(X)
Purchases during the period	$\underline{X}$

4.2 Suppose that a business had trade creditors of £3,728 on 1 October 20X7 and £2,645 on 30 September 20X8. If payments to trade creditors during the year to 30 September 20X8 were £31,479, then purchases during the year can be derived as follows.

	£
Payments to trade creditors	31,479
Plus closing balance of trade creditors	2,645
Less opening balance of trade creditors	(3,728)
Purchases	30,396

4.3 The same calculation could be made in a **ledger account**, with purchases being the balancing figure to complete the account.

CREDITORS

	£		£
Cash payments	31,479	Opening balance b/d	3,728
Closing balance c/d	2,645	Purchases (balancing figure)	30,396
	34,124		34,124

Control account

4.4 Once again, various **complications** can arise in the purchase ledger control account which you may have to consider.

PURCHASE LEDGER CONTROL ACCOUNT

	£		£
Opening debit balances (if any)	X	Opening credit balances	X
Cash paid	X	Purchases and other expenses	X
Discounts received	X	Cash received clearing debit	
Returns outwards	X	balances	X
Contras with S/L control a/c	X	Closing debit balances	X
Allowances on goods damaged	X		
Closing credit balances	X		
	X		X

Activity 10.3

Joe Clinton has not kept a proper set of accounting records during 20X7 due to the prolonged illness of his bookkeeper. However, the following information is available.

	£
Cash purchases in year	5,850
Cash paid for goods supplied on credit	41,775
Creditors at 1 January 20X7	1,455
Creditors at 31 December 20X7	1,080

Calculate Joe Clinton's purchases figure for the trading account for 20X7.

5 PURCHASES, STOCKS AND COST OF SALES

Purchases: use of mark up

5.1 When the **value of purchases is not known,** a different approach might be required to find out what they were, depending on the nature of the information given to you.

5.2 One approach would be to use information about the cost of sales, and opening and closing stocks. This means that you would be using the **trading account** rather than the total creditors account to find the cost of purchases.

FORMULA TO LEARN

		£
Since:	opening stocks	X
	plus purchases	X
	less closing stocks	(X)
	equals the cost of goods sold	X
then:	the cost of goods sold	X
	plus closing stocks	X
	less opening stocks	(X)
	equals purchases for the period	X

5.3   Suppose that the stock in trade of a business on 1 July 20X6 has a balance sheet value of £8,400, and a stock taking exercise at 30 June 20X7 showed stock to be valued at £9,350. Sales for the year to 30 June 20X7 are £80,000, and the business makes a mark up of 25% on cost of sales for all the items that it sells. What were the purchases during the year?

5.4   To answer this, we use what we know about the **relationship between sales, cost of sales and gross profit.**

KEY TERMS

- **Mark up** is the term use to describe **gross profit's** relationship with **cost of sales** – usually expressed as a percentage of cost.

- **Margin** is the term used to describe **gross profit's** relationship with **sales** – expressed as a percentage of sales.

Term	Relationship	100% figure
Mark up on cost	Gross profit/ cost of sales	Cost of sales
Margin on sales	Gross profit/sales	Sales

5.5   To calculate cost of sales using what we know about the **mark up** the business operates means we have to manipulate the following relationship.

	£	%	
Sales	X	125	balancing figure
Cost of sales	(X)	(100)	
Gross profit	X	25	

The cost of goods sold is 80% (100% ÷ 125%) of sales value.

5.6   The cost of sales can therefore be derived from the value of sales, as follows.

		£
Sales	(125%)	80,000
Gross profit	(25%)	16,000
Cost of sales	(100%)	64,000

And so we can derive purchases:

	£	£
Opening stock		8,400
Add: purchases (balancing figure)	64,950	
Less: closing stock	(9,350)	
		55,600
Cost of sales		64,000

5.7   Let us now use the same figures in paragraph 5.3, but supposing we are told that the business operates on a 30% **margin**. To calculate the cost of sales using **margin** we have to manipulate the following relationship:

	£	%	
Sales	X	100	
Cost of sales	(X)	70	balancing figure
Gross profit	X	30	

5.8   As before, the cost of sales can now be derived from the value of sales:

		£
Sales	(100%)	80,000
Profit	(30%)	24,000
Cost of sales	(70%)	56,000

And now we can derive purchases:

	£	£
Opening stock		8,400
Add: purchases (balancing figure)	56,950	
Less: closing stock	(9,350)	
		47,600
Cost of sales		56,000

Activity 10.4

An extract from a business's trading account stood as follows for the year ended 31 March 20X7.

	£	£
Sales		150,000
Opening stock	12,000	
Purchases	114,500	
	126,500	
Closing stock	14,000	
		112,500

(a)   Calculate the gross profit mark up on cost of sales.
(b)   Calculate the gross profit margin on sales.

Stolen goods or goods destroyed

5.9   A similar calculation is required to derive the value of **goods stolen or destroyed**. An example will show how to determine the cost of an unknown quantity of goods lost.

5.10   EXAMPLE: STOCK LOST IN A FIRE

Fairmount Boutique sells fashion clothes. On 1 January 20X7, it had stock in trade which cost £7,345. During the nine months to 30 September 20X7, the business purchased goods from suppliers costing £106,420. Sales during the same period were £154,000. The shop makes a mark-up of 40% on cost for everything it sells. On 30 September 20X7, there was a fire in the shop which destroyed most of the stock in it. Only a small amount of stock, known to have cost £350, was undamaged and still fit for sale.

How much stock was lost in the fire?

5.11 SOLUTION

		£
(a)	Sales (140%)	154,000
	Gross profit (40%)	44,000
	Cost of goods sold (100%)	110,000

		£
(b)	Opening stock, at cost	7,345
	Plus purchases	106,420
		113,765
	Less closing stock, at cost	350
	Equals cost of goods sold and goods lost	113,415

		£
(c)	Cost of goods sold and lost	113,415
	Cost of goods sold	110,000
	Cost of goods lost	3,415

5.12 EXAMPLE: STOCK STOLEN

Ashley Guerrard runs a jewellery shop in the High Street. On 1 January 20X7, his stock in trade, at cost, amounted to £4,700 and his trade creditors were £3,950.

During the six months to 30 June 20X7, sales were £42,000. Ashley Guerrard makes a margin of $33^{1}/_{3}$% on everything he sells.

On 30 June, there was a burglary at the shop, and all the stock was stolen.

In trying to establish how much stock had been taken, Ashley Guerrard was able to provide the following information.

(a) He knew from his bank statements that he had paid £28,400 to creditors in the six month period to 30 June 20X7.

(b) He currently owed creditors £5,550.

Required

(a) Calculate how much stock was stolen.
(b) Prepare a trading account for the six months to 30 June 20X7.

5.13 SOLUTION

Step 1   We must establish some 'unknowns' before we can calculate how much stock was stolen. The first 'unknown' is the amount of **purchases** during the period.

CREDITORS

	£		£
Payments to creditors	28,400	Opening balance b/d	3,950
Closing balance c/d	5,550	Purchases (balancing figure)	30,000
	33,950		33,950

Step 2 The **cost of goods sold** is also unknown, but this can be established from the gross profit margin and the sales for the period.

		£
Sales	(100%)	42,000
Gross profit	($33\frac{1}{3}$%)	14,000
Cost of goods sold	($66\frac{2}{3}$%)	28,000

Step 3 The **cost of the goods stolen** is as follows.

	£
Opening stock at cost	4,700
Purchases	30,000
	34,700
Less closing stock (after burglary)	0
Cost of goods sold and goods stolen	34,700
Cost of goods sold (see (ii) above)	28,000
Cost of goods stolen	6,700

Step 4 The cost of the goods stolen will *not* be a charge in the trading account (see paragraph 5.14), and so the trading account for the period is as follows.

ASHLEY GUERRARD
TRADING ACCOUNT FOR THE SIX MONTHS TO 30 JUNE 20X7

	£	£
Sales		42,000
Less cost of goods sold		
Opening stock	4,700	
Purchases	30,000	
	34,700	
Less stock stolen	6,700	
		28,000
Gross profit		14,000

Accounting for stock lost/stolen/destroyed

5.14 When stock is stolen, destroyed or otherwise lost, the loss must be accounted for somehow. Since the loss is **not a trading loss**, the cost of the goods lost is not included in the trading account, as the previous example showed. We therefore have to CREDIT Trading a/c. But where does the debit go to?

5.15 There are two possible accounts that could be **debited** with the other side of the accounting double entry, depending on whether or not the lost goods were **insured**.

(a) If the lost goods were **not insured** the business must bear the loss and the loss is shown in the profit and loss account.

DEBIT   Profit and loss account
CREDIT   Trading account

(b) If the lost goods were **insured** the business will not suffer a loss because the insurance will pay back all the cost of the lost goods. This means that there is no charge at all in the profit and loss account, and the appropriate double entry for the cost of the loss is as follows.

DEBIT   Insurance claim account (debtor)
CREDIT   Trading account

The insurance claim will then be a current asset, and shown in the balance sheet of the business as such. When the claim is paid, the account is then closed.

DEBIT   Cash
CREDIT   Insurance claim account (debtor)

Activity 10.5

Janey Jennings's business had opening stock of £71,300. Purchases and sales for 20X7 were £282,250 and £455,000 respectively. The gross profit margin is a constant 40% on sales. On 31 December 20X7 a fire destroyed all the stock on Janey Jennings's premises, except for small sundry items with a cost of £1,200.

Calculate the cost of the stock destroyed and prepare Janey's trading account for the period ended 31 December 20X7.

6   THE CASH BOOK

6.1   The construction of a cash book, **largely from bank statements** showing receipts and payments of a business during a given period, is often an important feature of incomplete records problems. The purpose of an incomplete records exercise is largely to test your understanding about how various items of receipts or payments relate to the preparation of a final set of accounts for a business.

6.2   We have already seen in this chapter that information about cash receipts or payments might be needed to establish the amount of credit sales or of purchases during a period. **Other receipts or payments figures** might be needed to establish the following amounts.

- Cash sales
- Certain expenses in the profit and loss account
- Drawings by the business proprietor

6.3   It might therefore be helpful, if a business does not keep a cash book on a daily basis, to **construct a cash book** at the end of an accounting period. A business which typically might not keep a daily cash book is a shop.

(a)   Many sales, if not all sales, are for cash and payment is received in the form of notes and coins, cheques, or credit cards at the time of sale.

(b)   Some payments for purchases are made in notes and coins out of the till rather than by payment out of the business bank account by cheque.

6.4   Where there appears to be a sizeable volume of receipts and payments in cash then it is also helpful to construct a **two column cash book**. This is a cash book with one column for cash receipts and payments, and one column for money paid into and out of the business bank account. (Note that at Foundation Stage a two column cash book was taken to mean a cash book with a column for payments from the bank account and another for discounts received.)

BPP PUBLISHING

6.5 EXAMPLE: PREPARING A TWO COLUMN CASH BOOK

Franklin George owns and runs a bookshop, making a gross profit of 25% on the cost of everything he sells. He does not keep a cash book.

On 1 January 20X7 the balance sheet of his business was as follows.

	£	£
Net fixed assets		20,000
Stock	10,000	
Cash in the bank	3,000	
Cash in the till	200	
	13,200	
Trade creditors	1,200	
		12,000
		32,000
Proprietor's capital		32,000

You are given the following information about the year to 31 December 20X7.

(a) There were no sales on credit.

(b) £41,750 in receipts were banked.

(c) The bank statements of the period show these payments.

(i)	To trade creditors	£36,000
(ii)	Sundry expenses	£5,600
(iii)	In drawings	£4,400

(d) Payments were also made in cash out of the till.

(i)	To trade creditors	£800
(ii)	Sundry expenses	£1,500
(iii)	In drawings	£3,700

At 31 December 20X7, the business had cash in the till of £450 and trade creditors of £1,400. The cash balance in the bank was not known and the value of closing stock has not yet been calculated. There were no accruals or prepayments. No further fixed assets were purchased during the year. The depreciation charge for the year is £900.

(a) Prepare a two column cash book for the period.

(b) Prepare the trading, profit and loss account for the year to 31 December 20X7 and the balance sheet as at 31 December 20X7.

6.6 DISCUSSION AND SOLUTION

A two column cash book is completed as follows.

Step 1 Enter the **opening cash in hand and bank balances**.

Step 2 Enter the information given about **cash payments** (and any **cash receipts**, if there had been any such items given in the problem).

Step 3 The cash receipts banked are a '**contra**' entry, being both a debit (bank column) and a credit (cash in hand column) in the same account.

Step 4 Enter the **closing cash in hand** (cash in the bank at the period end is not known).

CASH BOOK

	Cash in hand £	Bank £		Cash in hand £	Bank £
Balance b/d	200	3,000	Trade creditors	800	36,000
Cash receipts			Sundry expenses	1,500	5,600
banked (contra)		41,750	Drawings	3,700	4,400
Sales	*48,000		Cash receipts banked		
Balance c/d		*1,250	(contra)	41,750	
			Balance c/d	450	
	48,200	46,000		48,200	46,000
* Balancing figures					

Step 5 The closing balance of cash at bank is a balancing figure (debit).

Step 6 Since all sales are for cash, the balancing figure that can be entered in the cash in hand debit column is **sales**.

6.7 Notice that since not all receipts from cash sales are banked, the value of cash sales during the period has to be **'grossed up' for cash payments** and the difference between opening and closing cash in hand.

	£
Receipts banked	41,750
Plus expenses and drawings paid out of the till in cash	
£(800 + 1,500 + 3,700)	6,000
Plus any cash stolen (here there is none)	0
Plus the closing balance of cash in hand	450
	48,200
Less the opening balance of cash in hand	(200)
Equals cash sales	48,000

6.8 The cash book constructed in this way has enabled us to establish both the closing balance for **cash in the bank** and also the volume of **cash sales**. The trading, profit and loss account and the balance sheet can also be prepared, once a value for purchases has been calculated.

CREDITORS

	£		£
Cash book:		Balance b/d	1,200
payments from bank	36,000	Purchases (balancing figure)	37,000
Cash book:			
payments in cash	800		
Balance c/d	1,400		
	38,200		38,200

The mark up of 25% on cost indicates that the cost of the goods sold is £38,400, as follows.

	£
Sales (125%)	48,000
Gross profit (25%)	9,600
Cost of goods sold (100%)	38,400

The closing stock amount is now a balancing figure in the trading account.

FRANKLIN GEORGE TRADING, PROFIT AND LOSS ACCOUNT
FOR THE YEAR ENDED 31 DECEMBER 20X7

	£	£
Sales		48,000
Less cost of goods sold		
Opening stock	10,000	
Purchases	37,000	
	47,000	
Less closing stock (balancing figure)	8,600	
		38,400
Gross profit (25/125 × £48,000)		9,600
Expenses		
Sundry £(1,500 + 5,600)	7,100	
Depreciation	900	
		8,000
Net profit		1,600

FRANKLIN GEORGE
BALANCE SHEET AS AT 31 DECEMBER 20X7

	£	£
Net fixed assets £(20,000 – 900)		19,100
Stock	8,600	
Cash in the till	450	
	9,050	
Bank overdraft	1,250	
Trade creditors	1,400	
	2,650	
Net current assets		6,400
		25,500
Proprietor's capital		
Balance b/d		32,000
Net profit for the year		1,600
		33,600
Drawings £(3,700 + 4,400)		(8,100)
Balance c/d		25,500

Theft of cash from the till

6.9   If cash is stolen, the amount stolen will be a credit entry in the cash book, and a debit in either the profit and loss account or insurance claim account, depending on whether the business is **insured**. The missing figure for cash sales, if this has to be calculated, must take account of cash received but later stolen: see Paragraph 6.7.

Using a debtors account to calculate both cash sales and credit sales

6.10   Another point which needs to be considered is how a missing value can be found for **cash sales and credit sales**, when a business has both, but takings banked by the business are not divided between takings from cash sales and takings from credit sales.

6.11   EXAMPLE: DETERMINING THE VALUE OF SALES DURING THE PERIOD

Suppose that a business had, on 1 January 20X7, trade debtors of £2,000, cash in the bank of £3,000, and cash in hand of £300.

During the year to 31 December 20X7 the business banked £95,000 in takings. It also paid out the following expenses in cash from the till.

Drawings	£1,200
Sundry expenses	£800

On 29 August 20X7 a thief broke into the shop and stole £400 from the till.

At 31 December 20X7 trade debtors amounted to £3,500, cash in the bank £2,500 and cash in the till £150.

What was the value of sales during the year?

6.12 SOLUTION

If we tried to prepare a debtors account and a two column cash book, we would have insufficient information, in particular about whether the takings which were banked related to cash sales or credit sales.

DEBTORS

	£		£
Balance b/d	2,000	Payments from debtors	
Credit sales	*Unknown*	(credit sales)	*Unknown*
		Balance c/d	3,500

CASH BOOK

	Cash £	Bank £		Cash £	Bank £
Balance b/d	300	3,000	Drawings	1,200	
			Sundry expenses	800	
Debtors: payments		*Unknown*	Cash stolen	400	
Cash sales		*Unknown*	Balance c/d	150	2,500

All we do know is that the combined sums from debtors and cash takings banked is £95,000.

The value of sales can be found instead by using the **debtors account**, which should be used to record cash takings banked as well as payments by debtors. The balancing figure in the debtors account will then be a combination of credit sales and some cash sales. The cash book only needs to have single columns.

DEBTORS

	£		£
Balance b/d	2,000	Cash banked	95,000
Sales to trading account	96,500	Balance c/d	3,500
	98,500		98,500

CASH (EXTRACT)

	£		£
Balance in hand b/d	300	*Payments in cash*	
Balance in bank b/d	3,000	Drawings	1,200
Debtors a/c	95,000	Expenses	800
		Cash stolen	400
		Balance in hand c/d	150
		Balance in bank c/d	2,500

The remaining 'undiscovered' amount of cash sales is now found as follows.

	£
Payments in cash out of the till	
Drawings	1,200
Expenses	800
	2,000
Cash stolen	400
Closing balance of cash in hand	150
	2,550
Less opening balance of cash in hand	(300)
Further cash sales	2,250

(This calculation is similar to the one described in Paragraph 6.7.)

Total sales for the year	£
From debtors account	96,500
From cash book	2,250
Total sales	98,750

Activity 10.6

Blissetts Ltd is a retail company and sales are all on cash terms. During 20X4 their bank account shows cash banked of £142,950 which included £660 in respect of the repayment of a director's loan. About £450 was taken from the till every month for wages and £60 was taken weekly for sundry expenses. The cash in the till amounted to £930 on 1 January 20X4 and £780 on 31 December 20X4.

Calculate the sales figure for Blissetts Ltd for 20X4.

7 ACCRUALS AND PREPAYMENTS

7.1 Where there is an **accrued expense or a prepayment**, the charge made in the profit and loss account should be found from the opening balance b/d, the closing balance c/d, and cash payments for the item during the period. The charge in the profit and loss account is perhaps most easily found as the **balancing figure in a ledger account.**

7.2 Suppose that on 1 April 20X7 a business prepays rent of £700. During the year to 31 March 20X8 it pays £9,300 in rent, and at 31 March 20X8 the prepayment of rent is £1,000. The cost of rent in the profit and loss account for the year to 31 March 20X8 would be the balancing figure in the following ledger account. (Note that a prepayment is a current asset, and so is a debit balance brought down.)

RENT

	£		£
Prepayment: balance b/d	700	P & L account (balancing figure)	9,000
Cash	9,300	Prepayment: balance c/d	1,000
	10,000		10,000
Balance b/d	1,000		

7.3 Similarly, if a business accrues telephone expenses as at 1 July 20X6 of £850, pays £6,720 in telephone bills during the year to 30 June 20X7, and accrues telephone expenses of £1,140 as at 30 June 20X7, then the telephone expense to be shown in the profit and loss account for the year to 30 June 20X7 is the balancing figure in the following ledger account. (Note that an accrual is a current liability, and so is a credit balance brought down.)

TELEPHONE EXPENSES

	£		£
Cash	6,720	Balance b/d (accrual)	850
Balance c/d (accrual)	1,140	P & L a/c (balancing figure)	7,010
	7,860		7,860
		Balance b/d	1,140

8 DRAWINGS

8.1 In the case of a sole trader, drawings would not normally present a problem in preparing a set of final accounts from incomplete records, but it is not unusual for questions to involve the following situations.

(a) The business owner **pays income into his bank account** which has nothing whatever to do with the business operations. For example, the owner might pay dividend income or other income from investments into the bank, from stocks and shares which he owns personally, separate from the business itself.

(b) The business owner **pays money out of the business bank account** for items which are not business expenses, such as life insurance premiums or a payment for his family's holidays.

(c) The owner takes **stock for his personal use**.

8.2 These personal items of receipts or payments should be dealt with as follows.

(a) **Receipts should be set off against drawings**. For example, if a business owner receives £600 in dividend income from investments not owned by the business and pays it into the business bank account, then the accounting entry is as follows.

DEBIT   Cash
CREDIT   Drawings

(b) **Payments of cash for personal items should be charged to drawings.**

DEBIT   Drawings
CREDIT   Cash

(c) **Goods taken for personal use (drawings of stock)**: the traditional way of dealing with this has been to charge the goods to drawings at cost. The required entries are:

DEBIT   Drawings
CREDIT   Purchases

However, the recommended treatment, according better with modern practice and the requirements of HM Customs & Excise, is as follows.

DEBIT   Drawings at selling price (including VAT)
CREDIT   Sales
CREDIT   VAT

> ## CENTRAL ASSESSMENT ALERT
>
> - If a question states that a proprietor's drawings during a given year are 'approximately £40 per week' then you should assume that drawings for the year are £40 × 52 weeks = £2,080.
>
> - However, if a question states that drawings in the year are 'between £35 and £45 per week', do not assume that the drawings average £40 per week and so amount to £2,080 for the year. You could not be certain that the actual drawings did average £40, and so you should treat the drawings figure as a missing item that needs to be calculated.

9   INCOMPLETE RECORDS IN YOUR CENTRAL ASSESSMENT

9.1   Past Central Assessments have generally contained an incomplete records element, so it is as well to know what to expect. Your incomplete records task will be broken down into several sub-tasks. In other words, you won't have to prepare the trading account from scratch, but will get there step by step.

9.2   Another feature of your central assessment tasks is that they will generally incorporate aspects of manufacturing accounts, covered in Chapter 11. We will give you one such incomplete records question in the next chapter when you have covered manufacturing accounts. The example below is taken from a past AAT Central Assessment and is typical.

9.3   EXAMPLE: TYPICAL INCOMPLETE RECORDS TASKS

During Colin Drew's early years in business trading as Drew Installations, he had very little administrative help and kept minimal records. A number of queries have now arisen and it has become necessary to calculate some figures relating to the year ended 31 October 20X2. You have been asked to provide assistance. The information available from Drew Installations is as follows.

(a)   Assets at 1 November 20X1:

	£	£
Stock		30,400
Debtors		22,800
Motor vehicles at cost	8,750	
Less provision for depreciation	2,690	
		6,060
Equipment at cost	5,200	
Less provision for depreciation	840	
		4,360

(b)   Liabilities at 1 November 20X1:

	£
Creditors	15,600
Bank overdraft	4,300
Accrued expenses	1,000

(c)   Payments made during the year ended 31 October 20X2:

	£
To creditors	120,750
Expenses	52,800
Equipment purchased 30 April 20X2	4,500
Drawings	unknown

(d) Receipts during the year ended 31 October 20X2:

	£
From debtors	unknown

(e) Profit margin 50% on all sales

(f) Depreciation calculated on a monthly basis was provided as follows:

Motor vehicles - 20% per annum straight line method
Equipment - 10% per annum reducing balance method

(g) Assets at 31 October 20X2

	£
Stock	32,700
Debtors	21,700
Motor vehicles at cost	8,750
Equipment at cost	9,700
Bank	15,850
Prepaid expenses	1,500

(h) Liabilities at 31 October 20X2

	£
Creditors	16,850

Tasks

1 Calculate the cost of goods sold during the year ended 31 October 20X2.

2 Calculate the gross profit for the year ended 31 October 20X2.

3 Calculate the sales for the year ended 31 October 20X2.

4 Calculate the receipts from debtors for the year ended 31 October 20X2.

5 Calculate the drawings made by Colin Drew during the year ended 31 October 20X2.

6 Calculate the net profit for the year ended 31 October 20X2.

9.4 SOLUTION: TYPICAL INCOMPLETE RECORDS TASK

Task 1

	£
Opening stock	30,400
Purchases (120,750 + 16,850 – 15,600)	122,000
	152,400
Closing stock	32,700
Cost of goods sold	119,700

Task 2
Cost structure

Sales	100%
Cost of sales	50%
Gross profit	50%
Gross profit	£119,700

Task 3

	£
Cost of goods sold	119,700
Gross profit	119,700
Sales	239,400

Task 4

	£
Sales	239,400
Add opening debtors	22,800
	262,200
Less closing debtors	21,700
Receipts from debtors	240,500

Task 5

BANK

	£		£
Debtors	240,500	Balance b/d	4,300
		Creditors	120,750
		Expenses	52,800
		Equipment	4,500
		Drawings	42,300
		Balance c/d	15,850
	240,500		240,500

Task 6

	£	£
Gross profit		119,700
Expenses (52,800 – 1,000 – 1,500)	50,300	
Depreciation: motor vehicles	1,750	
Depreciation: equipment (W)	661	
		(52,711)
Net profit		66,989

Working: equipment depreciation

	£
Equipment held for entire year (5,200 – 840) × 10%	436
Equipment held for 6 months (4,500 × 10% × 6/12)	225
	661

9.5 Now try the following activity, which comes from a past AAT Central Assessment.

Activity 10.7

Lucy Barber previously worked full-time for a furniture manufacturing company. Approximately two years ago, however, she decided to set up a part-time business making and selling speaker stands for hi-fi systems. She now has an arrangement to sell exclusively to Electronics World Ltd and you have been asked to assist her in preparing her accounts for the year ended 30 April 20X7.

The following information is available.

(a) Tools and equipment costing £3,000 were purchased for the business on 31 July 20X5.

(b) A van costing £4,800 was purchased on 31 October 20X5, again for use in the business.

(c) Lucy Barber rents a small workshop on a light industrial estate. The rent payable was £100 a month until 31 October 20X6 but then it was increased to £120 a month and this remains as the current rate. On 30 April 20X6 one month's rent was owing to the landlord.

(d) During Lucy Barber's first period of trading, which ended on 30 April 20X6, all of the transactions were for cash. On 30 April 20X6 the cash balance of the business was £4,250. On 1 May 20X6 she opened a business bank account and a private bank account. The £4,250 was paid into the business account but no funds were paid at that time into the private account. From 1 May 20X6 all business transactions passed through the business bank account with the exception of some cheques from Electronics World Ltd (see below).

(e) From 1 May 20X6 sales to Electronics World Ltd were on credit as were purchases from her supplier, Johnson Materials Ltd. Cheques received from Electronics World were all paid into the business bank account apart from three which Lucy Barber paid directly into her private account.

(f) Throughout the year ended 30 April 20X7 Lucy Barber withdrew £200 a month cash from her private account for personal spending. No other transactions passed through the account other than the three cheques paid in from Electronics World Ltd. On the 30 April 20X7 the balance of the account was £600.

(g) During the year ended 30 April 20X7 she made and sold 500 pairs of speaker stands. In determining the price charged for each pair she calculated the cost of materials used for the pair then doubled this figure.

(h) On 30 April 20X7.

   (i)   £4,400 was owed to the business by Electronics World Ltd.
   (ii) £1,500 was owed by the business to Johnson Materials Ltd.
   (iii) Materials were in stock to make 120 pairs of speaker stands.

(i) Lucy Barber does not have a record of the materials that were in stock on 30 April 20X6.

(j) The van is to be depreciated at 10% per annum on cost. The tools and equipment are to be depreciated at 20% per annum on cost.

(k) The following is a summary made by Lucy Barber of the entries which passed through the business bank account during the year ended 30 April 20X7.

	£
Money received	
Electronics World Ltd	17,600
Money paid out	
Rent	1,300
Johnson Materials Ltd	12,000
Tools and equipment	250
Electricity	640
Telephone	560

Tasks

1   Calculate the total sales made by Lucy Barber during the year ended 30 April 20X7.

2   Calculate the selling price for one pair of speaker stands.

3   Calculate the cost of materials used in making one pair of speaker stands.

4   Calculate the total cost of goods sold during the year ended 30 April 20X7 (ie the cost of materials used in making the sales calculated in Task 1).

5   Calculate the cost of materials purchased by Lucy Barber during the year ended 30 April 20X7.

6   Calculate the stock of materials held by Lucy Barber on 30 April 20X6.

7   Calculate the capital invested in the business by Lucy Barber on 30 April 20X6.

8   Calculate the figure for rent which would be included in the calculation of profit for the year ended 30 April 20X7.

Key learning points

- If the relevant information is available, an **opening balance sheet** should be prepared.

- **Debtor and creditor accounts** can be used to find balancing figures.
    - ° Opening debtors and creditors
    - ° Closing debtors and creditors
    - ° Cash paid/cash received
    - ° Credit sales/purchases

- Information about **margin and mark up** can be used to find either sales or cost of sales figures, to help particularly in identifying stock stolen or destroyed.

- The **cash book** should be divided into cash and bank balances where appropriate.

- **Accruals and prepayments** can be used to help find a profit and loss account expense figure: add the balance b/d on a ledger account to cash paid in the period, deduct the balance c/d (the accrual or prepayment) and you have your P&L charge.

- **Proprietor's drawings** often complicate incomplete record questions, regarding non-business cash income, non-business cash expenses and drawings of stock.

Quick quiz

1 In the absence of a sales account or sales day book, how can a figure of sales for the year be computed?

2 In the absence of a purchase account or purchases day book, how can a figure of purchases for the year be computed?

3 What is the accounting double entry to record the loss of stock by fire or burglary?

4 If a business proprietor pays his personal income into the business bank account, what is the accounting double entry to record the transaction?

Answers to quick quiz_____

1 Sales can be found using the formula:

	£
Payments received from trade debtors	X
Plus closing balance of trade debtors	X
Less opening balance of trade debtors	(X)
Credit sales	X

2 Again, the following formula can be used.

	£
Payments to trade creditors	X
Plus closing balance of trade creditors	X
Less opening balance of trade creditors	(X)
Credit purchases	X

3 (a) If the good are not insured:

DEBIT   Profit and loss
CREDIT   Trading account

(b) If the loss is insured:

DEBIT   Insurance claim a/c
CREDIT   Trading account

4 For a receipt from a proprietor, the double entry is:

DEBIT   Cash
CREDIT   Drawings

11 Club accounts, manufacturing accounts and partnerships

This chapter contains

1 Club accounts

2 The receipts and payments account

3 Further aspects of club accounts

4 Manufacturing accounts

5 Partnership accounts

Learning objectives

- Record information for the organisational accounts of partnerships, clubs and manufacturers as well as sole traders

- Understand the structure of club accounts, manufacturing accounts and partnership accounts

- Understand the function and form of the income and expenditure account and balance sheet for clubs, and the P&L account and balance sheet for partnerships

- Identify the function and form of final accounts for clubs, partnerships and manufacturers

- Appreciate that any organisation's accounting systems are affected by its structure, administrative systems and transactions

- Appreciate the need to present accounts in the correct form

Knowledge and understanding

Methods of recording information for the organisational accounts of: sole traders; partnerships; manufacturing accounts; club accounts

Understanding the structure of the organisational accounts of: sole traders; partnerships; manufacturing accounts; club accounts

The need to present accounts in the correct form

Methods of analysing income and expenditure

Function and form of accounts for income and expenditure

Function and form of a trial balance, profit and loss account and balance sheet for sole traders, partnerships, manufacturing accounts and club accounts

Function and form of final accounts

Understanding of the ways the accounting systems of an organisation are affected by its organisational structure, its administrative systems and procedures and the nature of its business transactions

1   CLUB ACCOUNTS

ASSESSMENT ALERT

You must be aware of the systems, methods of accounting and final accounts appropriate to partnerships, clubs and manufacturers as well as for sole traders, but you will not be asked to prepare final accounts for any of them. You may be given one of these bodies, rather than a sole trader, in any part of the central assessment.

Why do clubs need final accounts?

1.1   So far you have dealt with the accounts of businesses. In the first three sections of this chapter we consider **clubs**, that is organisations which are not incorporated and whose objectives are to provide services to their members or the pursuit of one or a number of activities rather than the earning of profit.

1.2   Such entities may be, and often are, very **small** in both membership and wealth. However, they can also be very large like the RAC.

1.3   So long as subscriptions are charged, there will be a need for some financial records, the minimum possible being a cash book and petty cash book. **Clubs** which rely on this minimum package often confine their annual accounts to a **receipts and payments account**. This is simply a summary of cash received and paid for a period, and is discussed in Section 2 of this chapter.

Cash or accruals accounting?

1.4   A receipts and payments account may be adequate for some clubs, but it has important deficiencies when used by clubs with substantial assets (in addition to cash) and liabilities. The arguments in favour of **accruals based accounting** apply to clubs as well as profit making entities. Most large clubs do produce final accounts based on accruals accounting. Many clubs produce what is basically a profit and loss account but they call it an **income and expenditure account.** This is covered in Section 3 of this chapter.

1.5   A club **does not exist to make a profit,** so it is wrong to refer to its 'profit and loss' account. However, a club must be able to pay its way, and so it is important to ensure that income covers expenses. An **income and expenditure account,** together with a **balance sheet,** is an important report for judging the financial affairs of the club. The principles of **accruals accounting** (the matching concept) are applied to income and expenditure accounts in the same way as for profit and loss accounts.

The income and expenditure account

> **KEY TERM**
>
> An **income and expenditure account** is the name that is given to what is basically the profit and loss account of a club It is also relevant for charities.

1.6   There are differences between the final accounts of a club and those of a business.

   (a)   Since clubs do not exist to make profits, the difference between income and matching expenditure in the **income and expenditure account** is referred to as a **surplus** or a **deficit** rather than a profit or loss.

   (b)   The capital or proprietorship of the organisation is referred to as the **accumulated fund,** rather than the capital account. In addition, other separate funds might be kept by the organisation (see Paragraph 1.10).

   (c)   There is usually **no separate trading account**. Instead, it is usual to net off expenditure against income for like items. To explain this point further, it will be useful to consider the sources of income for a club in further detail.

> **KEY TERM**
>
> The **accumulated fund** is a form of capital account for a club.

Sources of income for clubs

1.7   Clubs vary in purpose and character, but we shall concentrate here on sports clubs, social clubs or societies. These will obtain their income from various sources which include the following.

   •   **Membership subscriptions** for annual membership of the club (and initial joining subscriptions for first year members)

   •   Payments for **life membership**

   •   'Profits' from **bar sales**

   •   'Profits' from the sale of **food** in the club restaurant or cafeteria

   •   'Profits' from **social events,** such as dinner-dances

- **Entrance fees** paid by members, and **donations** for specific causes, or for general use.

- **Interest** received on investments

1.8 **Netting off expenditure against income** for like items means that where some sources of income have associated costs, the net surplus or deficit should be shown in the income and expenditure account.

   (a) If a club holds an annual dinner-dance, the income and expenditure account will net off the costs of the event against the revenue to show the surplus or deficit.

   (b) If a club has a bar, the income and expenditure account will show the surplus or deficit on its trading. Although the organisation itself does not trade, the bar within the organisation does, and so it is correct to refer to 'profits' from the bar.

1.9 Where there is trading activity within a club (eg bar sales, cafeteria sales etc), so that the organisation must hold stocks of drink or food etc, it is usual to prepare a **trading account** for that particular activity, and then to record the surplus or deficit from trading in the income and expenditure account. An example is shown below.

BURNLEY BRIDGE CLUB
BAR TRADING ACCOUNT FOR THE YEAR TO 31 DECEMBER 20X7

	£	£
Sales		28,000
Less cost of goods sold		
Bar stocks 1 January 20X7	2,200	
Purchases	25,400	
	27,600	
Less bar stocks at 31 December 20X7	2,600	
		24,000
Bar profit (taken to income and expenditure account)		4,000

Club funds

1.10 The following funds are typical of a club:

Fund	Set up	Contains
Accumulated	On founding	Original capital plus surplus/less deficits over time.
Life membership	Once life memberships are offered	Life membership subscriptions by various members of the club. The money paid is commonly invested outside the organisation (for example in a building society account). The investment then earns interest for the organisation.
Building	To set aside money for a new building/extension	This money will be invested outside the organisation, earning interest, until it is needed for the building work. It might take several years to create a fund large enough for the building work planned.

1.11 The basic principles of **accounting for special funds** are as follows.

(a) When money is put into the fund:

DEBIT   Cash
CREDIT   Special-purpose fund

(b) When the cash is invested:

DEBIT   Investments (eg building society account)
CREDIT   Cash

(c) When the investments earn interest:

DEBIT   Cash
CREDIT   Interest received account (and subsequently the fund account, or possibly the income and expenditure account itself)

CENTRAL ASSESSMENT ALERT

You will not have to prepare a full income and expenditure account or balance sheet in your assessment.

2 THE RECEIPTS AND PAYMENTS ACCOUNT

2.1 Many small charities and clubs have little, if any, accounting expertise and keep records only of cash paid and received. The receipts and payments account is a summary of an organisation's cash book. To facilitate the production of such a financial statement an **analysed cash book** will probably be used. No balance sheet is produced with a receipts and payments account.

KEY TERM

A **receipts and payments account** is a summary of the cash book of a club or charity.

2.2 EXAMPLE: RECEIPTS AND PAYMENTS ACCOUNT

HAMILTON CRICKET CLUB
RECEIPTS AND PAYMENTS ACCOUNT
FOR THE YEAR ENDED 30 APRIL 20X7

Receipts	£	Payments	£
Balance b/d	216	Bar expenses	206
Bar takings	360	Rent	250
Subscriptions	728	Wages	340
		Postage	50
		Printing	180
		Affiliation fees to LTS	72
		Lawn mower*	85
		Heat and light	90
		Balance c/d	31
	1,304		1,304

*Item of capital expenditure

2.3 The advantages and disadvantages of a club producing a receipts and payments account are as follows.

Advantages	Disadvantages
It is very easy to produce and understand.	It takes no account of any amounts owing or prepaid.
It serves as a basis for the preparation of the income and expenditure account and balance sheet.	It includes items of capital expenditure and makes no distinction between capital and revenue items.
	It takes no account of depreciation of fixed assets.

2.4 For the layperson, particularly in the case of **small clubs** where transactions are simple and straightforward, a receipts and payments account will be sufficient.

The accounting records of a club

2.5 Although many clubs, due to their size, do not maintain full accounting records, in principle there is no reason why they should not. **The principles of double entry and ledger accounting apply equally well to a club**. The difference is that, instead of general ledger account balances being included in a balance sheet, and items of income and expense in a profit and loss account, the balances and items of income and expense appear in a balance sheet and an **income and expenditure account**.

2.6 Purchases could be accounted for using a **memorandum purchase ledger** and a total creditors account in the general ledger; members' annual subscriptions could easily be monitored using a **memorandum sales ledger** and a total debtors account.

3 FURTHER ASPECTS OF CLUB ACCOUNTS

3.1 You may be provided with a receipts and payments account, balances of assets and liabilities at the beginning of the period, and details of accruals and prepayments at the end of the period. You would be required typically to perform the following.

- Calculate the amount of membership subscriptions due for the year.

- Prepare a **trading account** for a particular activity for the period.

- Calculate the balance on the **accumulated fund** at the beginning of the year. This is simply assets less liabilities – more often than not, the task will ask you to calculate total assets and total liabilities or net assets.

3.2 Let us therefore look at each of the following items in some detail.

- Membership subscriptions
- Bar trading account
- Life membership

These are items which we have not yet come across in this Interactive Text, because they are not found in the accounts of businesses. We must not forget, however, that in many respects accounts of clubs are **similar to those of businesses** with fixed assets, a provision for depreciation, current assets and current liabilities, expense accounts (eg electricity, telephone, stationery etc), accruals and prepayments.

Membership subscriptions

3.3 Annual membership subscriptions of clubs are usually payable one year in **advance**.

A club or society receives payments from members for benefits which the members have yet to enjoy. **Payments in advance** by members are sometimes known as **prepaid subscriptions**, being receipts in advance by the club or society (or prepayments by the member). They will be shown in the balance sheet of the club as a **current liability**, to the extent that the year's membership has still to run as at the balance sheet date.

3.4 EXAMPLE: SUBSCRIPTIONS IN ADVANCE

The Redale Tennis Club charges an annual membership of £50 payable in advance on 1 October each year. All 40 members pay their subscriptions promptly on 1 October 20X6. If the club's accounting year ends on 31 December total subscriptions of 40 × £50 = £2,000 would be treated as follows:

(a) $40 \times \dfrac{9 \text{ months}}{12 \text{ months}} \times £50 = £1,500$ will appear in the balance sheet of the club as at 31 December 20X6 as a current liability '**subscriptions in advance**'. These subscriptions relate to the period 1 January to 30 September 20X7.

(b) $40 \times \dfrac{3 \text{ months}}{12 \text{ months}} \times £50 = £500$ will appear as income in the income and expenditure account for the period 1 October to 31 December 20X6.

3.5 When members are **in arrears** with subscriptions and owe money to the club or society, they are 'debtors' of the organisation and so appear as **current assets** in the balance sheet under 'subscriptions in arrears'. **These should be shown as a separate item in the balance sheet, and should not be netted off against subscriptions in advance.**

3.6 EXAMPLE: SUBSCRIPTIONS IN ARREARS

Suppose that the Nantwich Chess Club has 100 members, each of whom pays an annual membership of £60 on 1 November. Of those 100 members, 90 pay their subscriptions before 31 December 20X7 (for the 20X7/X8 year) but 10 have still not paid. If the club's accounting year ends on 31 December, then as at 31 December 20X7 the balance sheet of the club would include the following items.

(a) *Subscriptions in advance (current liability)*

$$90 \text{ members} \times \dfrac{10 \text{ months}}{12 \text{ months}} \times £60 = £4,500$$

(b) *Subscriptions in arrears (current asset)*

$$10 \text{ members} \times \dfrac{2 \text{ months}}{12 \text{ months}} \times £60 = £100$$

3.7 **Clubs often take no credit for subscription income until the money is received.** In such a case, any subscriptions in arrears are *not* credited to income and *not* shown as a current asset.

3.8 EXAMPLE: SUBSCRIPTIONS IN ADVANCE AND IN ARREARS

At 1 January 20X7, the Burneston Theatre Group had membership subscriptions paid in advance of £1,600, and subscriptions in arrears of £250. During the year to 31 December 20X7 receipts of subscription payments amounted to £18,400. At 31 December 20X7 subscriptions in advance amounted to £1,750 and subscriptions in arrears to £240.

What is the income from subscriptions to be shown in the income and expenditure account for the year to 31 December 20X7?

3.9 SOLUTION

The question does not say that subscriptions are only accounted for when received. You may therefore assume that the society takes credit for subscriptions as they become due, whether or not they are received. The income for the income and expenditure account would be calculated as follows.

		£	£
Payments received in the year			18,400
Add:	subscriptions due but not yet received (ie subscriptions in arrears 31 Dec 20X7)	240	
	Subscriptions received last year relating to current year (ie subscriptions in advance 1 Jan 20X7)	1,600	
			1,840
			20,240
Less:	subscriptions received in current year relating to last year (ie subscriptions in arrears 1 Jan 20X7)	250	
	subscriptions received in current year relating to next year (ie subscriptions in advance 31 Dec 20X7)	1,750	
			2,000
Income from subscriptions for the year			18,240

You may find it simpler to do this calculation as a ledger account.

SUBSCRIPTIONS ACCOUNT

	£		£
Subscriptions in arrears b/d	250	Subscriptions in advance b/d	1,600
I & E a/c (balancing figure)	18,240	Cash	18,400
Subscriptions in advance c/d	1,750	Subscriptions in arrears c/d	240
	20,240		20,240
Subscriptions in arrears b/d	240	Subscriptions in advance b/d	1,750

Activity 11.1

The following information relates to a sports club.

	£
20X6 subscriptions unpaid at beginning of 20X7	410
20X6 subscriptions received during 20X7	370
20X7 subscriptions received during 20X7	6,730
20X8 subscriptions received during 20X7	1,180
20X7 subscriptions unpaid at end of 20X7	470

The club takes credit for subscription income when it becomes due, but takes a prudent view of overdue subscriptions. What amount should be credited to the income and expenditure account for 20X7?

Activity 11.2

(a) A club takes credit for subscriptions when they become due. On 1 January 20X7 arrears of subscriptions amounted to £38 and subscriptions paid in advance were £72. On 31 December 20X7 the amounts were £48 and £80 respectively. Subscription receipts during the year were £790.

What amount would be shown for income from subscriptions in the income and expenditure account for 20X7?

(b) A club takes no credit for subscriptions due until they are received. On 1 January 20X7 arrears of subscriptions amounted to £24 and subscriptions paid in advance were £14. On 31 December 20X7 the amounts were £42 and £58 respectively. Subscription receipts during the year were £1,024.

What amount would be shown for income from subscriptions in the income and expenditure account for 20X7?

Bar trading account

3.10 If a club has a bar or cafeteria a separate trading account will be prepared for its trading activities. A bar trading account will **contain the following items**.

	£	£
Bar takings		X
Opening stocks of goods	X	
Purchases	X	
Closing stocks of goods	(X)	
Cost of bar sales		(X)
Gross profit		X
Other expenses directly related to the running of the bar, if any		(X)
Net profit / (loss)		X/(X)

The net bar **profit** is then included under **income** in the income and expenditure account. A **loss** on the bar would be included under **expenditure**.

Life membership

3.11 Some clubs offer life membership in return for a **lump sum subscription**. Life members, having paid this initial lump sum, do not have to pay any further annual subscriptions. In return the club receives a sum of money which it can then invest, with the annual interest from these investments being accounted for as income in the income and expenditure account.

3.12 The 'one-off' payments from life members are *not* income relating to the year in which they are received by the club, because the payment is for the life of the members, which can be a very long time to come. As they are long-term payments, they are recorded in the club accounts as an addition to a **life membership fund** as follows.

DEBIT   Cash
CREDIT   Life membership fund

ASSESSMENT ALERT

The life membership fund is shown in the balance sheet of the club immediately after the accumulated fund.

3.13 Life members enjoy the benefits of membership over their lives. **Accounting for life membership over time** can be explained with an example.

Suppose that Andrea pays a life membership fee of £500 to the Twitchers' Birdwatching Club. The £500 will initially be put into the club's life membership fund. This money is then invested by the club, and earns interest of £50 per annum.

3.14 There are **two ways** of accounting for the life membership fee.

(a) **Keep the fee in the life membership fund until the life member dies.** (Since the £500 earns interest of £50 pa this interest can be said to represent income for the club in lieu of an annual subscription.)

		£	£
Step 1	On payment of life membership fee of £500		
	DEBIT Cash	500	
	CREDIT Life membership fund		500
Step 2	On Andrea's death		
	DEBIT Life membership fund	500	
	CREDIT Accumulated fund		500
Step 3	Each year, as £50 interest is received		
	DEBIT Cash	50	
	CREDIT Income and expenditure account		50

(b) **Transfer a 'fair' amount from the life membership fund into the income and expenditure account each year.** This amount will represent the proportion of the total life membership payment which relates to the current year. We do not know how long any life member will live, but if an estimated average life from becoming a life member until death is, say, 20 years, it is reasonable to write off payments to the fund over a 20 year period. Each year, one-twentieth of life membership fees (£25) would be deducted from the fund and added as income in the income and expenditure account.

		£	£
Step 1	On payment of life membership fee of £500.		
	DEBIT Cash	500	
	CREDIT Life membership fund		500
Step 2	Each year, assuming life expectancy of 20 years		
	DEBIT Life membership fund	25	
	CREDIT Income and expenditure account		25
Step 3	Each year, as £50 interest is received		
	DEBIT Cash	50	
	CREDIT Income and expenditure account		50

At the end of 20 years, the net result is the same:

		(a) £	(b) £
Life membership fund:			
(a)	£500 – £500	0	
(b)	£500 – (20 × £25)		0
Income and expenditure fund:			
(a)	20 × £50	1,000	
(b)	(20 × £25) + (20 × £50)		1,500
Accumulated fund:			
(a)	£500	500	
(b)	Nothing directly; £500 life membership transferred as I&E surplus		0
		1,500	1,500

3.15 If method (b) is selected the payments could be written down by either a **straight line method or a reducing balance method**, in much the same way as fixed assets are depreciated - with the exception that it is a **capital fund** being written off, and the annual write-off is income to the club, and not an expense like depreciation.

3.16 A further feature of method (b) is that there is **no need to record the death of individual members** (unlike method (a)). The annual write-off is based on an average expected life of members, and it does not matter when or if any individual member dies. The same average write off each year will be used.

3.17 A reason for preferring method (b) is that life membership subscriptions eventually **pass through the income and expenditure account** as income of the club, since life members, although they pay a long time in advance, do eventually enjoy the benefits of membership in return for their payment. It is fair that, over time, life membership fees should be accounted for as income of the club, to boost the annual surpluses, or reduce the annual deficits.

CENTRAL ASSESSMENT ALERT

In spite of method (b)'s advantages, method (a) is still commonly used. In a central assessment question, unless you are told about a rate for 'writing off' the life membership fund annually, you should assume that method (a) should be used, where the question gives you information about the death of club life members.

BPP PUBLISHING

3.18 EXAMPLE: LIFE MEMBERSHIP FUND

The Swingers Line Dancing Club has a scheme whereby as an alternative to paying annual subscriptions, members can at any time opt to pay a lump sum which gives them membership for life. Lump sum payments received for life membership are held in a life membership fund but then credited to the income and expenditure account in equal instalments over a ten year period, beginning in the year when the lump sum payment is made and life membership is acquired.

The treasurer of the club, Hank Stetson, establishes the following information.

(a) At 31 December 20X6, the balance on the life membership fund was £8,250.

(b) Of this opening balance, £1,220 should be credited as income for the year to 31 December 20X7.

(c) During the year to 31 December 20X7, new life members made lump sum payments totalling £1,500.

Show the movements in the life membership fund for the year to 31 December 20X7, and in doing so, calculate how much should be transferred as income from life membership fund to the income and expenditure account.

3.19 SOLUTION

LIFE MEMBERSHIP FUND

	£	£
As at 31 December 20X6		8,250
New life membership payments received in 20X7		1,500
		9,750
Less transfer to income and expenditure account:		
out of balance as at 31 December 20X6	1,220	
out of new payments in 20X6 (10% of £1,500)	150	
		1,370
Fund as at 31 December 20X7		8,380

The income and expenditure account for the year would show:

Income from life membership		1,370

Activity 11.3

The following balances were extracted from the books of the Grand Slam Bridge Club as at 31 December 20X7.

	£
Tables and chairs	380
Playing cards and other accessories	102
Stock of reference books	130
Subscriptions in advance	80
Subscriptions in arrears	27
Life membership fund	300
Deficit for the year	117

Life membership funds are accounted for by crediting them to a life membership account, where they remain until the death of the member.

The only movement on the life membership account in 20X7 arose from the death of one of the five life members during the year. His subscription had been transferred to the accumulated fund before the above balances had been extracted.

(a) What was the balance on the accumulated fund at 31 December 20X7?
(b) What was the balance on the accumulated fund at 1 January 20X7?

Activity 11.4

For many years, life membership of the Ripon Poetry Association cost £100, but with effect from 1 January 20X7 the rate has been increased to £120. The balance on the life membership fund at 31 December 20X6 was £3,780 and membership details at that date were as follows.

	No of members
Joined more than 19 years ago	32
Joined within the last 19 years	64
	96

The Association's accounting policy is to release life subscriptions to income over a period of 20 years beginning with the year of enrolment.

During 20X7, four new members were enrolled and one other member (who had joined in 20X3) died.

What is the balance on the life membership fund at 31 December 20X7?

Activity 11.5

On 1 January 20X7 a club owed its suppliers £435 in respect of bar stocks; on 31 December 20X7 the amount was £363. The cash book showed payments to suppliers of £5,685 during the year. Opening stock amounts to £390. Bar sales are mostly on cash terms, though IOUs are occasionally accepted from members. IOUs outstanding at 1 January 20X7 amounted to £12; on 31 December 20X7 the figure was £8. The cash book shows that till receipts lodged in the bank during the year amounted to £6,064, but this was after paying the barman's wages of £20 per week in cash. Bar prices are fixed so as to earn a constant mark up of 25% on cost.

(a) Calculate the cost of closing stock at 31 December 20X7.

(b) What is the net profit on bar trading disclosed in the club's income and expenditure account for 20X7?

4   MANUFACTURING ACCOUNTS

ASSESSMENT ALERT

We now turn to a particular kind of statement produced by some businesses as part of their final accounts - a manufacturing account for businesses involved specifically with manufacture. These are very likely to come up in Central Assessments, so pay close attention!

4.1   A business's trading account usually includes a **cost of goods sold** derived as the total of opening stock plus purchases, less closing stock. This is suitable for a retail business which buys in goods and sells them on without altering their condition. But for a manufacturing company it would be truer to say that the cost of goods sold is as follows:

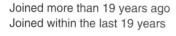

FORMULA TO LEARN

	£
Opening stock of finished goods	X
Plus factory cost of finished goods produced	X
	X
Less closing stock of finished goods	(X)
Cost of finished goods sold	X

KEY TERM

A **manufacturing account** is an account in which the costs of producing finished goods are accumulated. Eventually the '**factory cost of finished goods produced** in the period' is transferred to the trading account as part of the cost of finished goods sold; this is illustrated above.

Factory cost of finished goods produced

4.2 The costs accumulated in a manufacturing account to produce a **factory cost of resources consumed** are as follows.

(a) **The cost of raw materials consumed in the period**. This is the opening stock of raw materials, plus purchases of raw materials less closing stock of raw materials.

(b) **The cost of direct factory wages**. The total of (a) and (b) is often referred to as the **prime costs**.

(c) **Production overheads or factory overheads**.

An adjustment is then made for **work in progress** (see Paragraphs 4.4 and 4.5 below), so we can arrive at **factory cost of finished goods produced**.

4.3 A pro-forma manufacturing account is set out below with illustrative figures.

MANUFACTURING ACCOUNT
FOR THE YEAR ENDED 31 DECEMBER 20X7

	£	£
Raw materials		
Opening stock	4,000	
Purchases (net of returns)	207,000	
	211,000	
Less closing stock	23,000	
Cost of raw materials consumed in the period		188,000
Factory wages		21,000
Prime costs		209,000
Factory overheads		
Factory power	4,000	
Plant depreciation	3,000	
Plant maintenance	1,500	
Rates and insurance	2,500	
Light and heat	3,000	
Sundry expenses	5,000	
Factory manager's salary	9,000	
Building depreciation	1,000	
		29,000
Factory cost of resources consumed		238,000
Work in progress adjustment		
Opening stocks	8,000	
Closing stocks	(17,000)	
Increase in work in progress stocks		(9,000)
Factory cost of finished goods produced		229,000

Activity 11.6

(a) Which one of the following costs would *not* be shown in factory overheads in a manufacturing account?

    A   The cost of insurance on a factory
    B   The cost of an extension to a factory
    C   The cost of depreciation on a factory
    D   The cost of rent on a factory

(b) Which one of the following costs would be included in the calculation of prime costs in a manufacturing account?

    A   Factory rent
    B   Office wages
    C   Direct production wages
    D   Depreciation on machinery

Work in progress adjustment

KEY TERM

Work in progress (WIP) is a production item on which work has begun but not finished; it is part-complete at the balance sheet date. Since resources have been devoted to creating it, a value can be given to it and it can be included in stock. The resources used in bringing WIP to its current state are therefore **not** included in the trading account.

4.4 You may need to think carefully about the **adjustment for work in progress** near the end of the statement. When a business purchases raw materials they are issued to production departments as required. Production departments will work on the raw materials in order to convert them into finished goods ready for sale. At the balance sheet date, there will be work in progress in the production departments, ie items which have been partly converted but which are not yet finished goods.

4.5 The **value** of work in progress will include the cost of the raw materials, and the **wages of employees** who have worked on it **plus any attributable overheads**. It follows that the prime costs and factory overheads shown in the manufacturing account will not all have resulted in the production of finished goods, because some of the costs will have gone on work in progress. Depending on whether the value of WIP has increased or decreased from the previous year, an adjustment is made as follows:

Balance of work in progress from one year to the next	Adjustment to arrive at factory cost of finished goods produced
Increased	**Deduct increase** (closing less opening stock of WIP) from total costs incurred
Decreased	**Add decrease** (opening less closing stock of WIP) to total costs incurred

ASSESSMENT ALERT

Calculating the value of WIP is outside the scope of the Unit 5 Standards. If the point comes up in an assessment, you will be given the value of WIP to use.

4.6 EXAMPLE: MANUFACTURING, TRADING AND PROFIT AND LOSS ACCOUNT

A manufacturing company has its factory and offices at the same site. Its results for the year to 31 December 20X7 were as follows.

	£
Sales	179,000
Purchases of raw materials	60,000
Factory wages	70,000
Depreciation of equipment	10,000
Local authority rates	5,000
Depreciation of building	2,000
Heating and lighting	3,000
Telephone	2,000
Other manufacturing overheads	2,300
Other administration expenses	2,550
Other selling expenses	1,150

Shared overhead costs are to be apportioned as follows.

	Manufacturing	Administration	Selling
Depreciation of equipment	80%	5%	15%
Rates	50%	30%	20%
Depreciation of building	50%	30%	20%
Heating and lighting	40%	35%	25%
Telephone	-	40%	60%

The values of stocks are as follows.

	At *1 January 20X7* £	At *31 December 20X7* £
Raw materials	5,000	3,000
Work in progress	4,000	3,000
Finished goods	16,000	18,000

Prepare the manufacturing, trading and profit and loss account of the company for the period to 31 December 20X7.

4.7 SOLUTION

MANUFACTURING ACCOUNT FOR THE YEAR ENDED 31 DECEMBER 20X7

	£	£
Opening stock of raw materials		5,000
Purchases		60,000
		65,000
Closing stock of raw materials		3,000
Cost of raw materials consumed in the period		62,000
Factory wages		70,000
Prime costs		132,000
Factory overheads		
Depreciation of equipment (80% of £10,000)	8,000	
Rates (50% of £5,000)	2,500	
Depreciation of building (50% of £2,000)	1,000	
Heating and lighting (40% of £3,000)	1,200	
Other expenses	2,300	
		15,000
Factory cost of resources consumed		147,000
Work in progress adjustment		
Opening stock	4,000	
Closing stock	(3,000)	
Reduction of stock of work in progress		1,000
Factory cost of finished goods produced		148,000

TRADING AND PROFIT AND LOSS ACCOUNT
FOR THE YEAR ENDED 31 DECEMBER 20X7

	£	£	£
Sales			179,000
Opening stock of finished goods		16,000	
Factory cost of finished goods produced (from manufacturing account)		148,000	
		164,000	
Closing stock of finished goods		18,000	
Cost of goods sold			146,000
Gross profit			33,000
Selling expenses			
Depreciation of equipment (15% of £10,000)	1,500		
Rates (20% of £5,000)	1,000		
Depreciation of building (20% of £2,000)	400		
Heating and lighting (25% of £3,000)	750		
Telephone (60% of £2,000)	1,200		
Other expenses	1,150		
		6,000	
Administration expenses			
Depreciation of equipment (5% of £10,000)	500		
Rates (30% of £5,000)	1,500		
Depreciation of building (30% of £2,000)	600		
Heating and lighting (35% of £3,000)	1,050		
Telephone (40% of £2,000)	800		
Other expenses	2,550		
		7,000	
			13,000
Net profit			20,000

CENTRAL ASSESSMENT ALERT

You will not have to prepare a full statement as above, but you may have to do parts of it.

Activity 11.7

Ananda Carver is considering expanding her business, Automania, into the manufacture of car seat covers. The following estimated figures for the next financial period have been produced:

	£
Direct labour	26,000
Materials used	14,000
Production overheads	20,000
Closing stock – work in progress	2,000

Calculate the production cost of goods completed.

Activity 11.8

The following details are available in respect of a company's manufacturing operations during 20X7.

		£
Work in progress:	opening stock	42,920
	closing stock	39,610
Raw materials:	opening stock	12,940
	purchases in year	213,680
	closing stock	14,550
Carriage inwards		3,970
Carriage outwards		4,200
Wages and salaries:	factory supervisor	12,490
	direct production staff	96,380
	other factory staff	18,330
	administration staff	21,520
Other factory costs		63,310

The company transfers goods from factory to warehouse at a price which represents a profit to the factory of 15% on the transfer price.

Prepare the company's manufacturing account for 20X7, showing the following.

(a) Prime costs of production in 20X7
(b) Factory cost of finished goods produced in 20X7
(c) Factory profit on finished goods produced in 20X7

Manufacturing accounts with incomplete records

4.8 You may well find that aspects of manufacturing accounts are integrated with incomplete records tasks. The activity below is taken from a past AAT Central Assessment, and is typical of the sort of task you are likely to come across.

Activity 11.9

Jane Sutton obtains her supplies of bread and cakes mainly from a small bakery owned by Pat Day. The goods are sold to various caterers, retailers and direct to the public through a shop attached to the bakery and also owned by Pat Day. The bakery and the shop have both recently been put up for sale and Jane Sutton is interested in buying them. She has been able to obtain some figures from the agent acting for Pat Day and these relate to the year ended 31 December 20X7. Jane Sutton asks you to produce some information from these figures.

Figures for Pat Day's bakery and shop - available from the agent

(a) *Stocks*

	£
Stock of baking materials at 1 January 20X7	1,000
Baking materials purchased	84,000
Stock of baking materials at 31 December 20X7	3,000

All finished goods are sold and no finished goods are therefore held in stock.

(b) *Staff costs*

	£
Bakery production wages	44,000
Bakery supervisory wages	25,000
Shop wages	30,000

(c) *Business fixed assets*

	£
Bakery premises at cost 1 January 20V0	100,000
Shop premises at cost 1 January 20V0	80,000
Bakery equipment at cost 1 June 20X0	50,000
Shop equipment at cost 1 June 20X0	40,000

(d) *Depreciation - calculated on a monthly basis*

Premises 2% per annum straight line method

Equipment 10% per annum straight line method

(e) *Other business expenses*

Bakery overheads	22,000
Shop expenses	30,000

(f) *Sales*

Two thirds of production is sold with a 50% mark-up to caterers and retail outlets.
All these sales are on credit.
One third of production is passed to the shop to then be sold with a 100% mark up.
All these sales are for cash.

(g) *Debtors and creditors*

Debtors at 1 January 20X7	12,000
Creditors at 1 January 20X7	6,000
Debtors at 31 December 20X7	Unknown
Creditors at 31 December 20X7	7,000
Received from debtors during the year	179,500
Paid to creditors during the year	Unknown

Task 1

Calculate the prime cost of the goods produced by the bakery during the year ended 31 December 20X7.

Task 2

Calculate the total production cost of the goods made by the bakery during the year ended 31 December 20X7.

Task 3

Calculate the total combined gross profit made by the shop and the bakery during the year ended 31 December 20X7.

Task 4

Calculate the amount paid to creditors during the year ended 31 December 20X7.

Task 5

Calculate the sum of money owed by debtors on 31 December 20X7.

5 PARTNERSHIP ACCOUNTS

What is a partnership?

5.1 This is defined by the **Partnership Act 1890**.

> **KEY TERM**
>
> A **partnership** is the relationship which subsists between persons carrying on a business in common with a view of profit.

5.2 In other words, if two or more persons agree to join forces in some kind of business venture, then a partnership is the usual result. In a partnership:

(a) The **personal liability** of each partner for the firm's debts is **unlimited,** and so an individual's personal assets may be used to meet any partnership liabilities in the event of partnership bankruptcy.

(b) All partners usually **participate in the running of the business,** rather than merely providing the capital.

(c) Profits or losses of the business are **shared** between the partners.

(d) A **partnership deed** is usually (though not always) drawn up, detailing the provisions of the contract between the partners.

Preparation of partnership accounts

5.3 Partnership accounts are in many respects identical to those of sole traders, the principal **differences** being that:

(a) The partnership capital is contributed not by one, but by several proprietors, and **each partner's contribution** must be identified in the accounts.

(b) The net profit, once calculated, has to be **appropriated** between the partners. Any amount taken from the business, whether it is in the form of a salary or interest on capital, is treated as an appropriation of net profit.

Partnership capital

5.4 Just as capital contributed by a sole trader to his business is recorded in his capital account, the capital contributed to a partnership is recorded in a series of **capital accounts, one for each partner**. The amount of each partner's contribution usually depends upon the partnership agreement, and since each partner is ultimately entitled to repayment of his capital it is vital to keep a continuous record of his interest in the firm. Sometimes partners may be required to contribute equally to the capital fund.

With one or two exceptions (dealt with below) each partner's capital account balance normally **remains constant** from year to year.

5.5 A **current account** for each partner is maintained to record a wide range of items on a continuous basis, for example, to charge drawings and other personal benefits and to credit salaries, interest on capital, share of profits etc. In effect, a partner's current account is merely an extension of his capital account, its balance representing further funds invested by the partner in the firm.

5.6 Sometimes, as in sole traders' accounts, a **drawings account** is kept to record each partner's withdrawals (in money or money's worth) throughout the year.

		£	£
DEBIT	Drawings account (or current account)	X	
CREDIT	Bank account (or other asset accounts)		X
	Purchases (or cost of sales)		X

Being withdrawal of cash (drawings and/or salaries) or other assets (including goods originally purchased for resale) by the partner

5.7 The balance on the partner's drawings account is **debited to his current account at the end of the year**. If he has withdrawn more than his profit share the current account may show a debit balance. This disadvantages the other partners who have credit balances and who have to find the excess. To overcome this problem, the partnership agreement could be altered to give partners interest on their current accounts and/or charge interest where debit balances are outstanding at the end of the year.

5.8 Where an existing or previous partner makes a **loan to the partnership** he becomes a **creditor** of the partnership.

(a) If the partnership is **short of cash** (which often happens) and the existing partners do not wish to contribute further capital which would be tied up in the business for many years, one or more of them may be prepared to enter into a formal loan agreement for a specified period and at a realistic interest rate.

(b) When a partner **retires**, if there is insufficient cash to pay the balance owed to him (the total of his capital and current account balances), the amount which he cannot yet be paid is usually transferred to a loan account.

In the partnership balance sheet a loan is shown separately as a long-term liability (unless repayable within twelve months), whether or not the loan creditor is also an existing partner. Any such loan attracts interest at 5% per annum (Partnership Act 1890) unless there is agreement to the contrary.

5.9 When preparing the partnership accounts, the **assets employed** (assets less liabilities) side of the balance sheet is presented in the same way as in a sole trader's set of accounts. However, the **funds employed** (partnership capital) side, is shown in the following way.

	£	£
Capital accounts		
Jill	10,000	
Susan	6,000	
		16,000
Current accounts		
Jill	2,500	
Susan	(1,000)	
		1,500
		17,500

Note that, unlike in a sole trader's balance sheet, the profit and drawings figures are not shown separately. They have been absorbed into the current accounts and only the balances appear on the final accounts.

Appropriation of net profits

5.10 When a sole trader's net profit has been ascertained it is appropriated by him, ie credited to his capital account. He may or may not remove it from the business in the form of drawings. The net profit of a partnership is appropriated by the partners, according to whatever formula they choose, and the sharing out of profit between them is detailed in a **profit and loss appropriation account**.

ASSESSMENT ALERT

Appropriation is beyond the scope of the Unit 5 standards.

Key learning points

- In club accounts, the **receipts and payments account** is, in effect, a summary of the cash book. For small clubs with a few straightforward transactions, this statement may be sufficient. For larger concerns, however, the receipts and payments account will form the basis for the preparation of the income and expenditure account and balance sheet.

- An **income and expenditure account** is the equivalent of a profit and loss account for clubs.

- You should carry out the following when presenting income and expenditure accounts.

    ○ **Match the sources** of revenue with related costs to show net income from the organisation's various activities.

    ○ Treat **subscriptions received in advance** as a current liability and (unless the question states the contrary) treat **subscriptions in arrears** as a current asset.

    ○ Describe the result for the year as **surplus or deficit**, not as profit or loss.

    ○ Describe the **capital** of the organisation as the accumulated fund but remember that capital may also include other funds such as a life membership fund.

- **Manufacturing accounts** are prepared for internal management use only. Their purpose is to distinguish between the costs and profitability associated with manufacturing operations and those associated with trading (which are shown in the trading account).

- Manufacturing accounts highlight the following.

    ○ **Prime costs**: the cost of raw materials and direct labour employed in production.

    ○ **Factory cost of finished goods produced**: equal to prime costs plus indirect factory expenses and plus or minus any movement over the period in the cost of work in progress.

    ○ **Factory profit**: a notional profit earned in manufacturing operations, allowing the factory to 'share' some of the overall profit.

- This chapter has also introduced the basic principles of **accounting for partnerships**. In general, a profit and loss account may be prepared for a partnership in exactly the same way as for a sole trader. In the **profit and loss appropriation account** the net profit is then apportioned between the partners according to the partnership agreement.

- In the **partnership balance sheet,** net assets are financed by **partners' capital and current accounts.** Current accounts must be credited with the profits appropriated to each partner for the year, and debited with partners' drawings. It is essential to remember that drawings, salaries and interest on capital are not expenses. Drawings only affect the balance sheet. Salaries and interest on capital are appropriations of profit.

Quick quiz

1   What is the equivalent to profit/loss for a club?

2   What is the 'capital account' of a club called?

3   List five possible sources of income for a club.

4   Why might a building fund be set up?

5   What are the two ways of accounting for life membership receipts?

6   What is the accounting treatment for the profit or loss from the sale of a fixed asset which has *not* been depreciated through the income and expenditure account?

7   What is a manufacturing account?

8   In the balance sheet of a partnership, how is a loan from a partner shown?

Answers to quick quiz

1   The equivalent terms are surplus and deficit.

2   The accumulated fund.

3   (a)   Membership subscriptions
    (b)   Payments for life membership
    (c)   Profits from bar sales
    (d)   Profits from social events
    (e)   Interest on income from investments

4   A building fund would be used to save for the cost of a new building or extension.

5   (a)   Keep the money in the fund until the member dies.
    (b)   Write off the subscriptions by transfer to the income and expenditure account.

6   It should be credited/debited to the accumulated fund.

7   A manufacturing account is an account in which the costs of producing finished goods are accumulated.

8   A loan from a partner is shown separately as a long-term liability.

Part D

Preparing the extended trial balance

12 Extended trial balance

This chapter contains

1   The extended trial balance and its purpose

2   Preparing the extended trial balance

3   Some typical Central Assessment tasks

Learning objectives

- Enter totals from the general ledger or other records correctly on the ETB

- Identify, trace and refer to the appropriate authority material errors identified by the trial balance

- Enter adjustments not dealt with in ledger accounts correctly on the ETB

- Make adjustments relating to accruals and prepayments

- Enter the agreed valuation of stock correctly on the ETB

- Prepare ETBs, in accordance with the organisation's policies, procedures and timescales

- Identify and resolve (or refer to an appropriate person) discrepancies, unusual features or queries

- Extend and total the ETB accurately

Performance criteria

5.4.1 Totals from the general ledger or other records are correctly entered on the extended trial balance

5.4.2 Material errors disclosed by the trial balance are identified, traced and referred to the appropriate authority

5.4.3 Adjustments not dealt with in the ledger accounts are correctly entered on the extended trial balance

5.4.4 An agreed valuation of closing stock is correctly entered on the extended trial balance

5.4.5 The organisation's policies, regulations, procedures and timescales in relation to preparing extended trial balances are observed

5.4.6 Discrepancies, unusual features or queries are identified and either resolved or referred to the appropriate person

5.4.7 The extended trial balance is accurately extended and totalled

BPP
PUBLISHING

1   THE EXTENDED TRIAL BALANCE AND ITS PURPOSE

ASSESSMENT ALERT

All the activities for this chapter are grouped together at the end of the chapter, so that you can go through the preparation of an ETB step by step and then attempt one on your own in one go.

1.1   We have already seen what a **trial balance** is: it is a list of all the balances in the ledger accounts, made up before the preparation of the final accounts to check the accuracy of the double entry accounting. The final accounts (the profit and loss account or income and expenditure account, and the balance sheet) are drawn up using the balances in the trial balance.

1.2   This step of drawing up the final accounts from the trial balance involves adjusting a few of the balances in some way. For example:

- Correcting errors
- Recognising accruals and prepayments
- Providing for depreciation and doubtful debts, and writing off bad debts
- Adding in the closing stock figure.

1.3   In order to keep track of such adjustments and set out the necessary figures neatly, an **extended trial balance** is used.

KEY TERM

An **extended trial balance** is a worksheet, used to keep track of adjustments between the trial balance and the final accounts.

Format of an extended trial balance

1.4   The extended trial balance gives a vertical list of all the ledger account balances (the **trial balance**) with three further columns (debits and credits for: **adjustments**) and then columns which show whether figures go to the **profit and loss account** or the **balance sheet**.

1.5   Its column headings will look something like this:

Ledger account	Trial balance figure		Adjustments		Profit and loss a/c		Balance sheet	
	Dr £	*Cr* £	*Dr* £	*Cr* £	*Dr* £	*Cr* £	*Dr* £	*Cr* £

1.6 The preparation of the ETB draws on all the knowledge and skills you have gained in the first nine chapters of this text.

2 PREPARING THE EXTENDED TRIAL BALANCE

2.1 The best way to see how the extended trial balance works is to follow through an example.

2.2 EXAMPLE: EXTENDED TRIAL BALANCE

The ledger accounts of Rico Mays, a trader, as at 31 December 20X7 before any adjustments have been made to them, are as follows.

	£
Shop fittings: at cost	9,000
depreciation provision at 1.1.X7	450
Leasehold premises: at cost	56,000
depreciation provision at 1.1.X7	2,800
Stock in trade at 1.1.X7	117,000
Debtors at 31.12.X7	240,750
Provision for doubtful debts at 1.1.X7	4,320
Cash in hand	120
Cash at bank	18,300
Creditors for supplies	292,500
Proprietor's capital at 1.1.X7	120,000
Purchases	459,000
Sales	580,000
Wages	81,900
Advertising	10,350
Rates for 15 months to 31.3.X8	6,750
Bank charges	900

The adjustments Leigh needs to make to his accounts are as follows.

(a) Depreciation of shop fittings £450

(b) Depreciation of leasehold £2,800

(c) A debt of £2,250 is irrecoverable and is to be written off and the doubtful debts provision is to be increased to 2% of the year end debtors figure

(d) The stock in trade at 31 December 20X7 is valued at £135,000

(e) On 31 December 20X7, £540 was owed for advertising expenses but an invoice has not yet been received

You are required to give effect to these adjustments by using an extended trial balance and to prepare a trading and profit and loss account for the year ended 31 December 20X7 and a balance sheet as at that date.

2.3 SOLUTION

Draw up a **trial balance** from this list of balances and insert it in the first two columns of the extended trial balance.

Folio	Account	Trial balance		Adjustments		Profit & loss account		Balance sheet	
		DR £	CR £	DR £	CR £	DR £	CR £	DR £	CR £
1	Shop fittings: cost	9,000							
2	Shop fittings: dep'n provision		450						
3	Leasehold premises: cost	56,000							
4	Leasehold premises: dep'n prov		2,800						
5	Stock at 1.1.X7	117,000							
6	Sales ledger control	240,750							
7	Provision for doubtful debts		4,320						
8	Petty cash	120							
9	Bank	18,300							
10	Purchase ledger control		292,500						
11	Proprietor's capital at 1.1.X7		120,000						
12	Purchases	459,000							
13	Sales		580,000						
14	Wages	81,900							
15	Advertising	10,350							
16	Rates	6,750							
17	Bank charges	900							
18									
19									
20									
21									
22									
23									
24									
25	SUB-TOTAL	1,000,070	1,000,070	0	0	0	0	0	0
26	Profit for the year			0	0				
27	TOTAL	1,000,070	1,000,070						
28									

These are the debit and credit columns, and so first you must sort out the credit balances in the ledger accounts from the debit balances. If there are no errors in the accounts, the total of the debit and credit balances should be equal. The result of this process is shown on Page 258. You should note here that, although in earlier examples we balanced off expense accounts by posting the balance to the trading profit and loss account, in the ETB the **opening total profit and loss account ledger balance is not adjusted. This is to allow the final profit to be calculated on the ETB, rather than within the profit and loss ledger account.**

2.4 The next step is to make all the **various adjustments**. Note that each adjustment has to be put in twice, in accordance with the rule of double entry (the extended trial balance is like a handy listing of all the ledger accounts). The adjustments fall into three main types.

- Accruals and prepayments
- Adjustments to stock figure
- Other adjustments

2.5 To make the explanation easier to follow, we will to look at 'other adjustments' first.

Other adjustments

2.6 Other adjustments will be recorded in the **adjustments column** in the extended trial balance. In our example, there are five such adjustments.

(a) *Shop fittings depreciation of £450*

DEBIT   Depreciation expense (eventually a deduction in the profit and loss account)
CREDIT   Provision for depreciation: shop fittings

The depreciation expense account does not yet appear in the list of ledger accounts, so we will have to add it on; the credit increases the provision in the balance sheet.

(b) *Leasehold depreciation of £2,800*

DEBIT   Depreciation expense
CREDIT   Provision for depreciation: leasehold

(c) *Write off debt of £2,250*

DEBIT   Bad and doubtful debts (expense)
CREDIT   Sales ledger control a/c

The bad and doubtful debts account does not yet appear in the list of ledger accounts, so we will have to add it on.

(d) *Increase bad debt provision to 2% of debtors*

2% of debtors = 2% of £(240,750 – 2,250)   = £4,770
Increase is therefore £4,770 – £4,320   = £450

DEBIT   Bad and doubtful debts
CREDIT   Provision for doubtful debts

Adjustments to stock figure

2.7 The adjustment required to the stock figure is not quite the same type of adjustment as those described above. You must bring in the **closing stock figure**

from the stock account, which is drawn up specially for the preparation of final accounts.

2.8 The closing stock figure of £135,000 is entered into the **adjustments column** of the extended trial balance as follows.

DEBIT   Stock a/c (balance sheet)
CREDIT   Stock a/c (profit and loss account)

So the entries will eventually go into the **Debit** balance sheet column and the **Credit** profit and loss column. Both of these closing stock figures can be given their own ledger accounts and added on to the list of ledger accounts or simply entered in the opening stock account.

Accruals and prepayments

2.9 Advertising expenses of £540 are owed, but have not yet been recorded in the accounts as an invoice has not yet been received. The £540 is an accrued expense, and it is necessary to increase advertising expenses (**debit** advertising expenses) so that the £540 is debited in the profit and loss account just like any other expenses.

2.10 The 'other side' of the entry is that there should be an accrual of £540 shown in the current liabilities of the balance sheet. We therefore set up an accruals heading on the list of ledger accounts and credit the £540 in the adjustment column.

2.11 There is a prepayment adjustment that has to be made as well. Rates to 31 March 20X8 have been paid, so there is a prepayment of $3/15 \times £6,750 = £1,350$. The £1,350 is entered as a debit on the prepayments heading (which needs adding to the list of ledger accounts) and a credit against rates.

2.12 The results of entering the adjustments, accruals and prepayments are on Page 261.

- The total figures for depreciation expenses and bad and doubtful debts expenses have been entered, to make the workings neater.

- Every figure has been entered twice.

2.13 Now there is very little left to do.

(a) **Add up the adjustments column,** to ensure that debits equal credits and that you have filled in the adjustments correctly.

(b) **Add the figures across the extended trial balance.** For example, shop fittings is just £9,000 and will be a balance sheet figure (fixed asset). Provision for depreciation will become £900 (£450 + £450) and is also a balance sheet figure.

(c) **Add up the profit and loss debits and credits.** The difference between them is the profit (or loss) for the year.

(d) **Take the profit (or loss) into the balance sheet** and then **add up the debits and credits in the balance sheet** to make sure that they do, in fact, balance.

The results of these procedures are shown on Page 262.

Folio	Account	Trial balance DR £	Trial balance CR £	Adjustments DR £	Adjustments CR £	Profit & loss account DR £	Profit & loss account CR £	Balance sheet DR £	Balance sheet CR £
1	Shop fittings: cost	9,000							
2	Shop fittings: dep'n provision		450		450				
3	Leasehold premises: cost	56,000							
4	Leasehold premises: dep'n prov		2,800		2,800				
5	Stock at 1.1.X7	117,000							
6	Sales ledger control	240,750			2,250				
7	Provision for doubtful debts		4,320		450				
8	Petty cash	120							
9	Bank	18,300							
10	Purchase ledger control		292,500						
11	Proprietor's capital at 1.1.X7		120,000						
12	Purchases	459,000							
13	Sales		580,000						
14	Wages	81,900							
15	Advertising	10,350		540					
16	Rates	6,750			1,350				
17	Bank charges	900							
18	Depreciation expense			3,250					
19	Bad and doubtful debts			2,700					
20	Stock (B/S)			135,000					
21	Stock (P&L)				135,000				
22									
23	Prepayments			1,350					
24	Accruals				540				
25	SUB-TOTAL	1,000,070	1,000,070	142,840	142,840	0	0	0	0
26	Profit for the year								
27	TOTAL	1,000,070	1,000,070	142,840	142,840				
28									

BPP PUBLISHING

Folio	Account	Trial balance DR £	Trial balance CR £	Adjustments DR £	Adjustments CR £	Profit & loss account DR £	Profit & loss account CR £	Balance sheet DR £	Balance sheet CR £
1	Shop fittings: cost	9,000						9,000	
2	Shop fittings: dep'n provision		450		450				900
3	Leasehold premises: cost	56,000						56,000	
4	Leasehold premises: dep'n prov		2,800		2,800				5,600
5	Stock at 1.1.X7	117,000				117,000			
6	Sales ledger control	240,750			2,250			238,500	
7	Provision for doubtful debts		4,320		450				4,770
8	Petty cash	120						120	
9	Bank	18,300						18,300	
10	Purchase ledger control		292,500						292,500
11	Proprietor's capital at 1.1.X7		120,000						120,000
12	Purchases	459,000				459,000			
13	Sales		580,000				580,000		
14	Wages	81,900				81,900			
15	Advertising	10,350		540		10,890			
16	Rates	6,750			1,350	5,400			
17	Bank charges	900				900			
18	Depreciation expense			3,250		3,250			
19	Bad and doubtful debts			2,700		2,700			
20	Stock (B/S)			135,000				135,000	
21	Stock (P&L)				135,000		135,000		
22									
23	Prepayments			1,350				1,350	
24	Accruals				540				540
25	SUB-TOTAL	1,000,070	1,000,070	142,840	142,840	681,040	715,000	458,270	424,310
26	Profit for the year					33,960			33,960
27	TOTAL	1,000,070	1,000,070	142,840	142,840	715,000	715,000	458,270	458,270
28									

From ETB to final accounts

2.14 Although to be competent in Unit 5 you do not have to prepare the balance sheet or profit and loss account from the ETB, it will be useful if you can see how the finished product is derived. The final step is to use the figures in the last four columns of the extended trial balance to draw up the balance sheet and profit and loss account. For this example, the result would be as follows.

RICO MAYS
TRADING AND PROFIT AND LOSS ACCOUNT
FOR THE YEAR ENDED 31 DECEMBER 20X7

	£	£
Sales		580,000
Less cost of sales		
Opening stock	117,000	
Purchases	459,000	
	576,000	
Less closing stock	135,000	
		441,000
Gross profit		139,000
Less expenses		
Wages	81,900	
Advertising	10,890	
Rates	5,400	
Bank charges	900	
Depreciation: fixtures and fittings	3,250	
Bad and doubtful debts expense	2,700	
		105,040
Net profit		33,960

RICO MAYS
BALANCE SHEET AS AT 31 DECEMBER 20X7

	£	£	£
Fixed assets	Cost	Dep'n	
Leasehold	56,000	5,600	50,400
Fixtures	9,000	900	8,100
	65,000	6,500	58,500
Current assets			
Stock		135,000	
Debtors	238,500		
Less provision for bad and doubtful debts	(4,770)		
		233,730	
Prepayments		1,350	
Cash at bank		18,300	
Cash in hand		120	
		388,500	
Current liabilities			
Trade creditors		292,500	
Accruals		540	
		293,040	
Net current assets			95,460
			153,960
Capital			
At 1 January 20X7			120,000
Profit for the year			33,960
At 31 December 20X7			153,960

> ## CENTRAL ASSESSMENT ALERT
>
> Fully extending the ETB is an excellent test of whether you are competent in distinguishing P&L and balance sheet items. However, you will not necessarily be asked to extend an ETB fully from scratch in a Central Assessment; you may just have to do the trial balance and adjustments, or alternatively, you may be given these and have to complete the P&L account and balance sheet columns.

Computerising the extended trial balance

2.15 Like other accounting activities, the extended trial balance can be **computerised**.

(a) **The computer could be programmed to do all the work itself.** The trial balance would be input (or the computer might already have drawn it up from the ledger accounts) and then the individual corrections would be input. The computer would go ahead and produce the final accounts by itself (though, as with all outputs, it would need checking).

(b) **The extended trial balance could be prepared using a spreadsheet package.** That is, it would look just like the example in this chapter, but it would be on a screen instead of paper. It would be used just as a handwritten version would be used, except that numbers would be keyed in rather than written down. In this sort of 'computerised' extended trial balance, the computer would do some of the arithmetic, but the human operator would still be doing a lot of the work.

The extended trial balance and the journal

2.16 Normally, when an error is found, it is entered into the **journal** and then the correcting entries are made in the relevant ledger accounts. So in an ideal world, when the trial balance and the extended trial balance are drawn up, corrections of errors have already been incorporated into the ledger account balances.

2.17 In practice, some errors are not discovered until the last minute (for example, perhaps the auditors of the accounts, who often carry out their work at year-end, discover some errors). When this happens, the corrections are entered in the journal, and their effect must be noted on the extended trial balance, in the 'adjustments' column.

2.18 Now try an ETB preparation yourself. The blank ETB given on Page 266 can be used for your solution. Attempt the following six activities before looking at the answers.

Activity 12.1

You are assisting the accountant of Donnelly & Co in the preparation of the accounts for the year ending 31 December 20X7. The following list of balances has been extracted from the ledgers.

	£
Land and buildings (freehold)	120,000
Proprietor's capital at 1.1.X7	208,000
Sales	470,000
Purchases	246,000
Stock at 1.1.X7	79,500
Returns in	400
Returns out	1,800
Discounts allowed	4,000
Discounts received	2,100
Uniform business rate	27,450
Motor expenses	12,250
Salaries	103,500
Insurance	9,500
Trade debtors	32,300
Trade creditors	17,800
Carriage in	4,200
Carriage out	2,550
Motor vehicles	65,150
Bank balance (in credit at the bank)	7,800
Provision for depreciation	
Buildings	4,000
Motor vehicles	21,370
Bad debts	600

Enter the trial balance on the ETB and add it up.

BPP PUBLISHING

Account	Trial balance		Ref	Adjustments		Profit & loss account		Balance sheet	
	DR £	CR £		DR £	CR £	DR £	CR £	DR £	CR £
SUB-TOTAL									
Profit for the year									
TOTAL									

Activity 12.2

You should have realised by now that there is a difference on the trial balance. You should enter the difference in a suspense account.

On investigation, the following errors and omissions are found to have occurred.

(a) An invoice for £3,300 for general insurance has been posted to cash but not to the ledger account.

(b) A customer went into liquidation just before the year end, owing Donnelly & Co £1,300. The amount was taken off debtors but the corresponding entry to expense the bad debt has not been made.

(c) A cheque paid for purchases has been posted to the purchases account as £4,595, when the cheque was made out for £4,955.

(d) A van was purchased during the year for £2,455, but this amount was credited to the motor vehicles account.

Show the journal which will clear the suspense account, by dealing with the points noted above. Enter the journal on to the ETB.

Activity 12.3

No adjustments have yet been made for accruals or prepayments. The accountant asks you to search for any required accruals and prepayments and you find the following information.

(a) The bill for the Uniform Business Rate was received and paid on 1 April 20X7. The bill covers the period 1 April 20X7 to 31 March 20X8 and amounts to £21,600.

(b) The insurance bill (£3,300) which had originally been posted to the suspense account was for motor insurance, for the period 1 December 20X7 to 30 November 20X8.

(c) An invoice for carriage outwards was received after the year end for the period 1 November 20X7 to 31 January 20X8, amounting to £720 plus VAT of £126.

Calculate the necessary accruals or prepayments and enter them on the ETB.

Activity 12.4

The accountant tells you that the following adjustments need to be made.

(a) Depreciation is to be provided as follows.

Freehold buildings   2% on cost
Motor vehicles   20% on cost

The buildings element of the figure for freehold land and buildings is £40,000. A full year of depreciation is charged in the year of acquisition of any asset.

(b) A general provision for bad debts is to be made, at 1% of net trade debtors.

(c) The closing stock figure was agreed at £82,000.

Enter the necessary adjustments for the above items on to the ETB.

Activity 12.5

Extend and total the ETB.

CENTRAL ASSESSMENT ALERT

You are certain to be given an ETB in your central assessment. The principles are logical and straightforward, but you will not be able to master the technique with sufficient accuracy and speed without a great deal of practice.

2.19 Section summary

These are the steps to complete an extended trial balance.

Step 1   Draw up the trial balance, enter it on the ETB and add it up.

Step 2   If debits and credits are unequal in the trial balance, check all the entries are correct, then insert a suspense account.

Step 3   Make the various adjustments required in the question.

- Accruals and prepayments
- Adjustments to stock figures
- Other adjustments (ie dep'n, bad and doubtful debts)

Step 4   Check that the suspense account has been cleared by the adjustments you have made.

Step 5   Add up the adjustments columns and check all the entries are correct and debits equal credits.

Step 6   Add the figures across the ETB.

Step 7   Add up the profit and loss account debits and credits.

Step 8   Take the profit or loss for the year to the balance sheet columns

- **Profit** = DEBIT in P&L a/c = CREDIT in B/S

- **Loss** = CREDIT in P&L a/c = DEBIT in B/S

Step 9   Add up the debits and credits in the balance sheet and make sure they are equal. Investigate and resolve any differences.

3   SOME TYPICAL CENTRAL ASSESSMENT TASKS

3.1   Below are four ETB activities, all from past Central Assessments. In recent years such exercises have required you to fill in the adjustments column only, and not to extend the ETB. These more recent tasks are included in the BPP Assessment Kit for this Unit.

CENTRAL ASSESSMENT ALERT

If you are not asked for a full, eight column ETB, you will have less time to spend on this task and will be given an extra task such as a bank reconciliation or suspense account.

Activity 12.6

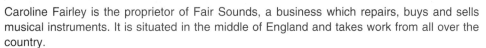

The suggested time allocation for this extended trial balance exercise is 70 minutes.

Caroline Fairley is the proprietor of Fair Sounds, a business which repairs, buys and sells musical instruments. It is situated in the middle of England and takes work from all over the country.

- You are employed by Caroline Fairley to assist with the bookkeeping.

- The business currently operates a manual system consisting of a general ledger, a sales ledger and a purchases ledger.

- Double entry takes place in the general ledger and the individual accounts of debtors and creditors are therefore regarded as memoranda accounts.

- Day books consisting of a purchases day book, a sales day book, a purchases returns day book and a sales returns day book are used. Totals from the various columns of the day books are transferred periodically into the general ledger.

At the end of the financial year on 30 April 20X8, the balances were extracted from the general ledger and entered into an extended trial balance as shown on Page 270.

Task 1

Make appropriate entries in the adjustment columns of the extended trial balance to take account of the following.

(a)   Depreciation is to be provided as follows:

Motor vehicles - 20% per annum reducing balance method
Equipment - 10% per annum straight line method

(b)   The £22,500 in the bank deposit account was invested on 1 July 20X7 at a fixed rate interest of 8% per annum.

(c)   On reviewing the debtors at 30 April 20X8, it was decided that one of them would probably not pay and the debt should be written off. The amount owing was £1,800. No entries have been made to reflect this. Any VAT implications are to be ignored.

(d)   The provision for doubtful debts should be adjusted to a figure of 5% of the outstanding debtors.

(e)   Closing stock was valued at cost at £43,795. However, this figure includes two items, cost price £175 each, which have been damaged in storage. It has been estimated that if a total of £35 was spent on repairing them, they could be sold for £140 each.

(f)   Insurance is paid quarterly in arrears on 31 January, 30 April, 31 July and 31 October each year. The instalment due on 30 April 20X8 was overlooked and a cheque, for £90, was not raised until 15 May 20X8.

Task 2

Extend the figures into the extended trial balance columns for the profit and loss and balance sheet. Total all of these columns, transferring the balance of the profit or loss as appropriate.

Extended trial balance at 30 April 20X8

DESCRIPTION	Ledger balance Debit £	Ledger balance Credit £	Adjustments Debit £	Adjustments Credit £	Profit and Loss a/c Debit £	Profit and Loss a/c Credit £	Balance Sheet Debit £	Balance Sheet Credit £
Purchases	127,680							
Sales		184,784						
Purchases returns		360						
Sales returns	502							
Stock at 1 May 20X7	40,650							
Salaries	22,590							
General expenses	14,580							
Insurance	270							
Motor vehicle (MV) at cost	9,600							
Provision for depreciation (MV)		4,685						
Equipment (EQ) at cost	17,100							
Provision for depreciation (EQ)		5,130						
Bad debt	2,025							
Provision for doubtful debts		1,485						
Debtors control account	31,200							
Creditors control account		25,232						
Drawings	17,892							
Capital		82,493						
Bank overdraft		261						
Cash	426							
VAT		1,685						
Bank interest received		900						
Bank deposit account	22,500							
Depreciation								
Closing stock - P&L								
Closing stock - balance sheet								
Bank interest owing								
Provision for doubtful debts - adjustment								
Other accruals								
Profit								
	307,015	307,015						

Activity 12.7

The suggested time allocation for this extended trial balance exercise is 80 minutes.

Andrew Hallgrove is the proprietor of Castle Alarms, which specialises in supplying domestic and commercial burglar alarm systems. Although the business operates throughout the UK, the offices and warehouse are located in the north of England.

You are employed within the business to assist with the bookkeeping. This is currently a manual system and consists of a general ledger, where double entry takes place, a sales ledger and a purchases ledger. The individual accounts of debtors and creditors are therefore regarded as memoranda accounts. Day books are used and totals from the various columns of these are transferred periodically into the general ledger.

At the end of the financial year of 31 October 20X6, the balances were extracted from the general ledger and entered into an extended trial balance as shown on Page 272.

Task 1

Make appropriate entries in the adjustment columns of the extended trial balance to take account of the following.

(a) Depreciation is to be provided as follows.

Motor vehicles: 20% per annum straight line method
Equipment: 10% per annum reducing balance method

(b) The bank loan of £50,000 was taken out on 31 January 20X6. The interest rate charged on the loan is fixed at 10% per annum.

(c) In August a system invoiced at £3,400 was installed at a local restaurant. Unfortunately no money was received in payment, the restaurant closed and the owner disappeared. A decision has now been made to write off the debt.

(d) Having written off all bad debts, the provision for bad debts is to be adjusted to 6% of remaining debtors.

(e) At the stocktake on 31 October 20X6 the stock was valued at £289,400 cost price. However, this figures includes the following.

(i) Five system costing £1,200 each which have now been replaced by improved models. It is thought that in order to sell them the price of each system will have to be reduced to £1,000.

(ii) A system costing £2,000 was damaged in the warehouse. Repairs will cost £200 before it can be used in an installation.

(f) The business took advantage of an offer to advertise on local radio during October 20X6 at a cost of £2,250. Although the invoice has now been received no entries have been made.

(g) Rent for the business property is £2,100 payable monthly in advance. This has been the figure payable over the last 12 months and a rent review is not due at the present time.

(h) On 30 October 20X6 £5,000 cash was withdrawn from the bank for use within the business. To date no entries have been made to reflect this transaction.

(i) A credit note received from Ashito Electronics and relating to goods returned has just been found in a pile of correspondence. The credit note, dated 20 October 20X6, is for £2,900 and has not been entered in any of the books of the business.

Task 2

Extend the figures into the extended trial balance columns for profit and loss and balance sheet. Total all of these columns, transferring the balance of the profit or loss as appropriate.

BPP
PUBLISHING

CASTLE ALARMS

Account	Trial balance Debit £	Trial balance Credit £	Adjustments Debit £	Adjustments Credit £	Profit and Loss a/c Debit £	Profit and Loss a/c Credit £	Balance Sheet Debit £	Balance Sheet Credit £
Sales		1,200,000						
Purchases	667,820							
Sales returns	96,570							
Purchases returns		52,790						
Opening Stock	301,840							
Debtors control account	189,600							
Cash	1,200							
Bank	25,300							
Creditors control account		95,000						
Provision for bad debts		12,000						
Bad debts	10,100							
Discount allowed	6,320							
Salaries	103,030							
Drawings	26,170							
Rent	27,300							
General expenses	14,310							
Capital		121,860						
VAT		22,600						
Bank loan		50,000						
Interest on bank loan	2,500							
Advertising	11,450							
Motor vehicles (cost)	32,600							
Equipment (cost)	48,860							
Motor vehicles (prov for depreciation)		4,100						
Equipment (prov for depreciation)		6,620						
Depreciation								
Loan interest owing								
Closing stock (P&L)								
Closing stock (B/S)								
Provision for bad debts (adjustment)								
Prepayments / accruals								
Subtotal	1,564,970	1,564,970						
Profit for the year								
TOTAL	1,564,970	1,564,970						

Activity 12.8

The suggested time allocation for this extended trial balance exercise is 85 minutes.

Melanie Lancton trades under the name of Explosives and operates out of a store and warehouse. She is a sole trader and has been in the clothes business for approximately ten years. Explosives deals mainly in jeans and speciality T shirts. All of the sales out of the store are for cash but the warehouse is used to supply other clothing retailers throughout the UK on a credit basis. Occasionally, orders are received on a limited scale from shops in northern France.

You are employed by Melanie to assist with the book-keeping. This is currently a manual system and consists of a general ledger, where double entry takes place, a sales ledger and a purchases ledger. The individual accounts of debtors and creditors are therefore regarded as memoranda accounts. Day books are used and totals from their various columns are transferred periodically into the general ledger.

The following balances were extracted from the general ledger at the end of the financial year on 31 May 20X6.

	£	£
Stock at 1 June 20X5	180,420	
Purchases	610,080	
Sales		840,560
Purchases returns		2,390
Sales returns	2,650	
Motor expenses	5,430	
Bank	20,415	
Cash	3,420	
Rent	11,000	
Lighting and heating	4,180	
Stationery and advertising	6,120	
Provision for bad debts		5,620
Debtors control account	120,860	
Creditors control account		102,860
Salaries	96,200	
Bad debts	7,200	
Drawings	31,600	
Discounts allowed	20,520	
Discounts received		18,400
Motor vehicles: at cost	60,480	
provision for depreciation		12,590
Office furniture and equipment: at cost	26,750	
provision for depreciation		3,170
VAT		10,260
Capital account at 1 June 20X5		211,475
	1,207,325	1,207,325

Having extracted the above figures, the following errors were found in the books.

(a)   The purchases day book totals for the month of March were as follows.

	£
Total	50,160
VAT	7,471
Net	42,689
Goods for resale	40,463
Other items	2,226

(i)   An invoice for £200 plus £35 VAT received from Just Jeans Ltd had been entered as £2,000 plus £35 VAT thus causing errors in both the net and total columns.

(ii)   The total of the net column was debited to the purchases account. An analysis of 'other items' showed £1,201 for lighting and heating and £1,025 for stationery and advertising. No entries had been passed in these accounts.

(b)   A credit note received from Astra Clothing for £40 plus £7 VAT had, in error, been left out altogether from the returns outwards day book.

273

(c)   Cash sales of £1,645 (inclusive of £245 VAT) had been entered as follows.

   Dr Cash book   £1,645
   Cr Sales   £1,645

(d)   An invoice had been received and correctly entered in the books from Kay Imports Ltd for £1,080 plus £180 VAT, total £1,260. A payment by cheque was made for £1,206 but the discount had been omitted from the discount column of the cash book.

The following adjustments also need to be taken into account.

(i)   Depreciation is to be provided as follows.

   Motor vehicles - 20% per annum on cost
   Office furniture and equipment - 10% per annum reducing balance method

   It should be noted that no depreciation is charged on assets in their year of purchase or in their year of sale. On 10 January 20X6 a new vehicle had been purchased for £9,800.

(ii)   Rent payable on the store and warehouse is £1,000 per month.

(iii) The stationery and advertising figure includes the sum of £1,560 paid to the Wise Advertising Agency for a series of newspaper advertisements covering all of Explosives' products and due to appear during the period October to December 20X6.

(iv)   Stock has been valued on 31 May 20X6 at £208,540. This figure excludes £2,300 of jeans (cost price) which had been damaged by a leak in the roof of the warehouse. The jeans were considered worthless and were thrown out. The Regal Insurance Company has agreed to pay a claim for the full cost of the jeans although as yet no payment has been received.

(v)   The provision for bad debts is to be adjusted to a figure representing 5% of debtors.

Task 1

Prepare journal entries to correct the errors (a) to (d) shown above. Dates and narratives are not required.

Use the blank journal on Page 275 for your answer.

Task 2

Enter the corrected balances into the first two columns of the extended trial balance provided on Page 276.

Note. It is the *corrected* balances that should be used, thus taking into account the journal entries prepared for Task 1. Total the two columns ensuring that the two totals agree.

Task 3

Make appropriate entries in the adjustment columns of the extended trial balance to take account of the adjustments (1) to (5) above.

Task 4

Extend the figures into the extended trial balance columns for profit and loss and balance sheet. Total all of these columns, transferring the balance of the profit or loss as appropriate.

JOURNAL		
Details	DR £	CR £

BPP PUBLISHING

EXPLOSIVES

Account	Trial balance		Adjustments		Profit and Loss a/c		Balance Sheet	
	Debit £	Credit £	Debit £	Credit £	Debit £	Credit £	Debit £	Credit £
Opening Stock								
Purchases								
Sales								
Purchases returns								
Sales returns								
Motor expenses								
Bank								
Cash								
Rent								
Lighting and heating								
Stationery and advertising								
Provision for bad debts								
Debtors control account								
Creditors control account								
Salaries								
Bad debts								
Drawings								
Discount allowed								
Discount received								
Motor vehicles (cost)								
Office furniture & equipment (cost)								
Motor vehicles (prov for depreciation)								
Office furniture & equipment (prov for depreciation)								
VAT								
Capital								
Depreciation								
Regal Insurance Company								
Closing stock (P&L)								
Closing stock (B/S)								
Provision for bad debts (adjustment)								
Prepayments / accruals								
Subtotal								
Profit for the year								
TOTAL								

Activity 12.9

The suggested time allocation for this extended trial balance exercise is 80 minutes.

Jason Brown is a sole trader who operates out of a warehouse in Nottingham. He buys and sells a range of office furniture and equipment and trades under the name J B Office Supplies. Most of his sales are made on credit to businesses in the Midlands area of England, although occasionally customers will call at his premises to make purchases for cash.

You are employed by Jason to assist with the bookkeeping. This is currently a manual system and consists of a general ledger, where double entry takes place, a sales ledger and a purchases ledger. The individual accounts of debtors and creditors are therefore regarded as memoranda accounts. Day books are used and totals from the columns of these are transferred periodically into the general ledger.

The following balances were extracted from the general ledger at the end of the financial year on 31 October 20X5.

	£
Purchases	170,240
Sales	246,412
Purchases returns	480
Sales returns	670
Stock at 1 November 20X4	54,200
Salaries	30,120
Rent	2,200
Insurance	360
Delivery vans at cost	12,800
Provision for depreciation - delivery vans	3,520
Equipment at cost	22,800
Provision for depreciation - equipment	5,760
Bad debts	2,700
Provision for doubtful debts	1,980
Debtors control account	41,600
Creditors control account	33,643
Drawings	10,522
Capital	83,171
Bank overdraft	348
Cash	568
VAT (credit balance)	2,246
Bank interest received	1,200
Bank deposit account	30,000
Suspense account	?

Task 1

Enter the above balances into the first two columns of the extended trial balance provided on Page 278. Total the two columns whilst at the same time entering an appropriate balance for the suspense account to ensure that the two totals agree.

JASON BROWN

Account	Trial balance Debit £	Trial balance Credit £	Adjustments Debit £	Adjustments Credit £	Profit and Loss a/c Debit £	Profit and Loss a/c Credit £	Balance Sheet Debit £	Balance Sheet Credit £
Purchases								
Sales								
Purchases returns								
Sales returns								
Opening Stock								
Salaries								
Rent								
Insurance								
Delivery vans (cost)								
Equipment (cost)								
Delivery vans (prov for depn)								
Equipment (prov for depn)								
Bad debts								
Provision for bad debts								
Debtors control account								
Creditors control account								
Drawings								
Capital								
Bank overdraft								
Cash								
VAT								
Bank interest received								
Bank deposit account								
Suspense account								
Depreciation								
Bank interest owing								
Closing stock (P&L)								
Closing stock (B/S)								
Provision for bad debts (adjustment)								
Prepayments / accruals								
Subtotal								
Profit for the year								
TOTAL								

Task 2

Unfortunately the errors causing the need for the suspense account cannot immediately be found and Jason is anxious that a draft extended trial balance should be produced as quickly as possible.

Make appropriate entries in the adjustment columns of the extended trial balance to take account of the following.

(a)   Depreciation is to be provided as follows.

Delivery vans: 20% per annum reducing balance method
Equipment: 10% per annum straight line method

(b)   The £30,000 in the bank deposit account was invested on 1 November 20X4 at a fixed rate of interest of 6% per annum. A cheque for £300 interest was received by J B Office Supplies on 2 January 20X5 and a further cheque for £900 on 3 July 20X5.

(c)   It is thought highly unlikely that £2,460 owed by M C Miller will be recovered and towards the end of October the decision was made for the debt to be written off. To date no entries have been passed. The provision on remaining debtors should be adjusted to a figure of 5%.

(d)   Closing stock has been valued at cost at £58,394. However, this figure includes four office chairs, cost price £230 each, which have been damaged in storage. It has been estimated that if a total of £40 was spent on repairing the worst of the damage then they could be sold for £190 each.

(e)   J B Office Supplies had sent a cheque for £1,260 to Metalux Imports, a supplier on 15 October 20X5. Unfortunately the cheque had not been signed and was returned in the post on 30 October. No entries have been passed.

(f)   Insurance is paid annually in advance on 1 April. The premium for the period 1 May 20X5 to 30 April 20X6 was £260.

(g)   The rent on the property used by J B Office Supplies was set on 1 January 20X4 at £200 per month payable in arrears. The next rent review has been scheduled to take place on 1 January 20X6.

Task 3

Extend the figures into the extended trial balance columns for profit and loss and balance sheet. Total all of these columns, transferring the balance of the profit or loss as appropriate.

Key learning points

- An **extended trial balance** is used to adjust trial balance figures for:
    - ° Errors
    - ° Accruals and prepayments
    - ° Provisions (depreciation, bad and doubtful debts)
    - ° Closing stock figures

- The extended trial balance is basically a worksheet representing all the ledger account balances and what happens to them.

- The ETB produces balances which can be taken directly to the balance sheet and profit and loss account.

- Since the ETB will be an important feature of your assessment it is important to practise ETB questions as much as possible, both manually and on a spreadsheet.

Quick quiz

1   Why is an ETB necessary?

2   What is the double entry to record closing stock on the ETB?

3   The P&L account columns should always add up to the same amount. True or false?

4   If the debit column total of the P&L account in the ETB is greater than the credit column, has the business made a profit or a loss?

5   In what ways can a computer help in the preparation of the ETB?

Answers to quick quiz

1   An ETB helps to keep track of adjustments between the trial balance and the final accounts.

2   DEBIT   Stock a/c (balance sheet)
     CREDIT   Stock a/c (P&L a/c)

3   False. The difference between the columns represents the profit/loss for the year.

4   A loss.

5   (a)   The computer does all the work itself by extracting the ledger balances.
     (b)   Use of a spreadsheet package.

Answers to activities

Answers to activities _____

Answer 1.1

(a)   Cash book
(b)   Sales day book
(c)   Purchase day book
(d)   Cash book
(e)   Sales (returns) day book
(f)   Purchase (returns) day book
(g)   Cash book

Answer 1.2 _____

	£
List price	30,000
Less 10% trade discount	3,000
	27,000
Less 2½% cash discount £27,000 × 2½%	675
	26,325

(a)   If Champer Ltd pays after 10 days it will receive only the trade discount. The company will therefore pay £27,000.

(b)   If payment is made within 10 days, the company will be able to take advantage of the cash discount and pay only £26,325.

Note. The cash discount is calculated as a percentage of the list price **net of trade discount**.

Answer 1.3 _____

(a)   The two sides of the transaction are:

  (i)   Cash is received (**debit** cash account)
  (ii) Sales increase by £37 (**credit** sales account).

CASH ACCOUNT

		£			£
07.12.X7	Sales a/c	37			

SALES ACCOUNT

					£
			07.12.X7	Cash a/c	37

(b)   The two sides of the transaction are:

  (i)   Cash is paid (**credit** cash account)
  (ii) Rent expense increases by £6,000 (**debit** rent account).

CASH ACCOUNT

		£			£
			07.12.X7	Rent a/c	6,000

RENT ACCOUNT

		£			£
07.12.X7	Cash a/c	6,000			

Tutorial note. This assumes that no rent liability had previously been recognised. If the expense had been posted already, the debit posting would be made to the creditors account.

(c)   The two sides of the transaction are:

  (i)   Cash is paid (**credit** cash account)
  (ii) Purchases increase by £1,250 (**debit** purchases account).

CASH ACCOUNT

	£	07.12.X7 Purchases a/c	£ 1,250

PURCHASES ACCOUNT

	£		£
07.12.X7 Cash a/c	1,250		

(d) The two sides of the transaction are:

(i) Cash is paid (**credit** cash account)
(ii) Assets increase by £4,500 (**debit** office furniture account).

CASH ACCOUNT

	£	07.12.X7 Office furniture a/c	£ 4,500

OFFICE FURNITURE (ASSET) ACCOUNT

	£		£
07.12.X7 Cash a/c	4,500		

Tutorial note. If all four of these transactions related to the same business, the cash account of that business would end up looking as follows.

CASH ACCOUNT

	£			£
07.12.X7 Sales a/c	37	07.12.X7	Rent a/c	6,000
			Purchases a/c	1,250
			Office furniture a/c	4,500

Answer 1.4

(a)	DEBIT	Machine account (fixed asset)	£6,400	
	CREDIT	Creditors (Angelo)		£6,400
(b)	DEBIT	Purchases account	£2,100	
	CREDIT	Creditors (Barnfield)		£2,100
(c)	DEBIT	Debtors (Carla)	£750	
	CREDIT	Sales		£750
(d)	DEBIT	Creditors (Daris)	£250	
	CREDIT	Cash		£250
(e)	DEBIT	Cash	£300	
	CREDIT	Debtors (Elsa)		£300
(f)	DEBIT	Wages expense	£5,000	
	CREDIT	Cash		£5,000
(g)	DEBIT	Rent expense	£1,000	
	CREDIT	Creditors (Graham)		£1,000
(h)	DEBIT	Creditors (Graham)	£1,000	
	CREDIT	Cash		£1,000
(i)	DEBIT	Insurance expense	£150	
	CREDIT	Cash		£150

Answer 1.5

		Original document	Book of prime entry	Accounts in general ledger to be posted to	
				Dr	*Cr*
(a)	Sale of goods on credit	Sales invoice	Sales day book	Total debtors	Sales
(b)	Allowances to credit customers	Credit note	Sales returns day book	Sales/Returns inward	Total debtors
(c)	Daily cash takings	Till rolls and/or sales invoices and receipts, bank paying-in book	Cash book	Cash	Sales

Tutorial note. All these transactions would be incorporated into the double entry system by means of periodic postings from the books of prime entry to the general ledger.

Answers to activities

Answer 2.1

	Account to be debited	Ledger	Account to be credited	Ledger
(a)	Rent	General	Bank	Cash book
(b)	R Sobers	Sales	Sales	General
(c)	Returns inwards	General	M Felix	Sales
(d)	Purchases	General	Rachet Ltd	Purchases
(e)	Fixed assets	General	Bank	Cash Book
(f)	Fixed assets	General	Bank	Cash Book
(g)	Rachet Ltd	Purchases	Bank	Cash Book

Answer 2.2

(a) Any five of the following.

- Plant and machinery
- Motor vehicles
- Stocks – raw materials
- Stocks – finished goods
- Total debtors
- Total creditors
- Wages and salaries
- Rent and rates
- Advertising expenses
- Bank charges
- Motor expenses
- Telephone expenses
- Sales
- Total cash or bank overdraft

(b) A control account is an account in which a record is kept of the total value of a number of similar but individual items. They are used to **check** that the sum of the individual balances in sales and purchase ledgers is correct.

It is the control account balance which will appear in the final accounts of the business; the sales ledger and purchase ledger act as **memoranda** for the lists of individual account balances.

Answer 2.3

(a) VAT for product A = 17.5/117.5 × £705 = £105. (So net price was £705 − £105 = £600.)
(b) VAT for product B = 0.175 × £480 = £84. (So gross price was £480 + £84 = £564.)

Answer 2.4

The ledger account will look like this.

VAT CONTROL ACCOUNT

	£		£
Creditors (purchases)		Balance b/d	2,165.00
17.5% × £4,500	787.50	Debtors (sales)	
Creditors (van)		17.5% × £(6,000 − 300)	997.50
17.5% × £10,460	1,830.50		
Balance c/d	544.50		
	3,162.50		3,162.50

Tutorial note. VAT on the purchase of a van is recoverable but VAT on the purchase of a company car is not recoverable.

Answer 2.5

VAT on the company car is irrecoverable. The company's other inputs amount to £(300,000 − £8,000) = £292,000. Of this, the proportion which is recoverable is given by the proportion of taxable sales (£525,000) to total sales (£600,000). Recoverable input tax is therefore £292,000 × 525/600 × 17.5% = £44,712.50.

Answer 2.6

(a)   The relevant books of prime entry are the cash book, the sales day book and the purchase day book.

CASH BOOK (RECEIPTS)

Date	Narrative	Total	Capital	Sales	Debtors
June		£	£	£	£
1	Capital	10,000	10,000		
13	Sales	310		310	
16	Waterhouses	1,200			1,200
24	Books & Co	350			350
		11,860	10,000	310	1,550

CASH BOOK (PAYMENTS)

Date	Narrative	Total	Fixtures and fittings	Creditors	Rent	Delivery expenses	Drawings	Wages
June		£	£	£	£	£	£	£
1	Warehouse Fittings Ltd	3,500	3,500					
19	Ransome House	820		820				
20	Rent	300			300			
21	Delivery expenses	75				75		
30	Drawings	270					270	
30	Wages	400						400
30	Big, White	450		450				
		5,815	3,500	1,270	300	75	270	400

SALES DAY BOOK

Date	Customer	Amount
June		£
4	Waterhouses	1,200
11	Books & Co	740
18	R S Jones	500
		2,440

PURCHASE DAY BOOK

Date	Supplier	Amount
June		£
2	Ransome House	820
9	Big, White	450
17	RUP Ltd	1,000
		2,270

(b) and (c)

The relevant ledger accounts are for cash, sales, purchases, creditors, debtors, capital, fixtures and fittings, rent, delivery expenses, drawings and wages.

CASH ACCOUNT

	£		£
June receipts	11,860	June payments	5,815
		Balance c/d	6,045
	11,860		11,860

SALES ACCOUNT

	£			£
		Cash		310
Balance c/d	2,750	Debtors		2,440
	2,750			2,750

PURCHASES ACCOUNT

	£		£
Creditors	2,270	Balance c/d	2,270

DEBTORS ACCOUNT

	£		£
Sales	2,440	Cash	1,550
		Balance c/d	890
	2,440		2,440

CREDITORS ACCOUNT

	£		£
Cash	1,270	Purchases	2,270
Balance c/d	1,000		
	2,270		2,270

CAPITAL ACCOUNT

	£		£
Balance c/d	10,000	Cash	10,000

FIXTURES AND FITTINGS ACCOUNT

	£		£
Cash	3,500	Balance c/d	3,500

RENT ACCOUNT

	£		£
Cash	300	Balance c/d	300

DELIVERY EXPENSES ACCOUNT

	£		£
Cash	75	Balance c/d	75

DRAWINGS ACCOUNT

	£		£
Cash	270	Balance c/d	270

WAGES ACCOUNT

	£		£
Cash	400	Balance c/d	400

(d)   TRIAL BALANCE AS AT 30 JUNE 20X7

Account	Dr £	Cr £
Cash	6,045	
Sales		2,750
Purchases	2,270	
Debtors	890	
Creditors		1,000
Capital		10,000
Fixtures and fittings	3,500	
Rent	300	
Delivery expenses	75	
Drawings	270	
Wages	400	
	13,750	13,750

Answer 2.7

SOCCO SHOPS					A/c no: SL 22
Date 20X7	**Details**	**Amount £**	**Date 20X7**	**Details**	**Amount £**
9/9	**Balance b/d**	**1,209.76**	10/9	Cash received	829.02
10/9	Invoice 540		10/9	Discount allowed	15.00
	(SDB 253)	207.45	10/9	Balance c/d	573.19
		1,417.21			1,417.21
10/9	Balance b/d	573.19			

Answer 2.8

REGALLY LTD					A/c no: PL 19
Date 20X7	**Details**	**Amount £**	**Date 20X7**	**Details**	**Amount £**
10/9	Cash paid	780.35	9/9	**Balance b/d**	**7,109.82**
10/9	Discount received	13.00	10/9	Purchases (PDB 258)	380.41
10/9	Balance c/d	6,696.88			
		7,490.23			7,490.23
			10/9	Balance c/d	6,696.88

Answer 2.9

SALES LEDGER CONTROL ACCOUNT					
Date 20X7	**Details**	**Amount £**	**Date 20X7**	**Details**	**Amount £**
9/9	Balance b/d	202,728.09	10/9	Receipts from debtors	1,768.11
10/9	SDB 253	2,773.04	10/9	Discount allowed	32.50
			10/9	Balance c/d	203,700.52
		205,501.13			205,501.13
10/9	Balance b/d	203,700.52			

PURCHASES LEDGER CONTROL ACCOUNT					
Date 20X7	**Details**	**Amount £**	**Date 20X7**	**Details**	**Amount £**
10/9	Payments to suppliers	6,659.36	9/9	Balance b/d	189,209.76
10/9	Discount received	83.00	10/9	PDB 258	827.99
10/9	Balance c/d	183,295.39			
		190,037.75			190,037.75
			10/9	Balance b/d	183,295.39

Answer 2.10

VAT ACCOUNT

Date 20X6	Details	Amount £	Date 20X6	Details	Amount £
18/6	Sales returns (SRDB)	1,261.72	17/6	Balance b/d	45,029.83
18/6	Purchases (PDB)	12,650.80	18/6	Sales (SDB)	9,227.43
18/6	Purchases (CB)	145.10	18/6	Purchases returns	
18/6	Purchases (PCB)	9.80		(PRDB)	2,675.28
18/6	Balance c/d	42,992.30	18/6	Sales (CB)	127.18
		57,059.72			57,059.72
			18/6	Balance b/d	42,992.30

SALES

Date 20X6	Details	Amount £	Date 20X6	Details	Amount £
18/6	Sales returns (SRDB)	7,209.87	17/6	Balance b/d	459,945.09
			18/6	Sales (SDB)	52,728.19
			18/6	Sales (CB)	726.76
18/6	Balance c/d	506,190.17			
		513,400.04			513,400.04
			18/6	Balance b/d	506,190.17

PURCHASES

Date 20X6	Details	Amount £	Date 20X6	Details	Amount £
17/6	Balance b/d	290,673.87	18/6	Purchases returns	
18/6	Purchases (PDB)	72,290.29		(PRDB)	15,287.35
18/6	Purchases (CB)	829.19	18/6	Balance c/d	348,562.00
18/6	Purchases (PCB)	56.00			
		363,849.35			363,849.35
18/6	Balance b/d	348,562.00			

DEBTORS CONTROL

Date 20X6	Details	Amount £	Date 20X6	Details	Amount £
17/6	Balance b/d	423,900.92	18/6	Sales returns (SRDB)	8,471.59
18/6	Sales (SDB)	61,955.62	18/6	Receipts from debtors	
				(CB)	72,109.29
			18/6	Balance c/d	405,275.66
		485,856.54			485,856.54
18/6	Balance b/d	405,275.66			

CREDITORS CONTROL

Date 20X6	Details	Amount £	Date 20X6	Details	Amount £
18/6	Purchases returns		17/6	Balance b/d	215,876.09
	(PRDB)	17,962.63	18/6	Purchases (PDB)	84,941.09
18/6	Payments to creditors				
	(CB)	45,290.02			
18/6	Balance c/d	237,564.53			
		300,817.18			300,817.18
			18/6	Balance b/d	237,564.53

PETTY CASH

Date 20X6	Details	Amount £	Date 20X6	Details	Amount £
17/6	Balance b/d	200.00	18/6	Purchases (PCB)	65.80
			18/6	Balance c/d	134.20
		200.00			200.00
18/6	Balance b/d	134.20			

CASH

Date 20X6	Details	Amount £	Date 20X6	Details	Amount £
17/6	Balance b/d	23,907.35	18/6	Purchases	974.29
18/6	Sales	853.94	18/6	Payments to creditors	45,290.02
18/6	Receipts from debtors	72,109.29			
			18/6	Balance c/d	50,606.27
		96,870.58			96,870.58
18/6	Balance b/d	50,606.27			

Answer 2.11

The main advantage of computerised accounting systems is that a large amount of data can be processed very quickly. A further advantage is that computerised systems are more accurate than manual systems.

Lou's comment that 'you never know what is going on in that funny box' might be better expressed as 'lack of audit trail'. If a mistake occurs somewhere in the system it is not always easy to identify where and how it happened.

Answers to activities

Answer 3.1

An **enterprise** is the most general term, referring to just about any organisation in which people join together to achieve a common end. In the context of accounting it can refer to a multinational conglomerate, a small club, a local authority and so on.

A **business** is a general term, but it does not extend as widely as the term 'enterprise':, it would not include a charity or a local authority. Any organisation existing to trade and make a profit could be called a business.

A **company** is an enterprise constituted in a particular legal form, usually involving limited liability for its members. Companies need not be businesses; for example, many charities are constituted as companies.

A **firm** is a vaguer term. It is used loosely in the sense of a business or a company. Some writers try to restrict its meaning to that of an unincorporated business (ie a business not constituted as a company, ie a partnership).

Answer 3.2

The missing words are:

separate; owners; all; company; owners; limited.

Answer 3.3

Transaction	Assets	=	Capital	+	Liabilities
(a)			Increase		Decrease
(b)	Decrease				Decrease
(c)			Decrease		Increase
(d)	Decrease		Decrease		
(e)	Increase		Increase		
(f)	Increase				Increase

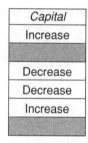
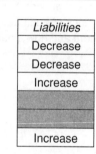

Answer 3.4

We have assets of £2,500 (cash), balanced by liabilities of £2,500 (the amounts owed by the business to Ann and Tim).

- The £1,750 owed to Ann is clearly **capital**, because it is a sum owed to the owner of the business.

- To classify the £750 owed to Tim, we need to know more about the **terms of his agreement** with Ann.

- If they have effectively gone into **partnership**, sharing the risks and rewards of the business, then Tim is a proprietor too and the £750 is 'capital' in the sense that Ann's £1,750 is.

- If Tim has no share in the profits of the business, and can expect only a repayment of his 'loan' plus some interest, the amount of £750 should be classified under **liabilities**.

Answer 3.5

(a) Assets (cash) increase by £5,000; liabilities (amount owed to the bank) increase by £5,000

(b) Assets (cash) decrease by £800; assets (stock) increase by £800

(c) Assets (cash) decrease by £50; capital decreases by £50 (the proprietor has taken £50 drawings for her personal use; in effect, the business has repaid her part of the amount it owed)

(d) Assets (cash) increase by £440; assets (stock) decrease by £300; capital (the profit earned for the proprietor) increases by £140.

(e) Assets (cash) decrease by £5,270; liabilities (the bank loan) decrease by £5,000; capital decreases by £270 (the proprietor has made a 'loss' of £270 on the transaction).

Answer 3.6

CASH (BANK)

		£			£
1/9	Capital	5,000	3/9	Fixed assets (database)	1,600
10/9	Sales	1,500	3/9	Purchases	720
17/9	Sales	4,200	3/9	Petty cash	180
17/9	Capital	150	10/9	Drawings	500
23/9	Capital	500	11/9	Purchases	2,000
23/9	Loan creditor (Gary)	1,000	17/9	Wages	250
23/9	Sales	11,340	17/9	Drawings	500
			17/9	Lockup cost	150
			23/9	Purchases	1,000
			23/9	Purchases	5,000
			23/9	Drawings	700
			23/9	Wages	250
				Balance c/d	10,840
		23,690			23,690
23/9	Balance b/d	10,840			

CAPITAL

		£			£
23/9	Balance c/d	5,650	1/9	Cash	5,000
			17/9	Cash	150
			23/9	Cash	500
		5,650			5,650
			23/9	Balance b/d	5,650

RETAINED PROFIT

		£			£
10/9	Drawings	500	10/9	Profit	780
17/9	Drawings	500	17/9	Profit	1,800
23/9	Drawings	700	23/9	Profit	5,680
23/9	Balance c/d	6,560			
		8,260			8,260
			23/9	Balance b/d	6,560

FIXED ASSETS

		£			£
3/9	Cash	1,600	23/9	Balance c/d	2,800
23/9	Creditor (van)	1,200			
		2,800			2,800
23/9	Balance b/d	2,800			

PETTY CASH

		£			£
3/9	Cash	180	23/9	Balance c/d	180
23/9	Balance b/d	180			

LOAN CREDITOR (GARY)

		£			£
23/9	Balance c/d	1,010	23/9	Cash	1,000
			23/9	Interest	10
		1,010			1,010
			23/9	Balance b/d	1,010

DEBTOR (VIV)

		£			£
23/9	Sales	1,600	23/9	Balance c/d	1,600
23/9	Balance b/d	1,600			

CREDITOR (VAN)

		£			£
23/9	Balance c/d	1,200	23/9	Fixed assets	1,200
			23/9	Balance b/d	1,200

CREDITOR (PURCHASES)

		£			£
23/9	Balance c/d	1,000	23/9	Purchases	1,000
			23/9	Balance b/d	1,000

PROFIT

		£			£
10/9	Purchases	720	10/9	Sales	1,500
	Capital (profit for week)	780			
		1,500			1,500
17/9	Purchases	2,000	17/9	Sales	4,200
	Wages	250			
	Lockup	150			
	Capital (profit for week)	1,800			
		4,200			4,200
23/9	Purchases	7,000	23/9	Sales	12,940
	Wages	250			
	Interest	10			
	Capital (profit for week)	5,680			
		12,940			12,940

SALES

		£			£
10/9	Profit	1,500	10/9	Cash	1,500
17/9	Profit	4,200	17/9	Cash	4,200
23/9	Profit	12,940	23/9	Debtor (Viv)	1,600
			23/9	Cash	11,340
		12,940			12,940

PURCHASES

		£			£
3/9	Cash	720	10/9	Profit	720
11/9	Cash	2,000	17/9	Profit	2,000
23/9	Cash	1,000	23/9	Profit	7,000
	Cash	5,000			
	Creditor	1,000			
		7,000			7,000

LOCKUP

		£			£
17/9	Cash	150	17/9	Profit	150

WAGES

		£			£
17/9	Cash	250	17/9	Profit	250
23/9	Cash	250	23/9	Profit	250

INTEREST

		£			£
23/9	Creditor	10	23/9	Profit	10

COURTNEY
TRIAL BALANCE 23/9/X9

	DR £	CR £
Cash	10,840	
Capital		5,650
Retained profit		6,560
Loan creditor (Gary)		1,010
Debtor (Viv)	1,600	
Fixed assets	2,800	
Petty cash	180	
Creditor (van)		1,200
Creditor (purchases)		1,000
	15,420	15,420

Answer 3.7

COURTNEY
BALANCE SHEET AS AT 23/9/X9

	£	£
Fixed assets		2,800
Current assets		
Debtors	1,600	
Cash at bank and in hand (£10,840 + £180)	11,020	
	12,620	
Current liabilities		
Trade creditors (£1,200 + £1,000)	2,200	
Net current assets		10,420
Long-term creditors		(1,010)
		12,210
Capital		
Proprietor's capital		5,650
Retained profits		6,560
		12,210

Answer 3.8

(a) A **steel manufacturer** would have a high proportion of its asset values locked up in fixed assets (factory premises, heavy machinery). It might also hold large stocks of raw materials and finished goods, and the value of debtors might be significant too.

(b) A **bank's** main asset is its debtors, namely the people to whom it lends money. Curiously enough, cash holdings may be much smaller than debtor balances, because banks aim to *use* cash (ie lend it or invest it) rather than merely sitting on it. In the case of a bank with a large number of branches, land and buildings will also be a significant item, but still not as great as debtors.

Answers to activities

Answer 3.9

Asset	Business	Current or fixed
Van	Delivery firm	Fixed
Machine	Manufacturing business	Fixed
Car	Car trader	Current

Answer 3.10

	Fixed asset	Current asset	Liabilities
(a) A PC used in the accounts department of a retail store	✓		
(b) A PC on sale in an office equipment shop		✓	
(c) Wages due to be paid to staff at the end of the week			✓
(d) A van for sale in a motor dealer's showroom		✓	
(e) A delivery van used in a grocer's business	✓		
(f) An amount owing to a bank for a loan for the acquisition of a van, to be repaid over 9 months			✓

Answer 3.11

Assets	=	*Capital*	+	*Liabilities*
£(95,500 + 15,700)	=	£105,200	+	£6,000
£111,200	=	£111,200		

Answer 3.12

(a) Capital expenditure (enhancing an existing fixed asset)

(b) Revenue expenditure

(c) Revenue income

(d) Capital expenditure

(e) Revenue expenditure

Answers to activities

Answer 4.1

False. The prudence concept may conflict with the accruals/matching concept, in which case, practically speaking, the prudence concept prevails. For example, if stock held is expected to be sold for less than it cost to buy or make, then that 'loss' on the value of the stock (cost less selling price) should be recognised immediately. Under the accruals concept, the loss would be recognised when the sale is made.

Answer 4.2

Materiality as a 'fundamental accounting concept' does have strict limitations. It refers primarily to financial reporting, but has no bearing at all on detailed procedural matters such as bank reconciliations or statements of account sent to customers.

The statement sent to the customer must be accurate to the last penny, however large it is. If you receive a bill from a company for £147.50, you do not 'round it up' to £150 when you pay. Nor will the company billing you be prepared to 'round it down' to £145. A customer pays an agreed price for an agreed product or service. Paying more is effectively giving money away. Paying less exposes your creditor to an unfair loss.

If you are preparing a performance report comparing how well the company is doing in the UK and France, different considerations apply. There is little point in being accurate to the last penny or centime (and inconsistencies might occur from the choice of currency rate used). Senior management are interested in the broader picture, they are looking to identify comparisons between the overall performance of each division.

Assume that profits in France were £1,373,370.75 and UK profits were £1,233,750.57.

France	UK
£	£
1,373,370.75	1,233,750.57
or	*or*
£'000	£'000
1,373	1,234

The rounded figures are much easier to read, and so the relative performance is easier to compare. Considerations of materiality allow you to ignore the rounding differences, because they are so small and the information is used for comparative purposes only.

Answer 4.3

Accounting standards aim to prescribe a set of rules under which accounting statements should be prepared and presented by reporting entities. Working to a standard aids comparability of financial statements across different enterprises, and different time periods. In the UK, accounting standards are issued by the Accounting Standards Board (ASB) as Financial Reporting Standards (FRSs), although many of the old ASC's Statements of Standard Accounting Practice (SSAPs) have also been adopted by the ASB.

BPP PUBLISHING

Answers to activities

Answer 5.1

	MOTOR VEHICLES		NLM 2
	£		£
12 June Jnl 51	14,500		

	FURNITURE		NLF 1
	£		£
13 June Jnl 51	1,000		

	VAN GOGH LTD		SLV 6
£			£
	12 June Jnl 51		14,500

	SOFA MIREDO		BLS 12
£			£
	13 June Jnl 51		1,000

Answer 5.2

Depreciation is a measure of the wearing out of a fixed asset through use, time or obsolescence. It is charged in order to match revenue and expenses with one another in the same accounting period so that profits are fairly and consistently calculated. If the cost of fixed assets was not written off over time, there would be incomplete matching of revenue and expenses.

Answer 5.3

(a) **Straight line depreciation** will give the same charge each year for the four years of economic life.

$$\text{Annual depreciation} = \frac{\text{Cost minus residual value}}{\text{Estimated economic life}}$$

$$\text{Annual depreciation} = \frac{£1,800 - £0}{4 \text{ years}}$$

$$\text{Annual depreciation} = \underline{£450}$$

Annual depreciation charges are therefore £450 for each year from 20X2 to 20X5 inclusive.

(b) The **reducing balance method** at 60% per annum involves the following calculations.

	£	
Cost at 1.1.20X2	1,800	
Depreciation 20X2	1,080	60% × £1,800
Book value 1.1.20X3	720	
Depreciation 20X3	432	60% × £720
Book value 1.1.20X4	288	
Depreciation 20X4	173	60% × £288
Book value 1.1.20X5	115	
Depreciation 20X5 (Note)	115	(balance remaining)
Residual value at end of estimated economic life	-	

Annual depreciation charges are therefore 20X2: £1,080, 20X3: £432, 20X4: £173, 20X5: £115.

Note. At some point it will usually be considered a waste of time to carry on the depreciation calculations as the amounts involved will be immaterial. (Sometimes the asset is maintained in the books at £1.)

Answer 5.4

Workings

(1) *Brian car*   Annual depreciation $\dfrac{£(20,000 - 2,000)}{3 \text{ years}} = £6,000\text{pa}$

Depreciation	Monthly depreciation	£500
	1 June 20X2 to 28 February 20X3 (9 months)	£4,500
	1 March 20X3 to 28 February 20X4	£6,000

(2) *Bill car*   Annual depreciation $\dfrac{£(8,000 - 2,000)}{3 \text{ years}} = £2,000\text{pa}$

Depreciation 1 June 20X3 to 28 February 20X4 (9 months)   £1,500

MOTOR VEHICLES

Date		£	Date		£
1 June 20X2	Creditor (or cash) (car purchase)	20,000	28 Feb 20X3	Balance c/d	20,000
1 March 20X3	Balance b/d	20,000			
1 June 20X3	Creditors (or cash) (car purchase)	8,000	28 Feb 20X4	Balance c/d	28,000
		28,000			28,000
1 Mar 20X4	Balance b/d	28,000			

PROVISION FOR DEPRECIATION OF MOTOR VEHICLES

Date		£	Date		£
28 Feb 20X3	Balance c/d	4,500	28 Feb 20X3	Dep'n expense	4,500
			1 Mar 20X3	Balance b/d	4,500
28 Feb 20X4	Balance c/d	12,000	28 Feb 20X4	Dep'n expense £(6,000+1,500)	7,500
		12,000			12,000
			1 Mar 20X4	Balance b/d	12,000

BALANCE SHEET (WORKINGS) AS AT 28 FEBRUARY 20X4

	Brian car		Bill car		Total
	£	£	£	£	£
Asset at cost		20,000		8,000	28,000
Accumulated depreciation Year to:					
28 Feb 20X3	4,500		–		
28 Feb 20X4	6,000		1,500		
		10,500		1,500	12,000
Net book value		9,500		6,500	16,000

Answers to activities

Answer 5.5

Annual depreciation $\dfrac{\pounds(35{,}000 - 3{,}000)}{8 \text{ years}}$ = £4,000 per annum

Because the asset was purchased six months into the year only half a year's depreciation was charged in the first year.

	£	£
Fixed asset at cost		35,000
Depreciation in 20X4 (1 year)	2,000	
20X5, 20X6 and 20X7	12,000	
Accumulated depreciation		14,000
Net book value at date of disposal		21,000
Sale price	18,600	
Costs incurred in making the sale	(1,200)	
Net sale price		17,400
Loss on disposal		(3,600)

This loss will be shown as an expense in the profit and loss account of the business. It is a capital loss, not a trading loss, and it should not therefore be shown in the trading account.

Answer 5.6

MOTOR VEHICLES: COST

		£			£
1.6.X6	Balance b/d	124,000	1.8.X6	Disposals	54,000
1.8.X6	Bank	71,000	31.5.X7	Balance c/d	141,000
		195,000			195,000

MOTOR VEHICLES: PROVISION FOR DEPRECIATION

		£			£
1.8.X6	Disposals	49,000	1.6.X6	Balance b/d	88,000
31.5.X7	Balance c/d	74,700	31.5.X7	Depreciation (P&L) (W)	35,700
		123,700			123,700

DISPOSAL OF FIXED ASSETS

		£			£
1.8.X6	Motor vehicles: cost	54,000	1.8.X6	Motor vehicles: dep'n	49,000
			1.8.X6	Bank	3,900
			31.5.X7	Loss on disposal (P&L)	1,100
		54,000			54,000

Working: depreciation charge

	£
Assets bought in earlier years:	
Cost b/d	124,000
Less assets sold in year	54,000
Still owned at year end	70,000
Depreciation b/d	88,000
Less assets sold in year	49,000
	39,000
Net book value at 31.5.X7	31,000
Assets acquired in the year	71,000
	102,000
Depreciation for the year at 35%	35,700

PUBLISHING

Answer 5.7

(a)

		Ford		Lada	
		£	£	£	£
Cost			10,000		8,000
Depreciation:	year to June 20X6	1,000		-	
	year to June 20X7	900		800	
	year to June 20X8	810		720	
			(2,710)		(1,520)
Value as at 1 July 20X8			7,290		6,480

(b)

MOTOR VEHICLES ACCOUNT

		£			£
1 July 20X8	Balance b/d	18,000	14 Nov 20X8	Disposals	10,000
14 Nov 20X8	Purchase of				
	Skoda	15,500	30 June 20X9	Balance c/d	23,500
		33,500			33,500
1 July 20X9	Balance b/d	23,500			

PROVISION FOR DEPRECIATION: MOTOR VEHICLES

		£			£
14 Nov 20X8	Disposals	2,710	1 July 20X8	Balance b/d	4,230
30 Jun 20X9	Balance c/d	3,718	30 June 20X9	Profit and loss	2,198
				(1550+648)	
		6,428			6,428

MOTOR VEHICLES DISPOSALS

		£			£
14 Nov 20X8	Motor vehicles	10,000	14 Nov 20X8	Provision for	
				depreciation	2,710
			14 Nov 20X8	Motor vehicles	6,000
			30 June 20X9	P & L a/c	1,290
		10,000			10,000

Answer 5.8

(a)

ASSET DISPOSALS

		£			£
31.5.X7	Motor vehicles	30,000	31.5.X7	Provision for	
31.5.X7	Profit and loss a/c	3,000		depreciation	24,000
			31.5.X7	Cash	9,000
		33,000			33,000

(b)

PROVISION FOR DEPRECIATION: LAND AND BUILDINGS

		£			£
31.5.X7	Balance c/d	35,200	1.6.X6	Balance b/d	32,000
			31.5.X7	Profit and loss a/c	3,200
		35,200			35,200

(c)

PROVISION FOR DEPRECIATION: FIXTURES AND FITTINGS

		£			£
31.5.X7	Balance c/d	110,000	1.6.X6	Balance b/d	88,000
			31.5.X7	Profit and loss a/c*	22,000
		110,000			110,000

* Depreciation is calculated using the reducing balance method, ie 25% × £(176,000 − 88,000)
= £22,000.

Answers to activities

(d)   PROVISION FOR DEPRECIATION: MOTOR VEHICLES

		£			£
31.5.X7	Assets disposals	24,000	1.6.X6	Balance b/d	54,000
31.5.X7	Balance c/d	42,000	31.5.X7	Profit and loss a/c	12,000
		66,000			66,000

* Depreciation is calculated on the straight-line basis ie 20% × £(90,000 − 30,000) = £12,000.

Answers to activities _____

Answer 6.1

These are some of the main reasons for preparing accounts.

(a)   Periodic reports are needed to assess whether trading activities are successful or not.

(b)   Many businesses are managed by people other than their owners. The owners will wish to see how well their managers are performing.

(c)   Limited companies are obliged by law to prepare a set of accounts on a yearly basis and file them with a company report at Companies House with the Registrar of Companies, ie there is a statutory reason for preparing accounts. This applies to charities too.

(d)   Accounting profit is used as the basis for the calculation of tax due and also for other key numbers such as the profit due to individual partners in a partnership or the bonus due to managers.

Answer 6.2 _____

		£	£
DEBIT	Development expenditure (balance sheet)	200,000.00	
CREDIT	Research (profit and loss account)		200,000.00

Reclassification of expenditure incurred on successful product development in the year to fixed assets, to be depreciated or amortised over a suitable period during which the product is earning revenues.

A total of £500,000 will still be expensed as research expenditure in the period as it was incurred on pure and applied research, not on development.

Answers to activities

Answer 7.1

(a)

			SALES DAY BOOK		SDB 090

Date	Name	Folio	Total	Plants	Garden tools
20X7			£	£	£
Sept 3	H Duckworth	SL 028 Dr	170.00	170.00	
11	T Carter	SL 105 Dr	260.00		260.00
15	J Matthews	SL 017 Dr	330.00	330.00	
			760.00	500.00	260.00
			GL 200 Dr	GL 401 Cr	GL 402 Cr

POSTING SUMMARY 30/9/X7

			£	£
DEBIT	GL 200	Debtors control account	760	
CREDIT	GL 401	Sales: plants		500
	GL 402	Sales: garden tools		260

CASH BOOK EXTRACT

	RECEIPTS CASH BOOK: SEPTEMBER 20X7				CB 079

Date	Narrative	Folio	Total	Discount	Debtors
20X7			£	£	£
Sept10	H Duckworth	SL 028 Cr	150.00	20.00	170.00
18	T Carter	SL 105 Cr	108.00	12.00	120.00
28	J Matthews	SL 017 Cr	200.00	-	200.00
			458.00	32.00	490.00
			GL 100 Dr	GL 207 Dr	GL 200 Cr

Memorandum sales ledger

		H DUCKWORTH				A/c no: SL 028	

Date	Narrative	Folio	£	Date	Narrative	Folio	£
20X7				20X7			
Sept 3	Sales	SDB 090	170.00	Sept 10	Cash	CB 079	150.00
					Discount	CB 079	20.00
			170.00				170.00

		T CARTER				A/c no: SL 105	

Date	Narrative	Folio	£	Date	Narrative	Folio	£
20X7				20X7			
Sept 11	Sales	SDB 090	260.00	Sept 18	Cash	CB 079	108.00
					Discount	CB 079	12.00
				Sept 30	Balance	c/d	140.00
			260.00				260.00
Oct 1	Balance	b/d	140.00				

		J MATTHEWS				A/c no: SL 017	

Date	Narrative	Folio	£	Date	Narrative	Folio	£
20X7				20X7			
Sept 15	Sales	SDB 090	330.00	Sept 28	Cash	CB 079	200.00
				Sept 30	Balance	c/d	130.00
			330.00				330.00
Oct 1	Balance	b/d	130.00				

General ledger (extract)

TOTAL DEBTORS (SALES LEDGER) CONTROL ACCOUNT A/c no: GL 200

Date 20X7	Narrative	Folio	£	Date 20X7	Narrative	Folio	£
Sept 30	Sales	SDB 090	760.00	Sept 30	Cash and discount	CB 079	490.00
				Sept 30	Balance	c/d	270.00
			760.00				760.00
Oct 1	Balance	b/d	270.00				

Note. At 30 September the closing balance on the debtors control account (£270) is the same as the total of the individual balances on the personal accounts in the sales ledger (£0 + £140 + £130).

DISCOUNT ALLOWED — A/c no: GL 207

Date 20X7	Narrative	Folio	£	Date	Narrative	Folio	£
Sept 30	Debtors	CB 079	32.00				

CASH CONTROL ACCOUNT — A/c no: GL 100

Date 20X7	Narrative	Folio	£	Date	Narrative	Folio	£
Sept 30	Cash received	CB 079	458.00				

SALES: PLANTS — A/c no: GL 401

Date	Narrative	Folio	£	Date 20X7	Narrative	Folio	£
				Sept 30	Debtors	SDB 090	500.00

SALES: GARDEN TOOLS — A/c no: GL 402

Date	Narrative	Folio	£	Date 20X7	Narrative	Folio	£
				Sept 30	Debtors	SDB 090	260.00

(b)   'TRIAL BALANCE' AS AT 30/9/X7

	Debit £	Credit £
Cash (all receipts)	458	
Debtors	270	
Discount allowed	32	
Sales: plants		500
Sales: garden tools		260
	760	760

Tutorial note

The trial balance is shown here to emphasise the point that a trial balance **includes the balances on control accounts, but excludes the balances on the personal accounts** in the sales ledger and purchase ledger.

Answer 7.2

	£	£
Amounts due to creditors at 1 January (balancing figure)		19,330
Purchases in year		86,700
		106,030
Less: cash paid to creditors in year	83,000	
discounts received	4,130	
contra with debtors control	5,200	
		92,330
Amounts still unpaid at 31 December		13,700

Answer 7.3

A. The total of sales invoices in the day book is debited to the control account. If the total is **understated** by £1,000, the debits in the control account will also be understated by £1,000. Options B and D would have the opposite effect: credit entries in the control account would be understated. Option C would lead to a discrepancy of $2 \times £1,000 = £2,000$.

Answer 7.4

(a)

DEBTORS CONTROL (OR TOTAL) ACCOUNT

20X6		£	20X6		£
Oct 1	Balances b/d	20,347	Oct 1	Balances b/d	228
20X7			20X7		
Sept 30	Sales	176,429	Sept 30	Cash received from	
				debtors	148,481
	Balances c/d	228		Discount allowed	5,273
				Returns	3,180
				Bad debts written off	1,079
				Transfer creditors	
				control account	949
				Allowances on goods	
				damaged	553
				Balances c/d	37,261
		197,004			197,004

(b)

CREDITORS CONTROL (OR TOTAL) ACCOUNT

		£			£
20X6			20X6		
Oct 1	Balances b/d	319	Oct 1	Balances b/d	18,024
20X7			20X7		
Sept 30	Cash paid to		Sept 30	Purchases	108,726
	creditors	95,184		Cash	319
	Discount received	2,798			
	Returns outwards	1,417			
	Transfer debtors				
	control account	949			
	Balances c/d	26,402			
		127,069			127,069

Answer 7.5

(a)

SALES LEDGER CONTROL ACCOUNT

	£		£
Uncorrected balance b/d	12,550	Discounts omitted (d)	100
Sales omitted (a)	850	Contra entry omitted (f)	400
Bank – cheque dishonoured (l)	300	Bad debt omitted (g)	500
		Returns inwards omitted (j)	200
		Amended balance c/d	12,500
	13,700		13,700
Balance b/d	12,500		

Note. Items (b), (c), (e), (h), (i) and (k) are matters affecting the personal accounts of customers. They have no effect on the control account.

(b)   STATEMENT OF ADJUSTMENTS TO LIST OF PERSONAL ACCOUNT BALANCES

	£	£
Original total of list of balances		12,802
Add: debit balance omitted (b)	300	
debit balance understated (e)	200	
		500
		13,302
Less: transposition error (c): understatement of cash received	180	
cash debited instead of credited (2 × £250) (h)	500	
discounts received wrongly debited to Kenton (i)	50	
understatement of cash received (l)	72	
		802
		12,500

Answer 7.6

(a)   *Journal*

		£	£
DEBIT	Insurance	1,327.40	
	Bad debt expense	428.52	
	Purchases (£5,926.38 – £5,296.38)	630.00	
	Motor vehicles (£1,610.95 × 2)	3,221.90	
CREDIT	Suspense account		5,607.82

(b)   *In ledger account form*

SUSPENSE ACCOUNT

	£		£
Balance b/d	5,607.82	Insurance	1,327.40
		Bad debt expense	428.52
		Purchases	630.00
		Motor vehicles	3,221.90
	5,607.82		5,607.82

Answer 7.7

CASH ACCOUNT

	£		£
Transfer from deposit a/c	500	Balance b/d	150
		Charges	36
		Balance c/d	314
	500		500

	£
Balance per cash book	314
Add unpresented cheques	116
Less outstanding lodgements	(630)
Less error by bank	(400)
Balance per bank statement	(600)

Note that on the bank statement the account is overdrawn

Answer 7.8

	£	£
Balance per cash book		(610)
Items on statement, not in cash book		
Direct debits	(715)	
Investment income	353	
		(362)
Corrected balance per cash book		(972)
Item in cash book not on statement:		
Customer's cheque		(875)
Balance per bank statement		(1,847)

Answer 7.9

(a)
                             CASH BOOK

		£				£
31 Oct	Dividends received	2,728	31 Oct	Unadjusted balance b/d (overdraft)		14
			31 Oct	Bank charges		936
			31 Oct	Adjusted balance c/d		1,778
		2,728				2,728

(b) BANK RECONCILIATION STATEMENT
     AT 31 OCTOBER 20X2

	£
Balance as per bank statement	3,426
Unpresented cheques	(1,648)
Outstanding lodgements	0
Balance as per corrected cash book	1,778

Workings

1 Payments shown on bank statement but not in cash book*   £861
   £(421 + 73 + 155 + 212)

   * Presumably recorded in cash book before 1 October 20X2 but not yet
   presented for payment as at 30 September 20X2

2 Payments in the cash book and on the bank statement   £20,111
   £(3,146 + 55 + 3,106 + 39 + 78 + 3,029 + 3,217 + 91 + 1,782 + 134 + 929 +
   230 + 263 + 77 + 52 + 3,191 + 26 + 666)

3 Payments in the cash book but not on the bank statement = Total   £1,648
   payments in cash book £21,759 minus £20,111 =

		£
Alternatively	J & Sons	868
	K & Co	107
	O Ltd	112
	P & Sons	561
		1,648

4 Bank charges, not in the cash book   £936

5 Receipts recorded by bank statement but not in cash book: £2,728
   dividends on investments

6 Receipts in the cash book and also bank statement   £21,471
   (8 Oct £4,589; 11 Oct £5,324; 15 Oct £2,313; 22 Oct £1,202;
   26 Oct £3,857; 29 Oct £4,186)

7 Receipts recorded in cash book but not bank statement   None

Answers to activities _____

Answer 8.1

By classifying a liability as an asset the company has improved its profit figure. The amount of £375 has been treated as an increase in profit, instead of a £375 deduction from profit. The net effect is to overstate profit by £750 (£375 × 2).

Answer 8.2 _____

ADMINISTRATION COSTS

Date	Details	Amount	Date	Details	Amount
20X5		£	20X5		£
1/1	Prepayments b/d	500.00	1/1	Accruals b/d	240.00
	Cash paid in year	32,095.50	31/12	Prepayments c/d	825.00
31/12	Accruals c/d	530.00	31/12	Charge for the year	32,060.50
		33,125.50			33,125.50

Answer 8.3 _____

(a) *Year to 31 August 20X6* £

One months' rental (1/3 × £2,100) *   700
Accrued copying charges (1/3 × £1,500) **   500
Photocopying expense (P & L account)   1,200

*   From the quarterly bill dated 1 August 20X6
**   From the quarterly bill dated 1 November 20X6

There is a prepayment for 2 months' rental (£1,400) as at 31 August 20X6.

(b) *Year to 31 August 20X7*

	£	£
Rental from 1 September 20X6 - 31 July 20X7 (11 months at		
£2,100 per quarter or £700 per month)		7,700
Rental from 1 August - 31 August 20X7 (1/3 × £2,700)		900
Rental charge for the year		8,600
Copying charges:		
1 September - 31 October 20X6 (2/3 × £1,500)	1,000	
1 November 20X6 - 31 January 20X7	1,400	
1 February - 30 April 20X7	1,800	
1 May - 31 July 20X7	1,650	
Accrued charges for August 20X7 (1/3 × £1,950)	650	
		6,500
Total photocopying expenses (P & L account)		15,100

There is a prepayment for 2 months' rental (£1,800) as at 31 August 20X7.

Summary of year 1 September 20X6 - 31 August 20X7

	Rental charges	Copying costs
	£	£
Prepayments as at 31.8.20X6	1,400	
Accrued charges as at 31.8.20X6		(500)
Bills received during the year		
1 November 20X6	2,100	1,500
1 February 20X7	2,100	1,400
1 May 20X7	2,100	1,800
1 August 20X7	2,700	1,650
Prepayment as at 31.8.20X7	(1,800)	
Accrued charges as at 31.8.20X7		650
Charge to the P & L account for the year	8,600	6,500

	Rental charges £	Copying costs £
Balance sheet items as at 31 August 20X7		
Prepaid rental (current asset)	1,800	
Accrued copying charges (current liability)		650

Answer 8.4

		£	£
DEBIT	Prepayments	450.00	
CREDIT	Premises costs		450.00

Kincaid: prepayment of £450.00 business rates

		£	£
DEBIT	Prepayments	550.00	
CREDIT	Premises costs		550.00

Upright: prepayment of £600.00 × 11/12 insurance premiums

		£	£
DEBIT	Purchases	6,000.00	
CREDIT	Accruals		6,000.00

SurePatents: royalty paid is £5,000/£100,000 = 5%, so the royalty to be accrued is £120,000 × 5% = £6,000.00

		£	£
DEBIT	Prepayments	100.00	
DEBIT	Premises costs	10.00	
CREDIT	Accruals		110.00

Westheat Fuels: prepayment of £150.00 × 2/3 = £100.00, plus an accrual of £330.00 × 1/3 = £110.00

Answer 8.5

		£	£
DEBIT	Bad debts	19,621.95	
CREDIT	Sales ledger control		19,621.95
(CREDIT	Sales ledger account		19,621.95)

Being the write off of 60% of the debt of The House Building Company (0.6 × £32,703.25)

Answer 8.6

BAD DEBT EXPENSE

		£			£
20X5	Debtors control a/c	2,000	20X5	Profit and loss a/c	2,000
20X6	Debtors control a/c	2,500	20X6	Profit and loss a/c	2,500
20X7	Debtors control a/c	2,750	20X7	Profit and loss a/c	2,750

PROVISION FOR DOUBTFUL DEBITS

		£			£
			20X5	Doubtful debt expense ($£10,000 × 2^{1}/2\%$)	250
20X5	Balance c/d	250			
			20X6	Balance b/d	250
20X6	Balance c/d ($£13,000 × 2^{1}/2\%$)	325		Doubtful debt expense £(325 – 250)	75
		325			325
20X7	Doubtful debt expense	100	20X7	Balance b/d	325
	Balance c/d (£7,500 × 3%)	225			
		325			325

The provision required at the end of 20X7 is lower than that required in 20X6. The reduction in provision will be treated as sundry income in the profit and loss account.

BALANCE SHEET EXTRACTS AS AT 31 DECEMBER

	20X5	20X6	20X7
	£	£	£
Debtors	10,000	13,000	7,500
Less provision	(250)	(325)	(225)
	9,750	12,675	7,275

Answer 8.7

		£	£
DEBIT	Bad debts expense	6,540.65	
DEBIT	Doubtful debts expense *	3,878.03	
CREDIT	Sales ledger control		6,540.65
CREDIT	Doubtful debts provision		3,878.03
(CREDIT	Sales ledger account		6,540.65)

Being the write off of half the remaining debt of The House Building Company (0.5 × £13,081.30), plus the setting up of a general doubtful debt provision.

*(£206,983.00 – £13,081.30) × 2% = £3,878.03

Answers to activities

Answer 9.1

FREDDIE'S HEALTH FOOD STORE
TRADING ACCOUNT FOR THE YEAR ENDED 31 DECEMBER 20X7

	£	£
Sales		120,000
Opening stocks	10,000	
Add purchases	70,000	
	80,000	
Less closing stocks	22,000	
Cost of goods sold		58,000
Gross profit		62,000

Answer 9.2

Returns inwards are a reduction in sales and do not affect cost of sales. Carriage outwards is a distribution expense in the profit and loss account and is therefore irrelevant here.

Cost of sales

	£
Opening stock	5,700
Purchases	75,280
Carriage inwards	3,680
	84,660
Closing stock	(8,540)
Cost of sales	76,120

Answer 9.3

	£
Draft stock figure	28,850
(a) Overstatement due to wrong addition £(212 – 74)	(138)
(b) No change (note 1)	-
(c) Reduction to cost £(665 – 430) (note 2)	(235)
	28,477

Notes

1   A comparison of cost and net realisable value shows that cost is still lower:

   £460 < £(800 – 270)

   and therefore no adjustment is required.

2   It is correct to include such items in stock, to avoid anticipating profit, but at cost value. Using the selling price meant that the profit element had been included.

Answer 9.4

CASH

	£		£
Capital	4,000	Trade creditors	7,100
Debtors	6,000	Fixed assets	2,900
Balance c/d	1,600	Other expenses	1,600
	11,600		11,600
		Balance b/d	1,600

(b)   LIFO

		Quantity Move-ment	Balance	Movement Unit cost £		Movement Total value £
14 Jan	Receipt	280	280		24	6,720
22 Jan	Issue	(170)	110		24	(4,080)
30 Jan	Receipt	160	270		24	3,840
4 Feb	Issue	(140)	130		24	(3,360)
15 Feb	Receipt	300	430		25	7,500
18 Feb	Issue	(90)	340		25	(2,250)
26 Feb	Issue	(70)	270		25	(1,750)
3 Mar	Receipt	150	420		26	3,900
4 Mar	Issue	(110)	310		26	(2,860)
				20	24	
19 Mar	Issue	(200)	110	140	25	(5,020)
				40	26	
29 Mar	Receipt	240	350		26	6,240
30 Mar	Issue	(80)	270		26	(2,080)

	£
Total receipts	28,200
Total issues	(21,400)
Closing stock	6,800

Answer 9.7

(a)   It would be understated.
(b)   It would be overstated.

Answer 9.8

(a)   60 bushes @ £11 each = £660

(b)   20 bushes @ £6.5 = £130
       30 bushes @ £6 = £180

       Total closing stock = £310

(c)   40 bushes @ £6 = £240
       20 bushes @ £6.5 = £130

       Cost of sales = £240 + £130 = £370

       Or alternatively:

       Opening stock = 40 bushes @ £6.5 = £260

       Purchases =   40 bushes @ £6.5 = £260
                     30 bushes @ £6 = £180

       Closing stock = see (b) above = £310

       Cost of sales = 240 + 260 + 180 − 310 = £370

Answer 9.9

LIFO

Year 1

Purchases (units)	Sales (units)	Balance (units)	Stock value £	Unit cost £	Cost of sales £	Sales £
10		10	3,000	300		
12			3,000	250		
		22	6,000			
	8		(2,000)		2,000	3,200
		14	4,000			
6			1,200	200		
		20	5,200			
	12		(2,800)*		2,800	4,800
		8	2,400		4,800	8,000

* (6 @ £200) + (4 @ £250) + (2 @ £300) = £2,800

Year 2

Purchases (units)	Sales (units)	Balance (units)	Stock value £	Unit cost £	Cost of sales £	Sales £
B/d		8	2,400			
10			2,000	200		
		18	4,400			
	5		1,000		1,000	2,000
		13	3,400			
12			1,800	150		
		25	5,200			
	25		(5,200)		5,200	10,000
		0	0		6,200	12,000

FIFO

Year 1

Purchases (units)	Sales (units)	Balance (units)	Stock value £	Unit cost £	Cost of sales £	Sales £
10		10	3,000	300		
12			3,000	250		
		22	6,000			
	8		(2,400)		2,400	3,200
		14	3,600			
6			1,200	200		
		20	4,800			
	12		(3,100)*		3,100	4,800
		8	1,700		5,500	8,000

* (2 @ £300) + (10 @ £250) = £3,100

Year 2

Purchases (units)	Sales (units)	Balance (units)	Stock value £	Unit cost £	Cost of sales £	Sales £
B/f		8	1,700			
10			2,000	200		
		18	3,700			
	5		(1,100)*		1,100	2,000
		13	2,600			
12			1,800	150		
		25	4,400			
	25		(4,400)**		4,400	10,000
		0	0		5,500	12,000

* (2 @ £250) + (3 @ £200) = £1,100
** (13 @ £200) + (12 @ £150) = £4,400

Trading accounts

	LIFO		FIFO	
	£	£	£	£
Year 1				
Sales		8,000		8,000
Opening stock	0		0	
Purchases	7,200		7,200	
	7,200		7,200	
Closing stock	2,400		1,700	
Cost of sales		4,800		5,500
Gross profit		3,200		2,500
Year 2				
Sales		12,000		12,000
Opening stock	2,400		1,700	
Purchases	3,800		3,800	
	6,200		5,500	
Closing stock	0		0	
Cost of sales		6,200		5,500
Gross profit		5,800		6,500

BPP PUBLISHING

Answers to activities

Answer 10.1

DEBTORS

	£		£
Opening balance	6,700	Cash received (balancing figure)	72,900
Sales (on credit)	69,400	Closing balance c/d	3,200
	76,100		76,100

Answer 10.2

DEBTORS CONTROL ACCOUNT

	£		£
1 January balance b/d	42,800	Bank	204,000
Sales	240,200	Discounts allowed	16,250
		31 December balance c/d	62,750
	283,000		283,000

Answer 10.3

	£
Creditors b/d	(1,455)
Cash paid	41,775
Creditors c/d	1,080
Credit purchases	41,400
Add cash purchases	5,850
Total purchases	47,250

Answer 10.4

The gross profit is £150,000 – £112,500 = £37,500.

(a) The gross profit mark up on cost of sales is:

$$\frac{£37,500}{£112,500} \times 100\% = 33^1/_3\%$$

(b) The gross profit margin on sales is:

$$\frac{£37,500}{£150,000} \times 100\% = 25\%$$

Answer 10.5

The trading account of Janey Jennings will appear as follows.

	£	£
Sales		455,000
Less cost of sales		
Opening stock	71,300	
Purchases	282,250	
	353,550	
Closing stock (balance)	80,550	
		273,000
Gross profit (40% × £455,000)		182,000

Cost of stock destroyed = £80,550 – £1,200 = £79,350.

Answer 10.6

		£
Cash banked		142,950
Less: loan repayment		660
decrease in till balance (£930 – £780)		150
		142,140
Add: wages payments (12 × £450)		5,400
expense payments (52 × £60)		3,120
Sales		150,660

In ledger format

CASH ACCOUNT

	£		£
Balance b/d	930	Salaries	5,400
Loan repaid	660	Expenses	3,120
Sales (balancing figure)	150,660	Bank	142,950
		Balance c/d	780
	152,250		152,250

Answer 10.7

Task 1

Total sales: year ended 30 April 20X7

		£
Private bank account		
Balance b/f		-
Drawings (£200 × 12)		2,400
Balance c/f		600
Cheques from Electronics World		3,000

ELECTRONICS WORLD LTD

	£		£
Balance b/f	-	Cash received (business a/c)	17,600
Sales (bal fig)	25,000	Cash received (private a/c)	3,000
		Balance c/f	4,400
	25,000		25,000

Task 2

Selling price for 1 pair speaker stands

500 pairs sold for £25,000

$$\therefore \text{ Price per pair paid} = \frac{£25,000}{500} = £50$$

Task 3

Cost of materials for 1 pair speaker stands

$$\text{Cost per pair} = \frac{£50}{2} = £25$$

Task 4

Cost of goods sold

Total = £25.00 × 500 = £12,500

Answers to activities

Task 5

Purchases

JOHNSON MATERIALS LTD

	£		£
Cash paid	12,000	Balance b/f	-
Balance c/f	1,500	Purchases (bal fig)	13,500
	13,500		13,500

Task 6

Closing stock at 30 April 20X7 = 120 × £25 = £3,000

To find opening stock at 30 April 20X6:

	£
Opening stock (balancing figure)	2,000
Purchases (Task 5)	13,500
Less: closing stock at 30 April 20X7	(3,000)
Cost of goods sold (Task 4)	12,500

Task 7

Capital invested on 30 April 20X6

	£	£
Assets		
Tools and equipment	3,000	
Less depreciation (£3,000 × 20% × $9/12$)	(450)	
		2,550
Van	4,800	
Less depreciation (£4,800 × 10% × $6/12$)	(240)	
		4,560
Stock		2,000
Bank		4,250
		13,360
Rent owed		(100)
Capital		13,260

Task 8

Rent to 30 April 20X7

	£
1 May 20X6 - 31 October 20X6 (£100 × 6)	600
1 November 20X6 - 30 April 20X7 (£120 × 6)	720
Rent for year	1,320

Answers to activities _____

Answer 11.1

SUBSCRIPTIONS

	£		£
Balance b/d	410	Bank: 20X6	370
		20X7	6,730
∴ I & E account	7,200	20X8	1,180
		20X6 subs written off	40
Balance c/d: 20X8 subs prepaid	1,180	Balance c/d: 20X7 subs due	470
	8,790		8,790

Answer 11.2 _____

(a)

		£	£
Subscriptions received in 20X7			790
Less: amounts relating to 20X6		38	
Amounts relating to 20X8		80	
			118
Cash received relating to 20X7			672
Add: subs paid in 20X6 relating to 20X7		72	
20X7 subs still to be paid		48	
			120
			792

Alternatively, in ledger account format:

SUBSCRIPTIONS

	£		£
Balance b/d	38	Balance b/d	72
∴ Income and expenditure a/c	792	Cash	790
Balance c/d	80	Balance c/d	48
	910		910

(b)

	£
Subscriptions received in 20X7	1,024
Less amounts relating to 20X8	58
	966
Add subs paid in 20X6 relating to 20X7	14
	980

Alternatively, in ledger account format:

SUBSCRIPTIONS

	£		£
∴ Income and expenditure a/c	980	Balance b/d	14
Balance c/d	58	Bank	1,024
	1,038		1,038

Answer 11.3

(a) SUMMARY BALANCE SHEET AT 31 DECEMBER 20X7

	£
Net assets	
Tables and chairs	380
Playing cards and other accessories	102
Reference books	130
Subscriptions in arrears	27
	639
Subscriptions in advance	80
	559
Funds	
Accumulated fund	259
Life membership fund	300
	559

(b) ACCUMULATED FUND

	£
Balance at 31 December 20X7	259
Add back deficit for the year	117
	376
Less transfer from life membership fund	75
Balance at 1 January 20X7	301

Answer 11.4

	£	£
Balance at 1 January		3,780
New enrolments		480
		4,260
Less release to income:		
1 × £80	80	
63 × £5	315	
4 × £6	24	
		419
Balance at 31 December		3,841

Answer 11.5

(a)

CREDITORS

	£		£
Bank	5,685	Bal b/d	435
Bal c/d	363	∴ Purchases	5,613
	6,048		6,048

DEBTORS

	£		£
Bal b/d	12	Bank £(6,064 + 1,040)	7,104
∴ Sales	7,100	Bal c/d	8
	7,112		7,112

The trading account shows sales of £7,100 and so cost of sales are £5,680 (100/125 × £7,100). Since opening stock is £390 and purchases are £5,613, closing stock is £323.

(b) Sales are £7,100, cost of sales is £5,680, and so gross profit is £1,420. From this must be deducted barman's wages of £1,040, giving £380.

Answer 11.6

(a) B. The cost of an extension is capital expenditure, which would be shown as an asset in the balance sheet.

(b) C. Office wages are not a manufacturing cost; they would appear in the profit and loss account, not the manufacturing account. Factory rent and depreciation of machinery are factory overheads; they are included in factory cost of goods produced, but not in prime cost. Prime cost includes only direct materials and direct production wages.

Answer 11.7

	£
Direct labour	26,000
Direct materials	14,000
	40,000
Production overheads	20,000
	60,000
Less closing stocks	(2,000)
Production cost of goods completed	58,000

Answer 11.8

MANUFACTURING ACCOUNT FOR 20X7

	£	£
Raw materials		
Opening stock	12,940	
Purchases	213,680	
Carriage inwards	3,970	
	230,590	
Closing stock	14,550	
		216,040
Direct wages		96,380
Prime costs		312,420
Factory overheads		
Wages and salaries £(12,490 + 18,330)		30,820
Other factory costs		63,310
		406,550
Work in progress		
Opening stock	42,920	
Closing stock	39,610	
		3,310
Factory cost of finished goods produced		409,860
Factory profit (£409,860 × 15/85)		72,328
Transfer price of finished goods produced		482,188

Answer 11.9

Task 1

	£
Opening stock of baking materials	1,000
Baking materials purchased	84,000
	85,000
Closing stock of baking materials	3,000
Baking materials used	82,000
Baking production wages	44,000
Prime cost	126,000

Task 2

	£
Prime cost	126,000
Baking supervisory wages	25,000
Baking overheads	22,000
Depreciation bakery premises	2,000
Depreciation bakery equipment	5,000
Production cost	180,000

Answers to activities

Task 3

Cost of goods to shop	60,000
Profit on sales (100% mark-up)	60,000
Cost of goods to caterers and retailers	120,000
Profit on sales (50% mark-up)	60,000
Total gross profit	120,000

Task 4

Purchases	84,000
Add creditors 1 January 20X7	6,000
	90,000
Less creditors 31 December 20X7	7,000
Paid to creditors	83,000

Task 5

Credit sales	180,000
Add debtors at 1 January 20X7	12,000
	192,000
Less receipts from debtors	179,500
Debtors at 31 December 20X7	12,500

Answers to activities

Answer 12.1

The full ETB is shown below.

Account	Trial balance DR £	Trial balance CR £	Ref	Adjustments DR £	Adjustments CR £	Profit & loss account DR £	Profit & loss account CR £	Balance sheet DR £	Balance sheet CR £
Land and buildings	120,000							120,000	
Proprietor's capital at 1.1.X7		208,000							208,000
Sales		470,000	1				470,000		
Purchases	246,000			360		246,360			
Stock at 1.1.X7	79,500					79,500			
Returns in	400					400			
Returns out		1,800					1,800		
Discounts allowed	4,000					4,000			
Discounts received		2,100					2,100		
Uniform Business Rate	27,450				5,400	22,050			
Motor expenses	12,250					12,250			
Salaries	103,500					103,500			
Insurance	9,500		1	3,300	3,025	9,775			
Trade debtors	32,300							32,300	
Trade creditors		17,800							17,800
Carriage in	4,200					4,200			
Carriage out	2,550			480		3,030			
Motor vehicles	65,150		1	4,910				70,060	
Bank	7,800							7,800	
Provision for dep'n: buildings		4,000	2		800				4,800
Provision for dep'n: motor vehicles		21,370	2		14,012				35,382
Bad debts	600		1&3	1,623		2,223			
Provision for doubtful debts			3		323				323
Depreciation expense			2	14,812		14,812			
Suspense account	9,870		1		9,870				
Stock at 31.12.X7 (P&L)			4		82,000		82,000		
Stock at 31.12.X7 (B/S)			4	82,000				82,000	
Prepayments				8,425				8,425	
Accruals					480				480
SUB-TOTAL	725,070	725,070		115,910	115,910	502,100	555,900	320,585	266,785
Profit for the year						53,800			53,800
TOTAL	725,070	725,070		115,910	115,910	555,900	555,900	320,585	320,585

Answer 12.2

Journal 1

		£	£
DEBIT	Insurance	3,300	
	Bad debt expense	1,300	
	Purchases (£4,955 − £4,595)	360	
	Motor vehicles (£2,455 × 2)	4,910	
CREDIT	Suspense account		9,870

BPP PUBLISHING

In ledger account form:

SUSPENSE ACCOUNT

	£		£
Balance b/f	9,870	Insurance	3,300
		Bad debt expense	1,300
		Purchases	360
		Motor vehicles	4,910
	9,870		9,870

Answer 12.3

(a) UBR: prepaid 1 January to 31 March 20X8

$= {}^{3}/_{12} \times £21,600 = £5,400$

(b) Insurance: prepaid 1 January to 30 November 20X8

$= {}^{11}/_{12} \times £3,300 = £3,025$

(c) Carriage outwards: accrue 1 November to 31 December 20X7

$= {}^{2}/_{3} \times £720 = £480$

VAT is not accrued as the invoice was received after the year end. If it was accrued the entry would be Debit VAT rec 126
Credit Accruals 126

Answer 12.4

Tutorial note. When calculating the bad debt provision in (b) you do not need to deduct the bad debts written off from the year end debtors figure. This adjustment has already been made. The suspense account balance arose because the bad debt expense entry had not been made.

(a) *Depreciation*

Buildings: 2% × £40,000 = £800

Motor vehicles: 20% × £(65,150 + 4,910) = £14,012

Journal 2

DEBIT	Depreciation expense	£14,812	
CREDIT	Provision for depreciation		
	Buildings		£800
	Motor vehicles		£14,012

(b) *Bad debt provision*

Trade debtors		£32,300
General provision @ 1%		£323

Journal 3

DEBIT	Bad debts	£323	
CREDIT	Provision for bad debts		£323

(c) *Journal 4*

DEBIT	Closing stock (balance sheet)	£82,000	
CREDIT	Closing stock (P & L account)		£82,000

Answer 12.5

See ETB.

Answer 12.6

Tasks 1 and 2

Extended trial balance at 30 April 20X8

DESCRIPTION	Ledger balance Debit £	Ledger balance Credit £	Adjustments Debit £	Adjustments Credit £	Profit and Loss a/c Debit £	Profit and Loss a/c Credit £	Balance Sheet Debit £	Balance Sheet Credit £
Purchases	127,680				127,680			
Sales		184,784				184,784		
Purchases returns		360				360		
Sales returns	502				502			
Stock at 1 May 20X7	40,650				40,650			
Salaries	22,590				22,590			
General expenses	14,580				14,580			
Insurance	270		90		360			
Motor vehicle (MV) at cost	9,600						9,600	
Provision for depreciation (MV)		4,685		983				5,668
Equipment (EQ) at cost	17,100						17,100	
Provision for depreciation (EQ)		5,130		1,710				6,840
Bad debt	2,025		1,800		3,825			
Provision for doubtful debts		1,485	15					1,470
Debtors control account	31,200			1,800			29,400	
Creditors control account		25,232						25,232
Drawings	17,892						17,892	
Capital		82,493						82,493
Bank overdraft		261						261
Cash	426						426	
VAT		1,685						1,685
Bank interest received		900		600		1,500		
Bank deposit account	22,500						22,500	
Depreciation			2,693		2,693			
Closing stock - P&L				43,690		43,690		
Closing stock - balance sheet			43,690				43,690	
Bank interest owing			600				600	
Provision for doubtful debts - adjustment				15	15			
Other accruals				90				90
Profit					17,469			17,469
	307,015	307,015	48,888	48,888	230,349	230,349	141,208	141,208

Answer 12.7

Task 1

See extended trial balance on Page 329. Workings are as follows.

(a) *Depreciation*

Motor vehicles: £32,600 × 20% = £6,520
Equipment: £(48,860 – 6,620) × 10% = £4,224

Total depreciation = £10,744

(b) *Bank loan interest*

Interest for 9 months = £50,000 × 10% × 9/12
= £3,750

Accrued interest = £3,750 – £2,500 = £1,250

(c) and (d)

Bad debts

	£
Debtors control account balance	189,600
Debt written off: restaurant	3,400
	186,200

Provision required = 6% × £186,200 = £11,172

Adjustment required = £12,000 – £11,172 = £828

(e) *Stock*

	£
Stock at cost	289,400
Reduction to NRV of 5 system £(1,200 – 1,000) × 5	(1,000)
Damaged system	(200)
	288,200

(f) *Advertising*

DEBIT	Advertising	£2,250	
CREDIT	Accruals		£2,250

(g) *Rent*

Rent for year = £2,100 × 12 = £25,200

∴ £27,300 – £25,200 = £2,100 is prepaid

DEBIT	Prepayments	£2,100	
CREDIT	Rent		£2,100

(h) *Cash withdrawn*

DEBIT	Cash	£5,000	
CREDIT	Bank		£5,000

(i) *Credit note*

DEBIT	Creditor's control account	£2,900	
CREDIT	Purchases returns		£2,900

Task 2

See extended trial balance on Page 329.

CASTLE ALARMS

Account	Trial balance Debit £	Trial balance Credit £	Adjustments Debit £	Adjustments Credit £	Profit and Loss a/c Debit £	Profit and Loss a/c Credit £	Balance Sheet Debit £	Balance Sheet Credit £
Sales		1,200,000				1,200,000		
Purchases	667,820				667,820			
Sales returns	96,570				96,570			
Purchases returns		52,790		2,900		55,690		
Opening Stock	301,840				301,840			
Debtors control account	189,600			3,400			186,200	
Cash	1,200		5,000				6,200	
Bank	25,300			5,000			20,300	
Creditors control account		95,000	2,900					92,100
Provision for bad debts		12,000	828					11,172
Bad debts	10,100		3,400		13,500			
Discount allowed	6,320				6,320			
Salaries	103,030				103,030			
Drawings	26,170						26,170	
Rent	27,300			2,100	25,200			
General expenses	14,310				14,310			
Capital		121,860						121,860
VAT		22,600						22,600
Bank loan		50,000						50,000
Interest on bank loan	2,500		1,250		3,750			
Advertising	11,450		2,250		13,700			
Motor vehicles (cost)	32,600						32,600	
Equipment (cost)	48,860						48,860	
Motor vehicles (prov for depreciation)		4,100		6,520				10,620
Equipment (prov for depreciation)		6,620		4,224				10,844
Depreciation			10,744		10,744			
Loan interest owing				1,250				1,250
Closing stock (P&L)				288,200		288,200		
Closing stock (B/S)			288,200				288,200	
Provision for bad debts (adjustment)				828		828		
Prepayments / accruals			2,100	2,250			2,100	2,250
Subtotal	1,564,970	1,564,970	316,672	316,672	1,256,784	1,544,718	610,630	322,696
Profit for the year					287,934			287,934
TOTAL	1,564,970	1,564,970	316,672	316,672	1,544,718	1,544,718	610,630	610,630

Answer 12.8

Task 1

JOURNAL		Page 1
Details	**£**	**£**
(a) (i) DEBIT Creditors control a/c	1,800	
CREDIT Purchases		1,800
Being correction of overstatement of purchases and creditors		
(ii) DEBIT Light and heat	1,201	
DEBIT Stationery and advertising	1,025	
CREDIT Purchases		2,226
Being posting of other expenses from purchases		
(b) DEBIT Creditors control a/c	47	
CREDIT Purchase returns		40
CREDIT VAT		7
Being purchase return omitted		
(c) DEBIT Sales	245	
CREDIT VAT		245
Being correction of misposting of VAT		
(d) DEBIT Creditors control a/c	54	
CREDIT Discounts received		54
Being posting of omitted discount received		

Task 2

See extended trial balance on Page 332.

Task 3

See extended trial balance on Page 332. Workings are shown below.

(i)   *Depreciation*

Motor vehicles = 20% × £(60,480 − 9,800) = £10,136
Office furniture and equipment = 10% × £(26,750 − 3,170) = £2,358

Total depreciation = £(10,136 + 2,358) = £12,494

(ii)   *Rent*

An accrual is required as the rent expense for the year should be £1,000 × 12 = £12,000.

(iii)   *Stationery and advertising*

Advertising of £1,560 has been prepaid.

(iv)   *Stock and insurance*

The damaged stock is correctly excluded from the stock balance. The amount due from the insurance company is a debtor.

(v)   *Provision for bad debts*

	£
Debtors control account balance	120,860

	£
Provision required £120,860 × 5% =	6,043
Current provision	5,620
Adjustment required	423

Task 4

See extended trial balance on Page 332.

EXPLOSIVES

Account	Trial balance Debit £	Trial balance Credit £	Adjustments Debit £	Adjustments Credit £	Profit and Loss a/c Debit £	Profit and Loss a/c Credit £	Balance Sheet Debit £	Balance Sheet Credit £
Opening Stock	180,420				180,420			
Purchases	606,054			2,300	603,754			
Sales		840,315				840,315		
Purchases returns		2,430				2,430		
Sales returns	2,650				2,650			
Motor expenses	5,430				5,430			
Bank	20,415						20,415	
Cash	3,420						3,420	
Rent	11,000		1,000		12,000			
Lighting and heating	5,381				5,381			
Stationery and advertising	7,145			1,560	5,585			
Provision for bad debts		5,620		423				6,043
Debtors control account	120,860						120,860	
Creditors control account		100,959						100,959
Salaries	96,200				96,200			
Bad debts	7,200				7,200			
Drawings	31,600						31,600	
Discount allowed	20,520				20,520			
Discount received		18,454				18,454		
Motor vehicles (cost)	60,480						60,480	
Office furniture & equipment (cost)	26,750						26,750	
Motor vehicles (prov for depreciation)		12,590		10,136				22,726
Office furniture & equipment (prov for depreciation)		3,170		2,358				5,528
VAT		10,512						10,512
Capital		211,475						211,475
Depreciation			12,494		12,494			
Regal Insurance Company			2,300				2,300	
Closing stock (P&L)				208,540		208,540		
Closing stock (B/S)			208,540				208,540	
Provision for bad debts (adjustment)			423		423			
Prepayments / accruals			1,560	1,000			1,560	1,000
Subtotal	1,205,525	1,205,525	226,317	226,317	952,057	1,069,739	475,925	358,243
Profit for the year					117,682			117,682
TOTAL	1,205,525	1,205,525	226,317	226,317	1,069,739	1,069,739	475,925	475,925

Answer 12.9 _____

Task 1

See extended trial balance on Page 398.

Task 2

(a) *Depreciation*

Delivery vans: £(12,800 − 3,520) × 20% = £1,856
Equipment £22,800 × 10% = £2,280

Total depreciation = £4,136

(b) *Interest*

£30,000 × 6% = £1,800

∴£600 accrued interest is receivable.

(c) *Bad debts*

	£
Debtors control account balance	41,600
Debt written off: M C Millar	2,460
	39,140

Provision for doubtful debts required
= 5% × £39,140 = £1,957 ∴ reduce current provision of £1,980 by £23.

(d) *Stock*

The damaged chairs must be valued at the lower of cost and net realisable value.

		£
Cost (£230 × 4)		920
NRV:	selling price (£190 × 4)	760
	less repairs	40
		720

∴ Reduce stock by £(920 − 720) = £200
Closing stock is £(58,394 − 200) = £58,194

(e) *JB Office Supplies*

This payment has not in fact been made, so the original entry must be reversed.

DEBIT	Bank overdraft	£1,260	
CREDIT	Creditors control a/c		£1,260

(f) *Insurance*

Premium prepaid = £260 × 6/12 = £130

(g) *Rent*

Total rent payable = £200 × 12 = £2,400

∴ £200 must be accrued

Task 3

See extended trial balance on Page 334.

JASON BROWN

Account	Trial balance Debit £	Trial balance Credit £	Adjustments Debit £	Adjustments Credit £	Profit and Loss a/c Debit £	Profit and Loss a/c Credit £	Balance Sheet Debit £	Balance Sheet Credit £
Purchases	170,240				170,240			
Sales		246,412				246,412		
Purchases returns		480				480		
Sales returns	670				670			
Opening Stock	54,200				54,200			
Salaries	30,120				30,120			
Rent	2,200		200		2,400			
Insurance	360			130	230			
Delivery vans (cost)	12,800						12,800	
Equipment (cost)	22,800						22,800	
Delivery vans (prov for depn)		3,520		1,856				5,376
Equipment (prov for depn)		5,760		2,280				8,040
Bad debts	2,700		2,460		5,160			
Provision for bad debts		1,980	23					1,957
Debtors control account	41,600			2,460			39,140	
Creditors control account		33,643		1,260				34,903
Drawings	10,522						10,522	
Capital		83,171						83,171
Bank overdraft		348	1,260				912	
Cash	568						568	
VAT		2,246						2,246
Bank interest received		1,200		600		1,800		
Bank deposit account	30,000						30,000	
Suspense account		20						20
Depreciation			4,136		4,136			
Bank interest owing			600				600	
Closing stock (P&L)				58,194		58,194		
Closing stock (B/S)			58,194				58,194	
Provision for bad debts (adjustment)				23		23		
Prepayments / accruals			130	200			130	200
Subtotal	378,780	378,780	67,003	67,003	267,156	306,909	175,666	135,913
Profit for the year					39,753			39,753
TOTAL	378,780	378,780	67,003	67,003	306,909	303,909	175,666	175,666

List of key terms and index

List of key terms

Trade creditor, 63
Trade debtor, 63
Trading account, 74

VAT, 31

Work in progress, 243

REVIEW FORM & FREE PRIZE DRAW

All original review forms from the entire BPP range, completed with genuine comments, will be entered into one of two draws on 31 January 2003 and 31 July 2003. The names on the first four forms picked out on each occasion will be sent a cheque for £50.

Name: _____   Address: _____

_____

_____

How have you used this Interactive Text?
(Tick one box only)

☐ Home study (book only)

☐ On a course: college _____

☐ With 'correspondence' package

☐ Other _____

Why did you decide to purchase this Interactive Text? *(Tick one box only)*

☐ Have used BPP Texts in the past

☐ Recommendation by friend/colleague

☐ Recommendation by a lecturer at college

☐ Saw advertising

☐ Other _____

During the past six months do you recall seeing/receiving any of the following?
(Tick as many boxes as are relevant)

☐ Our advertisement in *Accounting Technician* magazine

☐ Our advertisement in *Pass*

☐ Our brochure with a letter through the post

Which (if any) aspects of our advertising do you find useful?
(Tick as many boxes as are relevant)

☐ Prices and publication dates of new editions

☐ Information on Interactive Text content

☐ Facility to order books off-the-page

☐ None of the above

Have you used the companion Assessment Kit for this subject?   ☐ **Yes**   ☐ **No**

Your ratings, comments and suggestions would be appreciated on the following areas

	Very useful	*Useful*	*Not useful*
Introductory section (How to use this Interactive Text etc)	☐	☐	☐
Chapter topic lists	☐	☐	☐
Chapter learning objectives	☐	☐	☐
Key terms	☐	☐	☐
Activities and answers	☐	☐	☐
Key learning points	☐	☐	☐
Quick quizzes and answers	☐	☐	☐
List of key terms and index	☐	☐	☐
Icons	☐	☐	☐

	Excellent	*Good*	*Adequate*	*Poor*
Overall opinion of this Text	☐	☐	☐	☐

Do you intend to continue using BPP Interactive Texts/Assessment Kits?   ☐ Yes   ☐ No

Please note any further comments and suggestions/errors on the reverse of this page.

The BPP author of this edition can be e-mailed at: katyhibbert@bpp.com

Please return to: Nick Weller, BPP Publishing Ltd, FREEPOST, London, W12 8BR

REVIEW FORM & FREE PRIZE DRAW (continued)

Please note any further comments and suggestions/errors below

FREE PRIZE DRAW RULES

1   Closing date for 31 January 2003 draw is 31 December 2002. Closing date for 31 July 2003 draw is 30 June 2003.

2   Restricted to entries with UK and Eire addresses only. BPP employees, their families and business associates are excluded.

3   No purchase necessary. Entry forms are available upon request from BPP Publishing. No more than one entry per title, per person. Draw restricted to persons aged 16 and over.

4   Winners will be notified by post and receive their cheques not later than 6 weeks after the relevant draw date.

5   The decision of the promoter in all matters is final and binding. No correspondence will be entered into.

See overleaf for information on other
BPP products and how to order

AAT Order

To BPP Publishing Ltd, Aldine Place, London W12 8AW
Tel: 020 8740 2211. Fax: 020 8740 1184
E-mail: Publishing@bpp.com Web:www.bpp.com

Mr/Mrs/Ms (Full name)
Daytime delivery address

Postcode

Daytime Tel

E-mail

	5/02 Texts	5/02 Kits	Special offer	8/02 Passcards	Tapes
FOUNDATION (£14.95 except as indicated)				Foundation	
Units 1 & 2 Receipts and Payments	☐	☐		£6.95 ☐	£10.00 ☐
Unit 3 Ledger Balances and Initial Trial Balance	☐				
Unit 4 Supplying Information for Mgmt Control	☐				
Unit 20 Working with Information Technology (£9.95) (6/02)	☐				
Unit 22/23 Healthy Workplace/Personal Effectiveness (£9.95)	☐				
INTERMEDIATE (£9.95)			All		
Unit 5 Financial Records and Accounts	☐	☐	Inter'te Texts	£5.95 ☐	£10.00 ☐
Unit 6 Cost Information	☐	☐	and Kits (£65)	£5.95 ☐	£10.00 ☐
Unit 7 Reports and Returns	☐	☐	☐	£5.95 ☐	
Unit 21 Using Information Technology	☐	☐		£5.95 ☐	
TECHNICIAN (£9.95)			Set of 12		
Unit 8/9 Core Managing Costs and Allocating Resources	☐	☐	Technician	£5.95 ☐	£10.00 ☐
Unit 10 Core Managing Accounting Systems	☐	☐	Texts/Kits		
Unit 11 Option Financial Statements (A/c Practice)	☐	☐	(Please	£5.95 ☐	£10.00 ☐
Unit 12 Option Financial Statements (Central Govnmt)	☐	☐	specify titles		
Unit 15 Option Cash Management and Credit Control	☐	☐	required)	£5.95 ☐	
Unit 16 Option Evaluating Activities	☐	☐	(£100)	£5.95 ☐	
Unit 17 Option Implementing Auditing Procedures	☐	☐	☐	£5.95 ☐	
Unit 18 Option Business Tax (FA02)(8/02 Text & Kit)	☐	☐		£5.95 ☐	
Unit 19 Option Personal Tax (FA 02)(8/02 Text & Kit)	☐	☐		£5.95 ☐	
TECHNICIAN 2001 (£9.95)					
Unit 18 Option Business Tax FA01 (8/01 Text & Kit)	☐	☐			
Unit 19 Option Personal Tax FA01 (8/01 Text & Kit)	☐	☐			
SUBTOTAL	£	£	£	£	£

TOTAL FOR PRODUCTS £ ☐

POSTAGE & PACKING

Texts/Kits

	First	Each extra
UK	£2.00	£2.00
Europe*	£4.00	£2.00 £ ☐
Rest of world	£20.00	£10.00 £ ☐
Passcards		
UK	£2.00	£1.00 £ ☐
Europe*	£2.50	£1.00 £ ☐
Rest of world	£15.00	£8.00 £ ☐
Tapes		
UK	£1.00	£1.00 £ ☐
Europe*	£1.00	£1.00 £ ☐
Rest of world	£4.00	£4.00 £ ☐

TOTAL FOR POSTAGE & PACKING £ ☐
(Max £10 Texts/Kits/Passcards)

Grand Total (Cheques to *BPP Publishing*) I enclose
a cheque for (incl. Postage) £ ☐
Or charge to Access/Visa/Switch
Card Number ☐☐☐☐ ☐☐☐☐ ☐☐☐☐ ☐☐☐☐

Expiry date _____ Start Date _____

Issue Number (Switch Only) ☐☐

Signature _____

We aim to deliver to all UK addresses inside 5 working days; a signature will be required. Orders to all EU addresses should be delivered within 6 working days. All other orders to overseas addresses should be delivered within 8 working days. * Europe includes the Republic of Ireland and the Channel Islands.